D0423090

Leadership for Learning in Music Education

Joseph W. Landon

EADERSHIP FOR LEARNING IN MUSIC EDUCATION
EADERSHIP FOR LEARNING IN MUSIC EDUCATION
EADERSHIP FOR LEARNING IN MUSIC EDUCATION
EADERSHIP FOR LEARNING IN MUSIC EDUCATION
EADERSHIP FOR LEARNING IN MUSIC EDUCATION
EADERSHIP FOR LEARNING IN MUSIC EDUCATION
EADERSHIP FOR LEARNING IN MUSIC EDUCATION
EADERSHIP FOR LEARNING IN MUSIC EDUCATION
EADERSHIP FOR LEARNING IN MUSIC EDUCATION
EADERSHIP FOR LEARNING IN MUSIC EDUCATION
EADERSHIP FOR LEARNING IN MUSIC EDUCATION
EADERSHIP FOR LEARNING IN MUSIC EDUCATION
EADERSHIP FOR LEARNING IN MUSIC EDUCATION
EADERSHIP FOR LEARNING IN MUSIC EDUCATION
EADERSHIP FOR LEARNING IN MUSIC EDUCATION
EADERSHIP FOR LEARNING IN MUSIC EDUCATION
EADERSHIP FOR LEARNING IN MUSIC EDUCATION
EADERSHIP FOR LEARNING IN MUSIC EDUCATION

CONTEMPORARY MUSIC EDUCATION SERIES

Michael D. Poland, Editor

Other books in the series

ACCOUNTABILITY AND OBJECTIVES
FOR MUSIC EDUCATION

* * * * * * * *

HOW TO WRITE
LEARNING ACTIVITY PACKAGES
FOR MUSIC EDUCATION

780.7
L244L

LEADERSHIP for LEARNING in MUSIC EDUCATION

by

JOSEPH W. LANDON

California State University, Fullerton
Fullerton, California

Educational Media Press
Costa Mesa, California

TABOR COLLEGE LIBRARY
Hillsboro, Kansas 67063

152115

Typography, layout and design by
L. R. Simmons Company, Downey, California

Copyright © 1975 by Educational Media Press, P. O. Box 1852, Costa Mesa, California 92626. All rights reserved. Printed in the United States of America. No part of this publication may be reproduced, stored in a retrieval system, or transmitted, in any form or by any means, electronic, mechanical, photocopying, recording, or otherwise, without prior written permission.

To
my wife, Sibyl
for her love, help and understanding - - -
and to two of the greatest teacher-leaders
in music education I have known,
Dr. Howard S. Swan and
the late Ralph E. Rush - - -
each of whom profoundly influenced
the ideas expressed in this book.

ACKNOWLEDGMENTS

The author expresses his grateful appreciation to Dr. Sherwood Cummings, Professor of English, California State University, Fullerton, colleague and friend--whose delightful wit, keen appreciation of music, and penetrating reading of the manuscript kept him "on the beam"--and, to his wife, Sibyl for proof-reading, correcting, and indexing in the final stages of the preparation of the book.

Appreciation is also acknowledged to the following persons and organizations for their contributions:

* Dr. Wesley R. Anderson, Principal, Highland High School, Kern School District, Bakersfield, California, for use of building plans and materials on "pontooning";

* Dr. Phillip A. Alfred, Associate Superintendent of Schools, San Bernardino City Unified School District, San Bernardino, California, for use of building plans, specifications, and curricular materials;

* Milton Blanchard, Coordinator, Office of Facility Planning (retired), California State University, Fullerton, for use of line drawings and specifications,

* Gelsomina Barton, Fine Arts Coordinator, Fullerton School District, Fullerton, California, for forms and materials used in the music program;

* Music Educators National Conference, Michele Brace, Director of Publications, for permission to reproduce line drawings and architectural-acoustical specifications; and, Malcolm E. Bessom, Editor, Music Educators Journal for permission to re-use the author's own article on Small-Group Music Strategies (SGMS) and Learning Activity Packages (LAPS);

* William C. Brown and Company, Publishers for permission to reproduce an architectural line drawing, and

To the following publishers for permission to quote materials used in the text:

Ginn and Company, Boston, Mass.
Harper and Row, Publishers, New York, N.Y.
McGraw-Hill Book Company, New York, N.Y.
Prentice-Hall, Inc., Englewood Cliffs, N.J.
Theodore Presser and Company (Oliver Ditson), Bryn Mawr, Pa.
Random-House, Inc., New York, N.Y.
TIME Magazine, New York, N.Y.
Vintage Books, New York, N.Y.

Most important of all, however, the writer will be eternally grateful to the many students and leaders in music whose lives have touched his--and who have helped mold his philosophy and understanding of what it is like to have the opportunity to teach and to lead.

INTRODUCTION

This book was written to articulate the nature of leadership in music education in human-behavioral terms. It resulted from a long-standing belief of the author that leadership is not the sole prerogative of official leaders, but that it may be exercised by any music educator--and, that the profession sorely needs persons whose vision and ability to influence others to do the things they want most to do is its most important characteristic. Leaders must have the capacity to help students as well as their own colleagues by deeply affecting the most important aspect of what this book is about--individual musical growth.

The title of this book should suggest its emphasis--Leadership for Learning in Music Education is not about administration per se (although administrative-managerial functions are included). Rather, it is about the inner essence of leadership by which total music teaching-learning may be effected.

The persons for whom this book is particularly intended are:

* college-university students of music education in general who are interested in the nature of their art and the dynamics of teaching-learning-leadership.
* upper division and graduate students in "methods" classes.
* externs and interns in schools who are on the threshold of their teaching careers.
* beginning teachers who are "re-learning what it is all about"--and who need specific guidance on the "what" and "how" of music education.
* experienced music educators who are anxious to further their own competence and expertise.
* persons who are preparing to assume official leadership roles in music education.
* department chairpersons, consultants, coordinators and directors of music who are interested in the art and science of leadership for learning in music education.

In a complex society such as ours, the content and process of learning is a growing, dynamic focal point in any discipline. The dynamics of change requires persons who understand how change must be rooted in total value systems, and how this is related to our society's educational institutions. The future of music education holds great promise--but that promise is more than a vision--it requires artisans who are professionally and personally prepared to cope with the total dimensions of their job.

There is a central theme which the reader will discover recurring throughout this book--that is, a music program is as good as the persons who most influence it--students, teachers, official leaders in music, and administrators. And, students will have the most influence on their own learning where they are led by capable professional music educators who know and care enough about their art to do something about it! Most important of all--the leader in music education understands that he/she does not operate in a vacuum--the dynamics of leadership must be exercised "in concert" by all persons concerned.

Joseph W. Landon

Fullerton, California
January, 1975

TABLE OF CONTENTS

PART ONE

FOUNDATIONS OF MUSIC EDUCATION (RATIONALE)

PART THREE

DIMENSIONS OF MUSIC LEADERSHIP (ORGANIZATION)

PART FOUR

THE MUSIC EDUCATOR AS A PROFESSIONAL LEADER (REALIZATION)

RESOURCES FOR MUSIC EDUCATION

PART ONE

foundations of music education — (rationale)

CHAPTER ONE

THE MUSIC EDUCATOR AS AN INSTRUCTIONAL LEADER

> **The final justification of all the billion-dollar programs, all the lofty educational policy, all the organizational efforts is that somewhere an individual child learns something that he might not have learned, or grows in understanding, or gains in skill or capacity or insight.**
>
> **John W. Gardner**

Music educators are no different in most respects than their counterparts in other fields of education. They are individuals who by interest, training and experience work with people engaged in the learning of music. They also select the content and strategies by which the learning of music is made possible. These choices are dictated by the attitudes, beliefs, professional expertise and personal competence of the music educator.

Good programs of music education are made possible where there are persons in the classroom and administration who *believe* in the importance of music as an academic discipline and aesthetic experience. Good programs also depend upon *what the music educator knows about his art* and *how effective he is in communicating this knowledge through the teaching-learning process.* The alchemy by which this occurs in the professional growth of music educators we shall call *the "Y" (why) Factor.* In terms of this book, this will also be known as *LEADERSHIP FOR LEARNING.*

Leadership For Learning – The "Y" (Why) Factor

The successful leader in music education must first be a competent teacher. This means that individuals who expect to be successful leaders must have a thorough knowledge of both content and process. They must also possess positive traits of personality which provide them with organizational ability as well as the warmth of persons who relate in a positive fashion to those with whom they are in contact. The title given to this individual is of less importance than *what the individual does.* In the terms of this book, however, the role of leadership in music education may be assumed by such persons as:

— the music specialist who instructs in several schools
— the music teacher who is a leader of students in any one school
— a department chairman
— an ad hoc chairman of any music committee (such as a city-wide music curriculum committee)
— a teacher-coordinator who is designated as a spokesman for his teacher colleagues in a school system
— the music consultant (any area, any level)
— the district music coordinator
— a director of music education or supervisor of music for a large school unit (such as a city, county or state)

Leadership qualifications place emphasis on persons who give evidence of a high degree of insight and skill in four principal areas; namely:

Professional competence
Personal qualities and relationships with others
Understanding of educational processes
Understanding the dynamics of change

Professional Competence of Leaders in Music Education

Understanding the art of music is the first requisite for a successful teacher or leader in music education. It is important that the very fabric of the art be understood as well as experienced--why music has unique qualities which make the teaching and learning of music different from other areas of human experience. This subject will be discussed in Chapter Two, *MUSIC: AN ART AND ACADEMIC DISCIPLINE.*

Understanding the implications of growth and development in learning is also an essential for music educators since this will provide the key to the selection and organization of material, teaching strategies, and tools of evaluation. Unless music educators are thoroughly aware of the educational implications arising from a knowledge of learners and learning process, no effective goals, objectives and teaching techniques can be applied. Music "facts" must be understood as being inseparable from experiencing music. Contrary to the misguided beliefs of latter-day educators who arbitrarily assigned certain types of music experience to fixed grade levels or acted on rather vague notions of what children and adolescents should be capable of performing at certain ages, there is a considerable amount of research which is available to guide our actions. We now know that *individuals grow and develop in music much in the same way as in any other area of learning*--it is principally the subject matter of music which differs. Thus, it is possible to know and utilize the ideas of Piaget, Gagné, Guilford and others--and to realize that such things as open education and individualization are equally valid for music. The strategies of the Contemporary Music Project and Manhattanville Music Curriculum Program now become viable alternatives to the dictum of arbitrary grade level learning which frequently created bored, frustrated and "drop-out" problem students. These implications for learning will also be discussed in later chapters, particularly Chapters Three and Four.

Professional preparation and competence include such things as knowledge of subject matter, breadth of general information, knowledge and handling of basic skills, and understanding of the teaching-learning process. In today's teacher education institutions, emphasis is placed upon *competency based instruction.* Thus, while state certification of teachers in each of the fifty states requires evidence of the completion of a stated degree and/or number of credits, the prima facie evidence of readiness to teach is gained through an assessment of the individual's *competence to handle the given subject matter in instructional situations.* These competencies are described by the Teacher Education Commission of the Music Educators National Conference, as follows:[1]

I. PERSONAL QUALITIES

1A. Qualities of leadership

1B. Intellectual curiosity

1C. Social commitment

1D. Role of the teacher

II. MUSICAL COMPETENCIES

2A. Musical competencies in producing sounds
Performance (principal instrument or voice)
Improvisation
Conducting
Ancillary instruments, singing ability, keyboard

2B. Musical competencies in organizing sounds
Composing — be able to use compositional skills
Arranging — arrange and adapt music for instruction

2C. Musical competencies in describing sounds
Analyzing — identify, explain structural forms & procedures

2D. Knowledge of history, repertoire, and performance practices
Repertoire — many media and compositional practices
History and styles — all principal eras, styles and practices
Non-Western music cultures

III. PROFESSIONAL QUALITIES

3A. Educational psychology — identify and explain principles of learning applied to music

3B. Philosophical and social foundations — be familiar with philosophical and social bases underlying music and education

3C. Individual differences — be able to assess differing backgrounds, abilities and interests of individuals and groups of students

3D. Professional growth — understand developmental process involved in becoming a successful teacher, applied to continuous study and self-evaluation

IV. GENERAL EDUCATION — study outside of music
- 4A. Arts, including areas of music not prescribed in major
- 4B. Humanities and social studies
- 4C. Physical and natural sciences
- 4D. Electives in liberal arts

Personal Qualities and Relationships With Others

Leadership in instruction, whether as a teacher or "status leader"[2] requires a variety of personal skills if ideas and music skills are to be communicated effectively. Whereas individuals may be reasonably effective in small group endeavors with a modicum of what may be described generally as a friendly, interacting personality and concern for others, these qualities alone are too generalized to be the sole agents for leadership in most instances simply because education now is a diverse, highly sophisticated operation. The older norms of appearance, alertness, voice-speech, emotional poise, flexibility and adaptability (sometimes described as "attitude") no longer can be taken as infallible criterion indices of personal qualifications of teachers and educational leaders, since we can find no evidence of fixed norms to which such terms may be applied. In their place, it is suggested that we substitute "situational" criteria for assessing personal factors. These criteria suggest ways of determining the effectiveness of individuals in meeting the demands of situations which may typically be found in education.

Personal qualities of music educators:[3]

Appearance, manner, bearing and impression on others — tactful, courteous, enthusiastic and forceful without undue aggressiveness; makes unusually favorable impression on others.

Mental alertness

— grasps ideas easily, has sound judgment, is exceptionally quick to understand; is creative and resourceful in a variety of situations.

Effectiveness of voice and speech

— voice is superior in quality and expressiveness; speaks distinctly; pronounces accurately.

Effectiveness of oral and written expression

— has extensive vocabulary; is concise, interesting and logical.

Emotional poise

— consistently acts decisively and with good judgment; has excellent self-control; appropriate sense of humor; inspires healthy pupil response.

Adaptability; resourcefulness; dependability

— highly adaptable; moves easily and comfortably to the new or unexpected; completely dependable in relationships and responsibilities; always well-prepared.

Professional attitude

— ethical and professional in all duties and relationships and is willing to extend self; sees teaching as more than just a classroom; has a broad view of the profession; accepts his roles and responsibilities and carries them out.

Ability to meet the physical demands of the job

— has great vitality; appearance and regular attendance to duties suggest optimum health.

Interpersonal and leadership qualities of music educators:

Self-motivated and personally organized

— is enthusiastic about and seeks ways to be more effective in educational duties; although not a "nit-picker" nor pigeon-holer, organizes work effectively and efficiently for optimum results.

Has purpose and sense of direction

— knows where he is going and the purpose of his

efforts; is able to write or verbalize about instructional objectives and priorities; can communicate these ideas to others with clarity and objectivity.

Is responsible

— can be counted upon to make decisions, accept responsibility and act accordingly; evaluates or accepts the evaluations of others in judging the educational product involved and in re-affirming or modifying the procedures utilized.

Is accepted by others

— is understanding and responsive to students and associates and takes this into account in his actions; is friendly and accepted as a fellow human being by associates; acts impartially and objectively after consultation with those who are affected by his actions.

Understands and utilizes efficient processes

— grasps the dynamics of group relationships and processes; is effective in organizing work with a minimum of wasted effort; can analyze job characteristics and plan efficient procedures to handle them; assists associates in working together to realize common goals.

Is accepted as a teacher

— is recognized as a master teacher of music by students and associates.

Understanding Educational Processes

One of the most important requisites of successful leaders in music education is the ability to understand and implement educational processes. This requires that such persons be competent to assess the learning needs of students in terms of their backgrounds, interests and capacities; be able to establish valid long and short-range educational goals in music; be able to translate these goals into behavioral terms for classroom instruction; know the necessary materials and personnel required to implement these behaviors and serve as a catalyst and organizer for such implementation; be able to plan instructional strategies for a variety of learners under various conditions and circumstances; and be able to establish procedures for evaluating the program and make the necessary changes and revisions where inadequacies are revealed.

The leader in music education must be a catalytic agent between his own art of music and the students in the music program. To be responsive to the type of students in the school, the leader must be able to assess the nature of the community in which the school or school system is located. The leader must know how to "listen" to its needs and educational aspirations, yet be able to lead where he understands how to effect better music education in the community's schools.

As an educational leader, the music educator also must know the overall philosophy and goals of the educational system as a whole and must serve in a larger sense to implement and support these objectives. This requires that the individual seeks to improve all avenues of communication between himself and colleagues at all levels in the educational system. It is important that music educators be as informed as possible about other disciplines and be ready to support their legitimate goals, as it would be hoped that music would be supported. The personal and professional rapport of the members of the total educational staff should be one of the first priorities of the music educator.

A unique aspect of the human organism is its adaptability and capacity for growth--*if given the opportunity.* Music educators must recognize this potential within themselves and be willing to discover ways to utilize their own capacities for personal and professional growth. This will require, in addition to other things, continuous involvement in music-making, as well as a systematic growth in a knowledge of materials and processes by which music is communicated to others.

Understanding the Dynamics of Change

So much has happened to profoundly affect education during the past two decades that the music educator whose head is buried in the sand has become quickly out of date. To understand how music is related to these events and influences, the music educator must be competent to understand and act in terms of the dynamics of change. While these changes have affected society as a whole, many are specific influences and trends within education in general and music education in particular. It is the latter with which we shall be concerned primarily.

One of the basic problems of institutions, including that of education, is that a great deal of their energies have been devoted to preserving the *status quo.* This is unfortunately true in terms of educational method and curriculum content--and, it is also true as applied to the way individuals work or do not work together to implement instruction. Unless inspired to function otherwise, many teachers tend to teach as they were taught, despite the wealth of research which could point the direction to a better way of doing things.

If it can be agreed that *education should serve the individuals within its societal structure,* and that *selective changes in both content and procedure may be desirable to sustain the learners who are growing up in that society,* we should begin to examine our priorities for education.

Goodlad suggests that unlike some former eras in the United States, our society now expects its learners to go on learning to the fullest of their potentials.[4] Society now has a complex array of communication systems which require that each person become familiar with the one belonging to his own system. We now are confronted by world-wide advances in technology. But our communication with other societies has now virtually outstripped our ability to effectively clarify our own role with individuals who are now our "world neighbors". The body of knowledge available to any person and the variety of techniques for exploring and developing this knowledge has long since outstripped our capacity to understand how to cope with this information.

One significant change is that of the length of the work week. In former days, leisure time was thought to be one of the luxuries of the aristocrat. Today, leisure has come within the grasp of workers and professional people in almost all segments of society. However, with the freeing of man from his labors, society has not kept pace with the ability to help individuals use that leisure time productively. Music education is in a position to fill this gap; consequently, leaders must accept the challenge and find ways of helping students of all ages find ways for productive self-fulfillment.

Figure 1

YOUTH VALUES IN CONTEMPORARY AMERICAN SOCIETY RE-AFFIRMED AND MODIFIED

(Havighurst Model)

	Personal Values	**Social Values**
Receding Values:	Individual saving and thrift Work as a major source of self-respect	Nationalistic, provincial and paraochial preferences
Stable Values:	Autonomy Rational conscience Rational foresight Instrumental activism Achievement motivation Productivity Worship	Loyalty to one's society Friendliness Social Responsibility Family interaction Social progress and social change
Emerging Values:	Expressive activity Aesthetic appreciation Widening and deeping of experience Tolerance of complexity and ambiguity	International and ecumenical cooperation Intranational opportunity and justice Agape--service in an open society Organizational loyalty and cooperation

It does not require a highly trained observer to note evidences of change. As educators, however, we should be acutely aware of those which are affecting students. In Figure 1, we note personal and social values of youth, both re-affirmed and modified, as adapted from Robert J. Havinghurst's youth value theorem.[5] What is generally spoken of as "the generation gap" often results from a failure to recognize what has happened to young people as a result of our vastly accelerated pace and many of the changes which have affected society as a whole. It is difficult, for instance, for many adults who grew up before the age of TV, space travel, and global communications to understand that static conditions can no longer cope with young people whose entire life style has changed from that of most adults over thirty years of age. Even in music education, the pervasive influences of electronic music and the rock culture, both slightly over ten years of age, have been far reaching. To ignore them in working with young persons is to suggest that neither has validity or relevance--an astonishing stance for any educator!

Students in the schools of the Seventies have different expectations and perceptions than those of the prior generation. Formerly students had few standards by which they might compare information, feelings, and judgments. Teaching which was acceptable a decade or two ago now may bore children of the television age who are used to the more sophisticated approach of the media, as exemplified in Sesame Street and the Electric Company. Yet, in all probability, today's generation of students is infinitely more attuned to the times--even more eager than former generations to learn.

Music and the arts have evolved from an elitist experience, oriented strictly in upper-class social structure and value systems, to a position where children of the "common man" may enjoy these influences *on their own terms.* Faced with massive population migrations, industrialization, technology and automation, our society has undergone wholesale changes in value systems--some subtle, but each being concerned with an increasing empathy for qualitative aspects of living. Although some artistic influences have deteriorated due to an over-emphasis on commercialism, much of significant and lasting value has been produced as a result of this concern. Whether these influences will prevail as a result of public education will depend largely upon the effectiveness of leadership in music education.

The following are some of the implications of change which should be understood by the music educator:

1. There should be an increased emphasis on music as a means of communicating human feelings. Thus, students should be exposed to the nature of music as a feelingful art and how it is related to the humanistic endeavors of mankind (including the present interests of youth).
2. The experiencing of music is a personal matter and individuals vary greatly in the way they learn and react to music--hence, greater emphasis should be placed upon individualized learning.
3. Since music is no longer an "elitist" subject, there should be ample opportunities *at all levels* for music experiences for *all* learners. This should include performance and "non-performance" classes for a wide spectrum of students in addition to the more traditional activities designed for those of higher motivation and skill.
4. Music curricula and the materials and techniques of instruction should be as innovative and imaginative as possible.
5. As early as possible in the student's exposure to music, he should have ample opportunity to *experience music on his own terms in a variety of ways,* including performing, composing, listening and conducting.
6. The subject matter of music, if it is to be truly representative of various styles, periods, and performance media, should include a wider spectrum of ethnic and contemporary music of all kinds.
7. Music should be a "vertical" curricular subject--that it to say, it should be available throughout the individual's entire formal schooling.
8. Music educators must begin to apply the results of research

which reveals that there are many forms of learning which affect music. It should be recognized that the individual's motivation, interest, and permanence of retention are greatly enhanced by discovery and inductive learning which is centered in the music itself (rather than peripheral activities). Consequently, the music educator should attempt to *guide and stimulate* rather than direct learning activities.

In terms of this book, it is suggested that leaders in music education consider the broad perspective of change in education. Although changes in society have had great influence on many of our institutions, succeeding generations of children must be aided in their understanding of the past as well as the present. Programs of music education must be broadly and eclectically conceived in order to reflect an interplay of the many musical functions and styles which have become important artistic forces in our society. With this in mind, music educators should explore all the possibilities for making music education a profound, individualized, subjective-feelingful experience.

Subsequent chapters in this Section will deal with Foundations of Music and Music Learning.

Summary

This Chapter has dealt with the successful leader in music education--whether teacher, department chairman, or "status" leader--emphasizing the importance of competence in instruction. To be such a leader, the music educator must possess a high degree of insight and skill in (a) professional competence; (b) personal qualities and relationships with others; (c) understanding of educational processes; and, (d) understanding the dynamics of change. The individual must be a competent musician who thoroughly *understands the art of music.* There must be a high degree of leadership ability, intellectual curiosity, social commitment and understanding of the role of the teacher. There must also be a high degree of competence in music and music-making, as well as the ability to communicate these ideas in contemporary pedagogical and personal ways.

Topics For Discussion

1. Construct a "model." list describing the attributes of an effective leader in music education, as contrasted with a less effective leader.
2. Discuss the importance of the "Musical Competencies" recommended by the MENC Commission on Teacher Education in your own professional preparation.
3. Think of some of the groups of individuals with whom you have been in contact recently. How do some of the people in the group "come across" as leaders? Is there a difference between "dominating" and "leading" groups?
4. Interview a successful music educator (either a teacher or "status" leader). You may devise your own interview structure; or, (a) ask the following structured questions: (1) What do you feel are the most important characteristics of leaders in music education? (2) Is it possible for persons to be successful leaders who are mediocre musicians and teachers? Why? (3) What organizational and social qualities should the leader possess? (4) Can you suggest some of the recent changes in education (and society) which you feel to have profound effect on music education?
5. Do you feel there are any persistent value conflicts between youth and those who govern and/or support public schools; and, if so, how are these manifested? Do you see some solutions to this?
6. As a leader in music education, how would you go about helping supporters of local schools feel a need for change? (Curriculum, method, or other.)
7. Which is the most important strategy for music educators in working on curriculum and other matters concerning the "educational structure"--is it more important to retain, modify, change, or supplant existing conditions? Can you apply all of these under certain circumstances?
8. Can the fulfillment of human potential be conceived in terms other than those of financial or vocational orientation? Is it possible that this also may be overshadowed by intrinsic aesthetic experience in music?

Suggested Readings

Association for Supervision and Curriculum Development. *To Nurture Humaneness: Commitment for the 70's,* 1970 Yearbook. Washington, D.C.: The Association, 1970. Qualities of humaneness discussed as a rationale for its nurture in education.

Bessom, Malcolm E., Alphonse M. Tatarunis and Samuel L. Forcucci. *Teaching Music in Today's Secondary Schools.* New York: Holt, Rinehart and Winston, Inc., 1974. Ch. I. discusses qualities of the successful music educator.

Goodlad, John I. *School, Curriculum, and the Individual.* Waltham, Mass.: Blaisdell Publishing Company, 1966.

Kroll, Arthur M. (Ed) *Issues in American Education.* New York: Oxford University Press, 1970. Humanistic approaches to schools, technology and education.

Leeper, Robert R. and Fred T. Wilhelms (Eds) *Supervision: Emerging Profession: Readings from Educational Leadership.* Washington, D.C.

Music Educators National Conference, Commission on Teacher Education. *Teacher Education in Music: Final Report.* Washington, D.C.: The Commission, 1972. A helpful list of competencies needed by the successful music educator.

CHAPTER TWO

MUSIC – AN ART AND ACADEMIC DISCIPLINE

Music is well said to be the speech of angels.
Carlyle

Since the launching of Sputnik in 1957, both the public and professional educators have examined the curriculum with increasing concern. Public education following that event was confronted by demands for better content and methodology. The initial impact of the pressure brought by forces outside the schools was to provide accelerated emphasis on mathematics and science. In time, the hue and cry resulted in a second look at other areas of the curriculum, including the social sciences and arts.

Although some governing boards were forced to curtail music offerings and services in the rush to find solutions which would appease the critics, the humanities and arts survived due to counter-pressures brought about by more rational minds. Among the supporters of music education were many prominent figures in American public and private affairs who pointed out that while some reforms were desirable, there must be balance in the curriculum--and, *the arts were essential in such a balance.*[1]

As a result of the re-evaluation forced on public education, musicians and music educators alike began to re-examine their art not as a foregone reality, but *in terms of the unique qualities which make music an important area of human experience.* Consequently, music educators and administrators have re-discovered the *raison d'être* for the existence of music in the school curriculum. From this new look have come several new beliefs about the nature of music as an art form as well as an understanding of the qualities of music which make it such a pervasive influence in the lives of youngsters and adults alike. These emerging considerations have begun to make music a more effective part of the total educational program of the public school.

The study of how music should affect learning experience at any level of education should begin with an understanding of (a) the nature of music as an art form; (b) the affective as well as cognitive aspects of musical learning; and, (c) how music is experienced in an institutional (i.e., school) setting.

The Nature Of Music As An Art Form

Music is an aural art which unfolds in tone and time through the sense of hearing. The professional music educator understands that the experience of music involves both affective and cognitive domains of learning. And, since music also involves physical responses as well, the psychomotor aspect of learning must also be included. In an educational setting, it is important that students be able to *respond to* as well as *comprehend musical experience* in a variety of satisfying ways, depending on the stimuli and circumstances involved. In this way, learners will understand the unique qualities and relationships which are essential to musical experience.

By defining music as a tonal and temporal art, we are reiterating the notion that it exists both in sound and in time. In addition, since it is an art work created by human beings, it expresses the feelings and creative energies of the persons who gave it birth. Whether good, bad, or indifferent, music communicates the subjective feelings of the subconscious which seeks a response from the apprehender in terms of a state of feeling or comprehending. This may be described as *mystical experience* in which the mystique is better known as *aesthetic experience.*

Kaplan suggests that music, as one dimension of aesthetics,

draws substantially from the realm of philosophy by means of its logical procedures as well as in its terminology.[2] However, this author cautions the reader not to be misled by the parallel which could lead in the direction of ontology, epistemology and axiology (meaning that which is considered to be real, true and of value). Rather, music should be approached in terms of its origin, nature, criteria and cultural manifestations--all values which are indigenous to the nature of true aesthetic expression. The focus should be placed on matters which govern the medium of musical experience, such as performance, composition, listening, conducting, criticism, and the like. In addition, theoretical problems which become the criteria by which musical values and tastes are derived should be explored. The foregoing are all aspects of musical experience and are all inherently bound to sound, symbolism, and the unique relationship of music to the senses and the intellect. Aesthetic experiencing occurs when the individual's beliefs, knowledge, feelings, critical judgments, and physique are combined as a totality. Thus, conditioned attitude and behavior, all important in the learning process, become components of aesthetic experience.

McLuhan proposes the idea that art imitates life and that art and technology are somehow related as extensions of some physical or psychic elements of man. This quality makes music assume the dimension of what he terms an "exploration in perception," which provides additional meaning for the structure of music in the school curriculum. No longer, says McLuhan, should music be considered as a luxury curricular item, since the arts ". . . now become a dynamic way of tuning up the sensorium and of providing fresh ways of looking at familiar things."[3]

Another dimension of music is provided by Meyer who points out that since it is man-made and man-controlled, music is not a natural system. By means of what is described as *designed uncertainty* (introduced by the composer), Meyer feels that music as an art form is able to combat the tendency toward the tedium of maximum certainty. Thus, *creative variety,* not possible in nature, becomes an essential ingredient of the act of musical creation.[4]

One of the six principal realms of meaning described by Phenix is that of aesthetics. This realm is conceptualized as including the visual arts, the arts of movement, literature and music. It is concerned with those contemplative perceptions of unique, particular significance. The other realms of meaning described by Phenix include those of symbolics (language and symbolic structures), empirics (physical and natural sciences), synnoetics (personal knowledge or cognition), ethics (moral meanings), and synoptics (comprehensively integrative meanings such as history, religion, and philosophy). All six realms provide the foundations for man's total experience and determine the quality of his life style. A well-rounded individual should be skilled in each of these realms in order to make use of such attributes and information and to be capable of ". . . creating and appreciating objects of aesthetic significance. . ."[5]

Creating and experiencing music are different acts. Reimer indicates that a person may have an extremely significant aesthetic experience either as a performer or listener, but only the composer is truly creative.[6] The act of *experiencing*, however, is particularly important in education--but it is not the exclusive way in which students should be exposed to music, since even very young children may also create. Again, it must be remembered that both experiencing and creating music are a form of aesthetic experience since they involve affective and cognitive qualities. In education, it should also be pointed out that true aesthetic meaning is gained by acquaintance with the substance of music--not by description. Much of the uniqueness of musical experience is brought about by the act of working with music in such a way that it is directly related to qualities within the music. Unlike other experience which may be induced by empirical knowledge or symbolism, music itself is "the message".[7]

The Form And Substance Of Music

It is perhaps the manner in which music is constructed--its unique "grammar" and "syntax"--which provides the substance of music as an art form. It is unfortunate that music is frequently described as a "language"--thus giving an inappropriate and untrustworthy analogy to our most common form of verbal communication. There are also those who would suggest that music provides a referential or trustworthy image of life, although it is well known that music probably is incapable of expressing any specific feelings associated with life. There probably is no precise analogy to language or specific human feeling, although both are involved with music in other ways. Certainly there is an absence of semantics which may convey either spoken meaning or the written symbolism of language. Even songs are not in themselves precisely a language, since the total sense impression conveyed by musical tone must be associated with words for a complete understanding of their meaning. The language of music is nondiscursive, non-symbolic, and non-metaphorical, and is indeed organized to a different logic than is found in such autonomous disciplines as English grammar, mathematics, and science.

The well-known American composer, William Schumann describes music as "an art of communication," and indicates that due to this phenomenon, music as an art form occupies a unique social position directly proportional to its role in contemporary life.[8] In large part, this suggests one of the reasons for the immediacy and popularity of folk and rock culture in contemporary life.

Language and music both contain patterned sound-sequences, but are differentiated in that the former (including its aural or symbolic state) reveals discursive meanings, whereas music communicates intellectual, emotional and qualitative meanings which provide us with what may be termed *musical feeling.* Dewey speaks of the unitary aspect of [musical] experience by means of which it attains aesthetic quality--which is, in a sense, the quality of *emotion.*[9] Probably it is this unifying quality which is of unique importance in any consideration of the art of music.

Since music is an aural experience, it follows logically that it also exists in terms of its acoustical properties. Broadly speaking, musical sound is vibration. Music also exists solely in a world of time which is revealed to the listener bit by bit. It is a bit like attempting to grasp the meaning of a picture by viewing it inch by inch. To make sense of the music, a listener must be able to make many meaningful connections between its various elements, including trying to recall sound previously heard and trying to anticipate that which is yet to come--meanwhile being immersed in attempting to grasp the sound of the immediate moment. Little wonder that the neophyte learner may say he does not like nor understand music on first hearing!

In order that some descriptive analysis of the substance be made, the following attributes of music are suggested:

1. Musical meanings will be derived in part by understanding the *scientific origins of music.*
2. Music experiencing may be viewed as an *aural translation of sound.*
3. Music is composed of a combination of *unique elements of sound.*
4. Music may be viewed as a form of communication of human feelings and emotions, which will be termed *the aesthetics of musical expression.*
5. Music may be described in terms of its *musical structures.*
6. Music may also be described in terms of either *referential* or *absolute meanings.*
7. Music should be viewed in terms of a Gestalt totality of *intellectual, physical, feelingful, and emotional qualities.*

In order that the reader may obtain a better idea of this construct describing the form and substance of music, let us first examine some of the aforementioned methods of descriptive analysis.

The Scientific Origins of Music help us to understand some of the sound and accoustical properties of music and to make traditional distinctions between "noise" and "musical tone", as well as helping us realize that some of the customary distinctions are completely lacking in contemporary usage. We know that sound, including musical tone, is produced by vibrations of varying speed and intensity. "Conventional" musical tone has definite pitch, intensity and color--and is generally expressed in a given duration. Contemporary usage provides the composer-performer-listener with a wider variety of sound, however. Nevertheless, the basic idiom of sound results from vibrations produced either in the human voice box or by mechanical or electronic means, as in instrumental or electronic music. Consequently, it is important for the music educator as well as the student to understand the physical elements of producing music either as a singer or instrumentalist.

To view music simply as a scientific experience, however, is to ignore the fact that art and science deal with different areas of human knowledge and experience. The practitioner of music may utilize some of the methods of the scientist, but when dealing with the subjective material of which music is made, he is far from the realm of science.

The Aural Translation of Sound, more specifically referred to here as non-musical symbolics (the printed notation of music), also appears to have little relationship with the actual form and substance of music. Although the symbolism of music is important in helping the performer "decode" the intent of the composer, the analogy of a musical language is actually false, since semantic meanings cannot be conveyed by musical sound. Its meaning is not verbal, tonal, nor emotional language per se, since its terms (sounds) defy precise definition or translation. Perhaps it is just the fact that *musical sounds are not conventional language conveyed by symbols of precise communication* provides us with the clue to the enormous power of music to reach our inner beings in a way in which language cannot.

Although symbolics are a dimension of re-creating music, the unique element of musical symbolism is *insight* rather than information. Reimer describes this quality of art-symbolism as *presentational* rather than discursive--the latter as in language where words, exemplified by sentence structure, are strung out like a "strand of pearls".[10] Instead, the symbolics of art have an "all-at-oneness" by which they assist us in becoming immersed in a total feelingful experience.

Referential, Absolute Meanings of Music, while valid for *some* music, do not seem appropriate as a complete description for reasons similar to the symbolics approach. If this statement were completely valid, music as a referential experience would need to have particular meanings, concepts, emotions, and qualities which are actually non-musical or extra-musical. *Absolutism* undoubtedly comes closer to the inner nature of music, since it deals with meanings obtained solely from the music itself. These meanings, however, fall short of providing a complete description of the art.

The Unique Elements of Sound provide an approach by which music may be analyzed in terms of its tone, duration, timbre and intensity.

The Gestaltist Totality of Intellectual, Physical, Feelingful, and Emotional Qualities of music provide us with a synthesizing, unifying approach which help to explain the unique expressional qualities by which musical feeling and ideas are communicated.

Music educators should thus learn to reject musical experiences which place undue emphasis on the science of sound, non-musical symbolics and referential meanings. In place of these, students should be helped to approach music as a totality of *intellectual, physical, feelingful, and emotional sensory impressions* (Figure 2). This concept would also include acoustics, musical elements, expression, structures (medium, form, style and design), symbolics, and referential meanings *only as appropriate to the total understanding of music.* This unified approach is what Dewey terms a *perceptual whole,* consisting of related parts in which no one single item is selected to further some "external" result.[11]

Figure 2

THE FORM AND SUBSTANCE OF MUSIC

Valid - Accept	Less Valid - Reject
Combination of elements	
Meaningful structures	Scientific dimension
Mode of expression	Non-musical symbolics
Intellectual-physical-feelingful and emotional qualities	Referential meanings

The construct which helps the individual "put music together" into a meaningful whole requires the person who is experiencing or creating music to make his own intellectual-emotional-sensory connections, just as a person would see-feel-and apprehend a brick wall to be a wall rather than a pile of bricks having only individual, non-connecting characteristics. In order that the individual be able to comprehend what his sensory and emotional impressions are, however, the person engaged in a musical experience must intellectually acquaint himself with those musical elements and structures which provide the total sensory impression. In this way, the unique totality of any musical experience may better be understood. Thus, education must provide the learner with the tools for musical experiencing and understanding.

Music And Meaning

In addition to the form and substance of music, there are other insights which are helpful in understanding music. These include a knowledge of (a) the elements of which music is composed; (b) how these elements are shaped into "patterns" and "forms"; (c) the historical setting in which music has been "put together"; (d) the persons who have produced our music over the ages; and, (e) the various media by which music is produced.

Being chiefly subjective in nature, music is also affected by value systems and musical taste. These are predicted upon the amount and quality of musical experience. Schwadron suggests that taste is a product of our response to varying musical stimuli, and is also a reflection of what has happened in that musical experience.[12] This includes the individual's capacity for symbolization and abstractness, cultural conditioning, and subjective likes and dislikes. This would suggest that there are various levels of meaning and understanding based not only on the nature of the experience, but the plurality of values and the valuing processes of the person involved.

The substance of music and other art forms may be viewed (or heard) in terms of commonalities as well as differences. In speaking of the commonalities of substance, Dewey suggests that every art product is "matter and matter only", whether it be pigments on canvas, words either spoken or written, or the energy and organization of musical sound.[13] Even on first apprehending a work of art, its total and massive quality has its own uniqueness, even though vague and undefined. The initial experiencing of music which will be discussed later as *perception* inevitably becomes the first stage in musical discrimination. Attention given to music or the art form cannot remain static, but is constantly moving and reacting. Yet the arts have a pervading quality of unity as well as variety since attention and experiencing can be controlled and operated within the art form itself.

Every work of art also is expressed by a particular medium which requires that the apprehender experience it by means of some specialized sensory organ. The basic situation is a *felt* relationship between doing and undergoing as the organism and environment react. The differences are those provided by the qualities of sound, form, texture, design, color, etc., which make music a singular and unique art.

Langer expresses musical meaning as a different interpretation of symbolism which gives "artistic truth" as a rationale for musical significance, expressiveness, and articulateness.[14]

Still another dimension of musical meaning is found in the realm of expectation which brings into clarity the psychologically affective state of music. This, according to Meyer, suggests that musical meaning which is embodied within the total experience of music is, in short, a product of one's expectation rather than rational logic.[15] This construct would lead to the belief that as a result of one's prior experience with music, the present musical stimulus would lead to an "expectation" of certain things to come, and in this sense meaning is obtained from the stimulus. Such a rationale forms the basis for an understanding of why some musical experience is totally meaningless, for, in order to be truly meaningful, it must be possible for a person to anticipate and comprehend the style and form of the experience which he is undergoing.

Britton emphasizes that the *sina qua non* of musical understanding is obtained by means of repeated musical listening.[16]

He further suggests that persons can begin to understand music by such devices as first sorting out musical phrases and carefully giving attention to this aspect of the unfolding music. Later, one should attempt to grasp other ways by which music is put together, attempting to see how music is extended in time and tone. To understand its meaning, we must begin to recognize music for what it really is--a totality of tonal nuance and color in many media, styles, and patterns. This obviously requires some understanding of the "grammar" and "syntax" of music, as well as numerous repetitions in hearing or performing music.

In its truest perspective, musical meaning is *affective* and *cognitive* rather than symbolic; *absolute-expressionism* rather than referential; *qualitative* rather than quantitative; *imprecise* and *generalized* rather than classified and specific; *subjective* rather than objective; and, in short is an *art form* rather than an exact science.

Experiencing Music

In order to gain a better understanding of how man perceives music, reference is again made to a dichotomy in musical meaning. Accordingly, the *absolutist* is a person who insists that musical meaning is wrapped up in the musical work itself and that meanings are obtained from the nature and relationships which occur strictly within the dimensions of the art form itself. Contrary to this idea, the *referentialist* believes that a musical work has particular meanings, concepts, emotions and qualities in addition to any abstract art qualities contained therein. Simplistic comparisons of these two positions should be avoided, since neither is found exclusive of the other. Thus, every musical work should have ideas, feelings, and functions which are indigenous in the work itself--but many of these influences will be brought to bear in terms of the human experience which results from its composition or performance.

Performance is sometimes considered erroneously to be a highly original and creative act. Although performance may be *sensitive* and *artistic,* it is not in and of itself a creative endeavor, unless highly unusual liberties are made by the performer--or unless the performance results in free improvisation. While performing requires a comparable amount of technical skill to composing, the performer actually is but the intermediary between the creator (composer) and the listener. His work is not truly original since it is actually a reflection of the created work.

The experiencing of music, particularly the new and untried, cannot be purely sensory in nature, for, as Meyer points out, ". . . music is directed not *to* the senses, but *through* the senses and *to the mind*."[17] The cognitive perception of an unfamiliar work, much like the repetitive apprehension suggested by Britton, requires a greater number of neural-mental decisions wherein relationships and implications are understood than that which is required when one is experiencing a familiar work or style. Since perception implies a recognizable sensation or impression received by the mind through the senses, it becomes evident that *perception is thus critically dependent upon learning.*

The way one perceives, understands and responds to music in terms of its content and organizational structure is established by means of the individual's own experiental background. Thus a type of learned behavior-response may become a form of *educated bias.* Experiencing or perceiving music can never be passive--certainly not indifferent.

Just as the various forms of human communication (i.e., verbal or written) depend upon an understanding of either the natural forces about us or of learned sign relationships, musical communication depends upon learning the subjective probabilities of musical content and style. These may be understood in terms of perceptions, cognition, feeling, expectation, habits and so on. Such phenomena may furnish a further explanation of why some musical experiences fail in educational settings while others outside of school succeed.

Obviously, some types of exposure to music are not really aesthetic experience--however, they may form the basis for it. It may be pointed out that the music instructor who insists on endless isolated drill and learning of facts, symbols, etc. is simply going about the motions of providing a musical experience. The truly aesthetic quality of musical experiencing involves a plurality of responses *directed toward* or *centered in* the actual music involved.

Although the subject of musical experience in an educational setting will be discussed later in PART TWO, the subject should not be left without some generalization of what has been said here. Perceptive experiencing demands a concentrated direction of attention toward music itself. An individual's sensitivity (roughly, the qualitative aspect of hearing music) depends on many factors, perhaps the most important of which involves the *way the individual apprehends music* directed toward *the awareness of meaningful structures which are unique elements in music.*

Music: Societal Need And Educational Imperative

Speaking to educators of the United States shortly after the advent of Sputnik, Finis E. Engleman, Executive Secretary of the American Association of School Administrators pointed out that while America and the world had been shaken by the physical accomplishments of men of science, other values were being neglected. Although new energies and technologies could literally move mountains or take man to the moon, the need to consider priorities which are not rooted in material values and technical skill is acute. ". . . the modern world has a particular need for men educated in science but also in the creative arts and humanities as well. Without either a horrible vacuum will occur."[18]

The point of view of this book is that music should not only be capable of yielding insights into the nature of art, but should also be relevant to our society and to the general conditions under which we live. Whereas some civilizations and nations have perverted art to serve anti-social goals, music best serves society when it is not designed to serve specific social objectives. Music and art must convey *aesthetic meanings* which are independent of moral, social, political, or semantic references.

The importance of the nurture of music and the arts knows no international boundaries. In terms of its institutional structures, the International Society for Music Education provides eloquent proof of the rising interest in sharing aesthetic values and educational technologies throughout a large segment of the civilized world. The author's own visits to music schools in Bulgaria, Portugal, Spain, Great Britain and Yugoslavia have yielded personal insights to support this belief. While developments in traditional countries studied in schools of this country are fairly well known, ethno-musicologists are discovering a vast storehouse of virtually untapped musical resources among the peoples of Africa, Asia and the South Pacific, to mention but a few. Even less-known materials are being uncovered constantly in our own country!

The Yale and Tanglewood meetings between concerned lay persons, musicians and educators brought into focus many of the issues related to the future of music education in the United States. These meetings also pointed out that this nation must not only make choices and assign priorities in politics and economics, but must become concerned over moral and aesthetic values which are important background for leaders in music education. Specifically calling upon administrators of the schools to act, the Tanglewood Symposium spoke in unmistakable terms when it recommended that ". . . we call for music to be placed in the core of the school curriculum."[19]

If music is to become a more effective force in society, music education will require wider applications in terms both of exposure at all educational levels and its availability to a greater number of individuals. If it is to become an important part of man's formal learning, music must be available with greater relevance and enjoyability for as many persons as possible.

Man cannot isolate himself from his arts in the Seventies. Aesthetic experience will continue to be an important aspect of human and societal development. The precise manner by which man and his music accomodates change and some of the recommendations of the aforementioned groups cannot be predicted with any degree of certainty. It seems likely that individuals in our society will continue to adopt many new modes of musical expression and to extend old ones. The challenge for music education is clear, however, for if we are to cope with change or to acquaint people with current or historically significant influences of music in our culture, it is obvious that schools, curricula, and educational leadership must show the way.

Summary

The success of music education depends upon the efforts of educators to convey successfully the unique qualities which are inherent within music itself. As a form of human aesthetic experience, music is important to the complete development of individuals within our society. The professional educator, therefore, must understand the nature of music, the range of aesthetic response which it can evoke, and must know the learning milieu in which music's aesthetic qualities are best developed.

As one of man's principal art forms, music is unique in that it exists solely in tone and in time. Its mode of communication, often inaccurately described as a "language", actually conveys feelings through personal experiental involvement as a performer, creator (composer), or listener. Musical meanings are derived from the unique control of sound, symbolism, and the relationship of these to the senses and intellect. As one of the principal "realms of meaning," music is concerned with experience which is immediate and directly related to qualities which provide a totality of intellectual-emotional-sensory impressions.

Musical meaning places emphasis on felt relationships which are both affective and cognitive. The stress is on immediate, subjective, generalized and feelingful qualities which are transmitted through the senses to the intellect. The development of musical sensitivity, therefore, depends not only on the *way* music is experienced but on our ability to become *aware of its unique, meaningful components.* Perceptive experiencing demands our attention be on the object--the music itself. It is essential that these qualities be uppermost in effective programs for music education.

Topics For Discussion

1. Discuss some of the most important affective and cognitive qualities of music which are particularly meaningful to you. In what way did you first apprehend these qualities and how have you subsequently modified your feeling with additional experience?
2. In the context of musical rather than extra-musical experience, what sort of vocabulary becomes increasingly more important as people work with music?
3. Why is referentialism dangerous territory when trying to recreate musical experience? Can you cite specific examples of this?

4. What is the relationship of symbolic to real experience in music?

5. What are some of the qualities of aesthetic experience which are said to be subjective rather than objective in nature? Are there any aspects of such experience, however, which may approach objectivity? How?

6. What implications for musical taste do you see as challenges to music education?

Suggested Readings

Cassidy, Harold C. *The Sciences and the Arts.* New York: Harper, 1962.

Dewey, John. *Art as Experience,* New York: Minton, Balch and Company, 1934.

Ernst, Karl D. and Charles L. Gary (Eds). *Music in General Education.* Washington, D.C.: Music Educators National Conference, 1965. See Ch. 4.

Kaplan, Max. *Foundations and Frontiers of Music Education.* New York: Holt, Rinehart and Winston, Inc., 1966. See Ch. 2.

Meyer, Leonard B. *Emotion and Meaning in Music.* Chicago: The University of Chicago Press, 1956. Should be read in its entirety.

Mursell, James L. *Education for Musical Growth.* New York: Ginn and Company, 1948. A milestone in the philosophy of musical growth.

Music Educators National Conference. *Toward an Aesthetic Education.* Washington, D.C.: Music Educators National Conference, 1971.

Reimer, Bennett. *A Philosophy of Music Education.* Englewood Cliffs, N.J.: Prentice-Hall, Inc., 1970. This entire book is one of the significant contributions to music and aesthetic education. See Ch. 2, 3, 5, 6 and 7.

Schwadron, Abraham A. *Aesthetics: Dimensions for Music Education.* Washington, D.C.: Music Educators National Conference, 1967. See Ch. 1.

CHAPTER THREE

VALUES AND VALUING: A PHILOSOPHICAL DIMENSION

It is only liquid currents of thought that move men and the world.
Wendell Phillips

Philosophy is that aspect of man's thinking which is concerned with his beliefs about knowledge, truth, beauty and all principles by which his conduct is governed. Man's belief about the universe and of his place in this cosmos reveals his total system of values. He philosophizes whenever he wishes to reflect or act upon those things which he believes to be important in his conduct as a rational being. Values are inseparable from living experience.

Valuing implies alternative-weighing as a system of governing behavior. By means of evaluating prior experience in terms of these alternatives, an individual may chart a future course of action which is felt to be most meaningful to him. It is this act of apprehending *what actually exists* by means of *what it is thought to be;* or, of *what it should be* rather than *what it actually is* which constitutes the philosophic orientation to man's behavior. As a process, it is *subjective* rather than *objective - - - normative* rather than *descriptive - - - belief* rather than *substance.* It is also individualized rather than collective valuing. Thus, individual beliefs which are not reconciled to group values become potential sources of controversy and lead to ineffectuality of effort.

There are five organically related processes of valuing which make philosophy important to educators, since by systematic valuing:

1. We obtain a better understanding of the various beliefs which motivate society in general.
2. We examine with care our own beliefs as well as those of others, and make appropriate, compatible decisions by which our actions will be governed.
3. We are able to focus on aims and total values affecting education and educational processes.
4. We formulate specific courses of action based upon these beliefs.
5. We evaluate the outcome of our thinking in terms both of present effectiveness and possible alternatives for goal-modification.

The Nature Of Values In Education

The many forces of contemporary society, including technology, science, abundance, poverty, warfare, urbanization, automation, population growth, ecological imbalance, etc., have had marked effect on man's view of his world and his institutions. No longer can he afford the luxury of viewing education as a passive, inert influence which exists primarily to communicate and to make a living. Rather, man is becoming increasingly concerned about *how* he lives and the *qualitative aspects of living.* Thus, the structure as well as the processes of education are vitally affected by both the quality and direction of these values.

According to Campbell and Gregg, there are four specific philosophic dimensions which relate to American education. These are:[1]

1. The School is a unique institution.
2. The School takes its direction from all community institutions.
3. The School is pointed directly toward people.
4. The School is at the vortex of conflicting values.

In addition to the foregoing, there are several beliefs commonly observed in American society which serve to influence our formal system of education. Some of these tenets are:

1. An inherent faith in man and in his democratic institutions.
2. The belief in the dignity and worth of the individual.
3. The promise of self-fulfillment for each individual in our society.
4. The availability of education for all persons.
5. The evolutionary nature of change and change-processes.
6. The importance of individual participation and involvement in learning activities.
7. The nurture of creative-diversity--developing unique potentials among a heterogeneous population.
8. The concept of education which is directed primarily toward values of "living a life" rather than those which are more specifically concerned with "making a living".
9. The importance of both general and specialized domains of learning.
10. The importance of humanistic and artistic experience in education.
11. The acquisition of the basic tools of communication.

In addition to these general beliefs, it seems advisable to define those principal "schools" of philosophy which have influenced man and his institutions. These are:

1. *Realism* — the doctrine that universals have objective reality; that objects exist in themselves apart from the mind's consciousness of them.
2. *Idealism* — the theory that objects of perception actually *are* ideas of the perceiving mind--that it is possible to know that reality exists only through the mind. Thus, values are embodied in reality itself, and man in his quest for values seeks to apprehend them as ideals or norms of behavior. Life becomes qualitative in direct proportion to one's success in apprehending and making appropriate responses to these self-existing ideals.
3. *Essentialism* — the belief which began with the Renaissance and flowered during the middle of the Nineteenth Century--that learning should be grounded on the "essentials",

that tried and tested heritage of skills, facts, and laws of knowledge which has come down to us throughout recorded civilization.

4. *Perennialism or Thomism* — by far the oldest system of values in its direct origins (dating to early Greece and attaining its widest influence in the 13th century A.D.)-- this philosophy maintains that there are universal concepts and basic truths by means of which one may extract from his experience a sense of the features of things as *they are.* In this theory, knowledge is attained as the individual develops an insight into consistent universal values. This is accomplished by means of insights into knowledge and the nature of things apart from the actual experience of the individual. The social heritage is of less importance than "external" principles of truth, goodness, and beauty. This philosophy also places stress on "The Great Books" and certain aspects of doctrinaire religion.
5. *Experimentalism* — the philosophy of education which considers changes in human behavior as creations of the individual's experience. Values are not insulated nor aloof, but exist in a pluralistic milieu by means of choices exercised by the individual in reacting to his environment. *A priori* knowledge gives way to scientific method in the development of knowledge. Humans are thus products of their own experiencing in a social environment. The responsibility of education is to help individuals discover information and to assume the responsibility for their own actions. Inevitably, the final consequences are a result of the person's *own* choices.
6. *Reconstructionism* — the view of persons who are not so much products of their environment as "shapers of society". This position accepts the naturalistic, this-worldly ontology of experimentalism, but places more stress on "structures of social reality in a crisis-culture". This construct considers the process of education not as impartial and aloof but as of actively participating in

> a learning experience which re-shapes and redirects an individual's unique resources. Reconstructionism also espouses the re-shaping of society by consensus and the widest use of technological tools, public services, and of human and natural resources.

It seems obvious that metaphysical and other outmoded structures of philosophy no longer provide a defensible viewing of man's needs and institutions. Advanced technology, scientific progress, and research in many fields such as anthropology, psychology, and sociology have rendered many such theories obsolete.

In terms of teaching strategies, Taba rejects (a) the simplistic notion of teaching to impart information; (b) the concept that the teacher's knowledge of subject matter bears a direct relationship to teaching effectiveness; (c) the notion that teaching consists of particular procedures to be employed in teaching specific subjects--that there is *a* or even *the* method of teaching history, mathematics, music, and so on; and, (d) the idea that teachers are born and not made and the secrets of teaching are tools of the art which "good" teachers grasp intuitively. On the other hand, Dr. Taba accepts the idea that good theories of education and instruction are derived from research, experimentation, and analysis which makes direct provision for the development of behavioral objectives, both cognitive and affective.[2]

To become effective forces for education, value systems must bring all fields of knowledge and experience into meaningful relationships and into direct application with society and its institutions. Brameld suggests that a viewing of culture must be a consideration of the several domains within it, and should include various clusters of institutional and behavioral experience.[3] These, although they are capable of differentiation, must be connected with larger clusters at many points. Inevitably, valuing becomes all-encompassing to include not only educational matters but life itself. As a totality, philosophy must consequently include:

1. Reality, knowledge, and value
2. The relations of these areas to one another

3. The relations of these areas, in turn, to all other fields

Forces Affecting Values

Man is never isolated in his quest for adequate value judgments as behavior-governing norms. Beliefs, however, are constantly besieged by internal as well as external forces, some dimensions of which (in terms of potential conflict) we shall discuss later in this chapter. The principal aspects of this interaction are shown in Figure 3 in which outputs in terms of values, value judgments, and action patterns result from multi-directional inputs which at once shape and in turn are shaped by the individual.

Figure 3

THE INTERACTION OF VARIOUS INFLUENCES IN INDIVIDUAL VALUE FORMATION

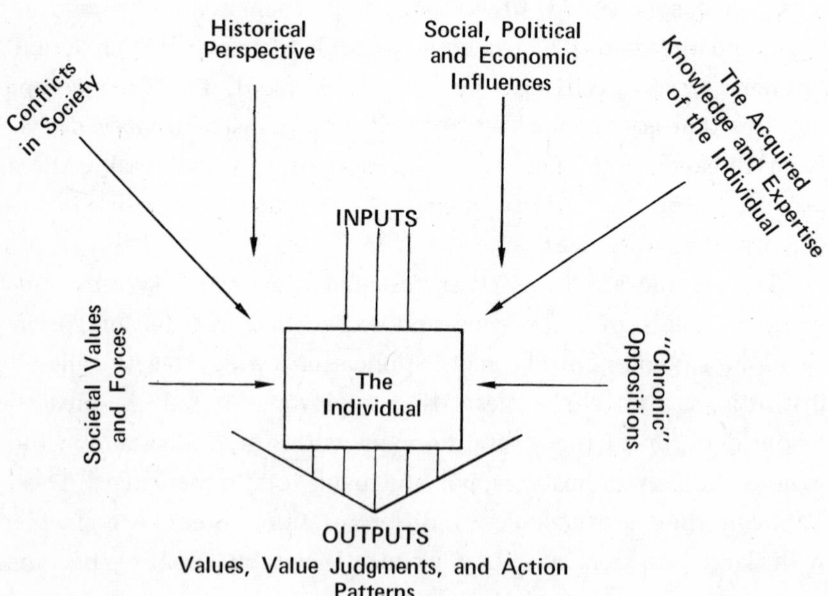

Some of the internal forces affecting values are described by Brameld as "chronic oppositions" within our "crisis-culture". These include:[4]

Self-interest versus social interest

Inequality versus equality

Planlessness versus planning

Nationalism versus internationalism

Absolutism versus experimentalism

Man-against-himself versus man-for-himself

The most significant forces of society currently affecting American public schools include the following:

1. The decline of prestige and political influence of the Caucasian peoples of the world.
2. The effects of international intimidation, conflict, "brinksmanship" and "limited warfare".
3. The abrupt explosion of science and technology which has carried civilization from the "atomic" to "space" age within a few brief years.
4. The development and utilization of electronics, computer technology, and automation in industry and business.
5. Recent conflicts in our views concerning the individual and his society and equality of opportunity regardless of socio-economic position.
6. The conflicting views of education for "utility" rather than for intrinsic values of learning.
7. The influence of legislation and court decisions on the public schools.
8. New national patterns of work and leisure which have drastically altered traditional norms.
9. Many changes in manpower needs in such fields as science, business, technology and entertainment.
10. Widespread effects of varied new media of communication.
11. The invention of sophisticated hardware which renders obsolete many of man's hand-performed activities.
12. Vast changes in global communication.
13. The explosion of the myth of abundance and the con-

TABOR COLLEGE LIBRARY
Hillsboro, Kansas 67063

comitant need for an expanding population, bringing implications for human and natural ecological systems.

Value Conflict And The "Ladder Of Abstraction"

The essential problem confronting the music educator is one of reconciling systems of valuing in a society in which cultural universals[5] are virtually non-existent. Conflicts inevitably arise when beliefs about what is "right", "good", or "moral" are rooted in diverse orientations. It is tempting to subsume taxonomies as philosophic positions, rather than as alternative-sorting devices. Prescriptions for action which are not founded on well-defined values also can lead to trouble.[6]

Early philosophies have been described as essentially monistic; that is, beliefs which viewed the universe in terms of a single principle, or a single conception of several principles. These ideas were essentially rationalistic, with the emphasis placed upon the human mind and its ability to acquire knowledge other than by means of direct observation. This position may be described as representing the "self-evident truths".

Later philosophic orientations, however, were both dualistic and pluralistic. They considered order in the universe as consisting of two or more forces which were not necessarily related. Such positions may best be described as being *empirical* in nature--that of believing that observable data is the most logical foundation for human knowledge and behavior. This concept views the universe as a constantly evolving totality in which human society, the laws of man (as opposed to natural laws) are not fixed but subject to modification and change. This places man in the peculiar position of having to re-evaluate his behavior in terms of value judgments which seem to be consistent with the mores of his society.

Perhaps one may assume that American education, on the whole, does not reflect extremes. Since there are many obvious conflicts in value, an examination of the so-called "cultural universals" may reveal significant problem areas which need to be resolved.

The "Ladder of Abstraction". Pluralistic and dualistic systems of valuing are generally adaptable to modification and change in modern society. One of the problems in any value system is, however, bridging the gap between theory and practice. In Figure 4, it will be noted that in translating general values (stated as "moral principles") into successively more precise behavioral terms, humans are continually affected by varying degrees of conflict. Conflicts should be resolved at intermediate levels instead of the areas of moral principle (on which there may be surface agreement) or human behavior which is in evident disagreement. Obviously, this is one of the primary problems in curriculum development as global objectives are subjected to translation into behavioral objectives and precise educational experiences.

Figure 4

CONFLICTS IN GENERAL PRINCIPLES

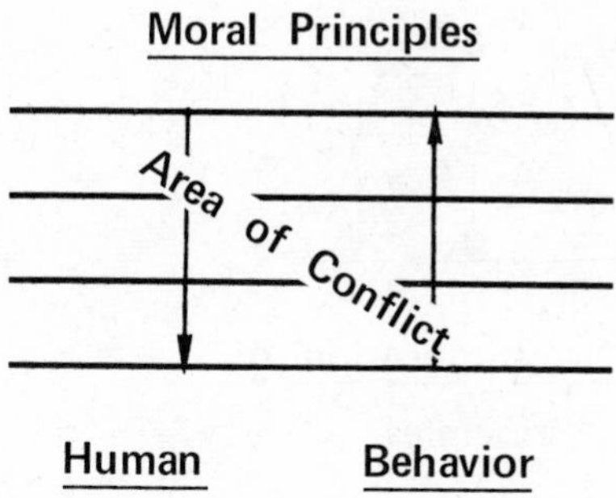

It is difficult for the observer to see the existence of intermediate levels of abstraction in moral behavior. In particular, the behavior of children presents too great a gap between absolute moral principles and behavior which is experienced.

In Figure 5, a "ladder of abstraction" is presented by which it becomes possible to view additional dimensions of potential conflict. In this theorem, a general principle (stated in this case as an abstraction) is subjected to progressively widening areas of validation until the ultimate specific application is reached. In order to perceive the difficulty of resolving with any degree of consistency a "universal" based on the United States Constitution and Bill of Rights, the following construct will be used to apply to the "ladder of abstraction".

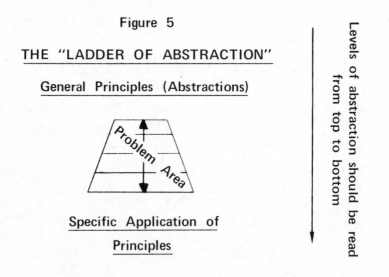

Figure 5

THE "LADDER OF ABSTRACTION"

General Principles (Abstractions)

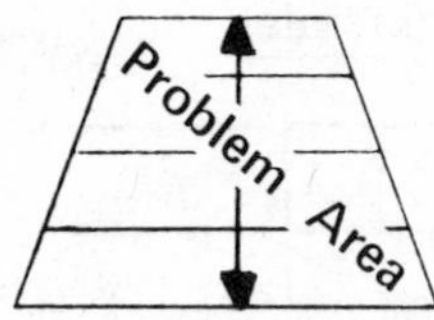

Specific Application of Principles

Levels of abstraction should be read from top to bottom

Theorem:

1. *Highest level of abstraction:* A widely accepted statement of "democratic" value presented in its most descriptive dimension. At this level, this principle or value will represent a "cultural universal".
2. *Intermediate level of abstraction A:* At this level, statements of educational policy which are consistent with No. 1 (the "universal") will be stated. These statements appear in a normative (valuative) dimension; thus, they should be read as declarations of conditions which "should be" to correspond with the original principle of abstract value.
3. *Intermediate level of abstraction B:* At the next point of interpretation, areas of conflict are noted which commonly occur from unresolved differences in valuation between abstraction A and the statement of value (position #1). These problems represent another level of abstraction stated as descriptive questions based on observed conflicts which exist in many American schools.
4. *Level of consensus:* The resolution of intermediate levels of abstraction A and B. (Note: This step will be achieved only in practice when human and situational variables are applied.)

Level 1 — *Statement of Value:* The right to govern and to be governed.

Level 2 — *Educational Policies Consistent With This Value:*

1. Men are capable of self-rule.
2. Men should be free to shape the purposes for which they live.
3. Living should not altogether be governed by a hierarchy of relationships between those who rule and those who are ruled.
4. Democratic principles may be transmitted by education.
5. Man may express his preference for a way of life which is consistent with both individual ideals as well as those of society.

Level 3 — *Problem Areas in Education Arising from the Application of this Principle:*

1. Disagreement on methods of discipline in the classroom.
2. Advisability of study of controversial issues in government; local, state, and national.
3. The rights of students to share in decisions relating to self-government.
4. Indecision concerning the propriety of student choices and input in curriculum and other phases of their learning.

It may be observed that cloudiness in resolving problems in the intermediate ranges of these levels of abstraction will inhibit the successful implementation of any educational program, no matter how good and how well accepted is the statement of general value. Thus, level 4, resolution by consensus, will be essential as a next step.

Let us now select a general principle and follow a construct through the intermediate levels of abstraction as it might be applied to music education.

Level 1 — *Statement of Value:* Music is for all persons.

Level 2 — *Educational Policies Consistent With This Value:*

1. Music is an academic discipline which is recognized part of the public school curriculum.
2. Music experiences should be provided at all school levels.
3. Music experiences should be available to all students.

Level 3 — *Problem Areas in Education Arising from the Application of this Principle:*

1. Fiscal priorities and budgetary cuts which eliminate music as an integral part of the school curriculum.
2. Problems arising from the type of music experience which is available to all students.
3. A disparity in the availability of music, often provided at *some* levels for *some* students.
4. Problems relating to music as a required versus elective subject.
5. Inequalities arising from undue emphasis on performance-oriented courses, in opposition to broader applications

of music education in the school curriculum.

6. Problems relating to the recognition or non-recognition of music as an academic discipline.
7. Problems of relevancy of content, including failure to recognize valid present-day cultural influences in the school music curriculum.
8. Problems generated by the public relations aspects of music which are in opposition to intrinsic educational values.
9. Controversies relating to teaching method.
10. Differences of opinion as to whether music should be taught by classroom teachers solely, or with the aid of music specialists (particularly at the elementary level).
11. Problems of inflexible curricula and scheduling which prevent students from electing music as a part of their school program.
12. Failure to provide for the needs of highly motivated and capable students in addition to those of average or below-average abilities and interests.
13. Problems created by the lack of opportunity to participate in music outside the acknowledged educational channels (an extended view of music education "for a lifetime").

From an examination of problem areas such as this, it is apparent that unless music educators can examine critically and begin to modify interpretations of general value, they will run into conflicts. Philosophical positions at intermediate levels of abstraction thus become areas of continual conflict rather than potential alternative-exploration areas directed toward the selection of appropriate action patterns. These intermediate levels must be flexible and capable of including a variety of inputs from the individuals involved. They will also vary by the nature of different applications and different sets of circumstances. It is imperative, however, that the final solutions be compatible with the original value or general principle.

In effect, music educators must be concerned with the consistency of valuing at all levels, the probing analysis and weighing of alternatives, and the closure which is accepted by consensus. Thus they will be able to develop a set of acceptable intermediate objectives (global or program objectives) by means of which the principal value statement is applied to a working framework for specific disciplines. The next step will be to develop specific course objectives, stated in terms of desirable behaviors for a specified group of students. It is in terms of *how* global and program objectives are translated into course and behavioral objectives that later sections of this book concerned with curriculum will be based.

Valuing As A Process Of Instructional Idealism

Education in the United States has not always been concerned with the inner nature of values and their application to teaching. William Carr, in a prefatory statement on values in the curriculum, suggests that expository method, long dominant as a method of instruction at all schools levels, is not in itself suited to the development of deeply held and rationally applied values.[7] Consequently, American public schools in particular, suffer from an impoverished system of values--with, too frequently, haphazard results.

Two basic distinctions may be made in value. O'Neill suggests that these are (a) the distinction between a value-experience, value object, and value-principle; and (b) the distinction between questions of subjective value in relation to the individual, of morality in terms of relations among individuals, and of ethics in terms of deliberate or unreflective behavior.[8]

Distinctions between values and goals, therefore, reflect on one hand the individual's idea of the interpretation of a principle, and on the other hand, the effect of this valuing on the behaviors of themselves and individuals with whom they are in contact. Learning ultimately is effected by means of solving problems and of satisfying needs in relation to goals. In formal education, it is important to consider belief as a function of behavior. Therefore, we must assume that "goal modification" rather than "goal edification" is the primary function of schooling. Education does not stress the primacy of beliefs other than in relation to behavior-modification.

Campbell and Corbally stress the importance of educational leadership as a decisive catalyst in the process of resolving value conflict. As has been noted, the public schools as well as other educational systems apply valuing at all levels of the process of education. By comparison with the "Ladder of Abstraction", Campbell and Corbally place broad values into an inverted pyramidal structure, beginning with the premise of "The Democratic Way of Life". This is next continued into the construct of "The Educative Process", "The Public School", and concluding with the focal point provided by "Administrative Leadership". In such a pattern, each descending level serves to sharpen the challenge, with educational leadership serving to assist participants in viewing alternative modes of behavior-modification and arriving at closure by means of consensus.[9]

Figure 6

The Challenge of Educational Administration in Goal-Modification

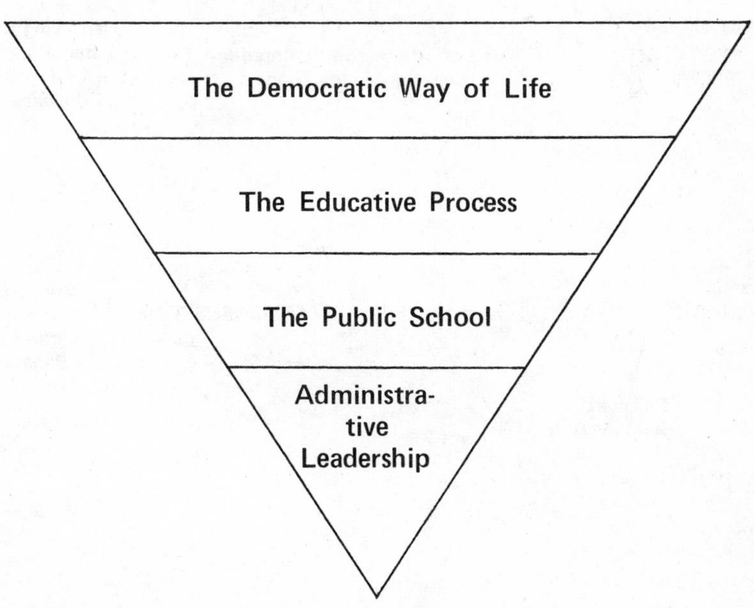

Figure 7 indicates how democratic group decisions which are made in the intermediate area of alternative-exploration may be used to achieve consensus and closure. It will be observed that once a general value is accepted, groups should explore many alternative applications of behavior which they feel to be consistent with this value. Some alternatives will be rejected--others will be accepted as group decisions. Ordinarily, the first decision will require more time than subsequent decisions. Once groups become accustomed to this process, decisions come with greater frequency and at shortened intervals of time. Ultimately, decisions narrow the gap of alternative-selection, and final consensus may be made by which the operational level of the group activity is achieved. In such a manner, the entire endeavor becomes a systematic process of democracy in an educational setting.

Figure 7

Decision-making as an Outgrowth of Consensus in Relation to Valuing Alternatives

Area of General Acceptance	Area of Alternative-Exploration (Behavior-Modification)	Narrowing of Alternatives Toward Operational Efficiency

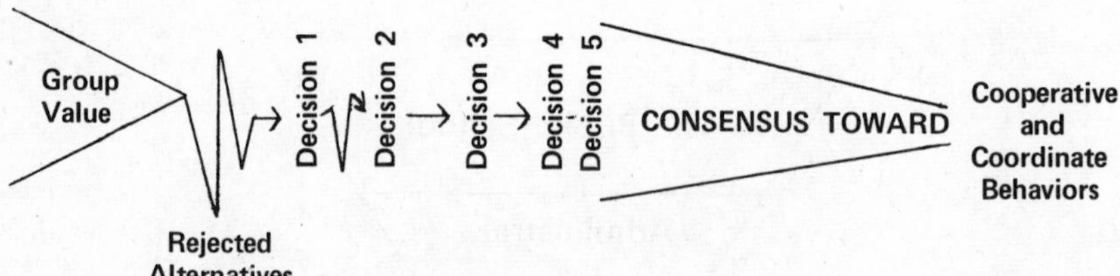

In terms of leadership strategies in applying the foregoing paradigm, individual valuating positions must be allowed to surface in the process of democratic decision-making. Likewise, the professional experience and potentials of individuals must be considered. The entire process of decision-making, consensus, and closure will also require a high degree of skill in group processes by individual members of the group as well as by its group leaders.

If instructional idealisms are to be translated effectively into patterns of behavior, a certain amount of structure is both desirable and necessary. The necessary dimensions of this structure, according to Halpin, are:[10]

1. The task
2. The formal organization to accomplish the task
3. The work group (or groups)
4. The leader (or leaders)

If education is to be responsive to the dynamic needs of society, it must remain fluid rather than static. The tasks of the educational structure will change according to emphasis or approaches desired in carrying out the group's values.

Certain taxonomies of process as related to various disciplines will be found helpful in pursuing a course from idealism to instructional operation. According to Cassidy, the essential taxonomies include:[11]

Analytic activities: observing, collecting, naming, reporting, making distinctions, dividing, classifying.

Synthetic activities: seeking relationships among facts and theories, deriving trends, hypotheses, theories, and laws.

Reduction to practice: returning from the general to the particular or the theoretical to the practical, putting ideas to use, making applications.

Applications To Music Education

The importance of a system of values in music education is essentially three-fold. First, it is important to one's beliefs about the nature of music as an art form; second, it clarifies the overall purposes of education in American society; and, finally, it serves to delineate the specific role music should play in the school curriculum and the total process of teaching-learning.

In this connection, Reimer emphasizes that:

> . . . the profession as a whole needs a formulation which can serve to guide the efforts of the group. The impact the profession can make on society depends in large degree on the quality of the profession's understanding of what it has to offer which might be of value to society. There is an almost desperate need for a better understanding of the value of music and of the teaching and learning of music.[12]

When aims, purposes, procedures and product are being considered in terms of educational "accountability", it behooves music education to share the general concerns of education as a whole. As an important ingredient of this notion, professional educators should understand why music education is a form of aesthetic education as well as knowing its specific contributions as an academic discipline. In addition, it is essential to have a clear-cut philosophy of learning and teaching which recognizes the needs of individuals and groups within a dynamic and complex society. Finally, it is necessary to understand the direction that music education must take to accomplish its task as an important segment of the school curriculum.

The particular functions of music must be viewed in terms of desired individual behaviors, as alternatives are explored and and group decisions made for arriving at the operational level of any program of music education. The dimensions of the desired behavior-modification should be pluralistic rather than monistic and must be compatible with the expressed value as well as the needs and potentials of individual students.

George F. McKay expresses one set of desirable ingredients as an extension of widely held aesthetic values in music education. It will be noted that he also rejects extramusicalities in stating intrinsic qualities which make music a unique art form. Music, when classified into what McKay terms "basic types of natural excitation, has its own typical conditions and shapings":[13]

1. The experience of music as song
2. The experience of music as dance
3. The excitement of sound in motion
4. Music experienced through declamation
5. Music as drama in action
6. Music as motive and development
7. Music as the result of architectural shaping
8. Music as related to mathematical order
9. The experience of music as pure harmony or as pure timbre

According to Reimer, a basic philosophic orientation which governs music as a form of aesthetic education is that, "All art serves the same function, which is to provide a means for exploring and understanding the nature of human feeling."[14] If this principle is accepted, behavior-modification (learning) must develop by means of experiences by which individuals are able to explore and develop understanding of their feelings in relation to music experienced. Accordingly, feeling and sensitivity are continually reinforced and aesthetic judgments are developed.

Smith and Smith provide three additional reasons for the validity of an art experience in an educational setting. These are: (a) aesthetic enjoyment (the provision of satisfactions which are intrinsically desired); (b) aesthetic experience (those pleasures which are unique to the specific aesthetic experience at hand); and, (c) aesthetic knowledge (those cognitive areas by which the ideals, norms or notions of human perfection are provided).[15]

Music and the Needs of Learners. Public education must of necessity be based on providing for broad as well as specific needs of many types of learners. This means that there must be *varied and qualitative experiences in music,* as in all areas of the school curriculum, which help to insure a balanced, meaningful music program for *all* learners. Not only must the average and subaverage student be considered, but also those with higher levels of interest and motivation.

It is important that there be music experiences provided in the school curriculum which challenge both the academically and artistically talented student. Potentially high academic achievers need the additional enrichment and aesthetic stimulation which music experiences provide, whereas these activities are essential to the intellectual-musical development of those who are artistically capable! Highly motivated and talented music students are capable of a high degree of musical response by which they are able to respond-understand-convey their own musical meanings and feelings.

Such programs must have the ingredients of breadth, depth, and continuity if the needs of all learners are to be served. Thus, similarly to programs in other academic disciplines, there must be adequate provision for musical experiences at *each* level of the public school. These programs must provide for the needs of the general student while at the same time providing musical challenges for the more capable learner.

Music Assists Individuals in Making Appropriate Aesthetic Judgments and in Establishing Standards of Taste. As noted in the previous chapter, aesthetics deals with art and beauty; hence, a judgment involves an opinion or estimate concerning the individual's responses to an art form such as music. A standard, on the other hand, is the establishment of a basis for the comparative measurement, in this case, of aesthetic values or of judging capacity. In a sense, the development of a standard of valuation might be considered to be a criterion or pattern by which the individual becomes capable of passing subjective opinion concerning the worth or excellence of an aesthetic or musical experience. The making of aesthetic judgments consistent with the standards one holds is, therefore, a lifelong process of continual valuative experience, hence of education.

Considerable distinction must be drawn between the *study of* and *making of* value judgments. The individual making empirical evaluations must decide about the presence or absence of certain properties or relations in terms of *his own* experience. Thus, as Feigl[17] points out, we must ourselves arrive at aesthetic judgments which are for ourselves concerned with the structure and content of works of art. The implications for the music educator are clear; we must help students develop the necessary personal skills of perception which will allow them to *know* and to *value* for themselves. It is not sufficient to tell or to read about music--one must actually *experience* music before this is possible.

It is necessary, therefore, that music education provide the learner with many, varied and qualitative musical experiences in order that the perception of musical principles and values be developed. In order to accomplish this, the learner must not only explore the media of musical sound, he must have a basic understanding of the corresponding musicological elements as well.

Thus, to meet the challenge, music educators must be concerned with providing students with an accurate and meaningful understanding of the music they experience. This cannot be done *for* the individual, but, rather by means of *self-motivated experiences* engendered by teaching which is also musically and aesthetically perceptive. This type of teaching also must recognize the various levels of developmental growth which are necessary ingredients in the process. Mursell[18] calls this a process of developing musical responsiveness--that of helping students respond emotionally, perceptually, and imaginally to the content of the music iteslf rather than to extraneous elements such as symbols or extra-musicalities. It should be clear that any attempt to develop values or standards of musical taste outside of musical experience is impossible.

Basic Values of Music Education. The following values expressed at the highest level of abstraction are examples of global objectives which are applicable to *all* music experience at *all* levels of music education.

It is our belief that:

1. Music is an art form which is important to society as a whole.
2. Music is a form of aesthetic experience which has unique qualities which are important to individuals within our society.
3. The unique qualities of music may be communicated and nurtured through the processes of education.[19]
4. Since the essential quality of music is musical feeling, music education should concern itself primarily with the

development of feelingful experience and aesthetic sensitivity.

5. Music should be viewed as a specific mode of communication of human experience and emotion, which may be described as musical expression.
6. The dimensions of musical experience are extremely broad and varied; thus, any program of music education must be eclectic and representative of the widest possible spectrum of valid musical experience. The essential criteria for the selection of experience content should be, (a) its validity as an art form; and, (b) its intrinsic aesthetic quality.
7. Music education should be concerned with an awareness of meaningful structures which are unique elements of music and these should be developed in a musical-aesthetic setting.
8. Each learner should be provided opportunities by which he may develop his own unique interests and potentials for music experience to its highest possible level.
9. Value judgments concerning musical feeling are essentially subjective and personal. Therefore, it is essential that individuals be allowed to experience music in ways which will assist them in making appropriate aesthetic judgments in the most meaningful way.
10. As an essential segment of total general education, music should be included in the school curriculum at all levels of education.[20]

If these ten values are accepted, consistent and parallel patterns of behavior-modification will be developed by means of behavioral objectives. Certainly, if rational man can be considered to be an organized totality, there is further need for an organic, comprehensive outlook toward music education. Consequently, the ideals relating to (a) what our schools should be; (b) the type of musical experiences which we hope to provide; and, (c) the component parts and operational patterns which govern how the curriculum will be effected each relate to the comprehensive aspects of our philosophy.

One of the most important aspects governing success or failure in achieving goals consonant with our philosophy hinges on the type of leadership exercised. To be effective, a program of music education requires leadership by persons who are:

1. Aware of and willing to support the basic values of music education in American schools.
2. Musically perceptive and aware of the need to strengthen their own values concerning music and aesthetic education.
3. Aware of the characteristics and needs of individuals who comprise the learners in the public schools.
4. Capable of transmitting their musical knowledge, thoughts and feeling to others by means of acceptable pedagogical procedures.
5. Aware of the value system of society and the part which music plays in this schema.
6. Knowledgeable about the fundamental principles of the learning process.
7. Skillful in instructional leadership.

An application of values and valuing processes as a taxonomy of objectives for music education will be developed in chapter five.

Summary

Values are extremely important to music educators since they provide direct insights into the beliefs which govern education and educational processes. As we examine various valuing systems, we become aware of alternatives for goal-modification which are essential to human behavior. Because music education is concerned with aesthetic and qualitative aspects of living, the structure and processes of education are directly affected by the quality and direction of these values.

The philosophic positions of realism, idealism, essentialism, perennialism, experimentalism, and reconstructionism provide many insights into the way in which man has shaped his institutions over the years. Effective valuing for contemporary learning brings all fields of knowledge into direct relationship with experience and with life itself. Man's behavior, although empirically based, interacts with many forces in society--causing individuals continually to examine and re-evaluate their actions. Conflicts between what man views to be his general principles and his personal and educational behavior should be resolved by consensus at intermediate levels of abstraction (the "Ladder of Abstraction"). Values and goals must therefore be compatible at each level as music educators strive for alternative modes of behavior-modification and closure.

Value systems are important to music education in that they assist in examining one's own beliefs about music; the purposes of education; and, the specific means of providing music experiences in the total school curriculum. Thus, it is not only important to understand the inner nature of music as an aesthetic experience, but the importance of appropriate ways in which the learner may be provided with many, varied, and qualitative music experiences.

Topics For Discussion

1. Discuss the role of values in contemporary society. State some of the commonly verbalized values which are frequently espoused and develop these in terms of a ladder of abstraction.
2. Point out what you consider to be further evidence of misunderstandings regarding commonly articulated goals and values in music education.
3. Trace at various levels of abstraction one or more of the basic values of music education, as stated in this chapter.
4. Cite specific conflicts with these values with which you are familiar.
5. Read and discuss in depth one or more of the "schools" of philosophy and its position concerning the forming of aesthetic value judgments.
6. How do the various basic educational philosophies differ in their approach to music education?
7. What is the importance of the values and principles presented in this chapter to the concept of leadership in music education?

Suggested Readings

Carr, William G. (Ed.) *Values and the Curriculum.* A Report of the Fourth International Curriculum Conference. Washington, D.C.: The National Education Association, Center for the Study of Instruction (CSI), 1970. William O'Neill chapter on "Behaving and Believing" is pertinent.

Glenn, Neal E., William B. McBride and George H. Wilson. *Secondary School Music: Philosophy, Theory, and Practice.* Englewood Cliffs, N.J.: Prentice-Hall, Inc., 1970. Summarizes several positions of valuing which are discussed in the foregoing chapter.

Henry, Nelson B. "Basic Concepts in Music Education", *Fifty-seventh Yearbook of the National Society for the Study of Education.* Chicago: The University of Chicago Press, 1958. See especially Ch. 1, 2, 3, 4, 5, 6 and 9.

Kaplan, Max. *Foundations and Frontiers of Music Education.* New York: Holt, Rinehart and Winston, Inc., 1966. See Ch. 2 and 3.

Leonhard, Charles, and Robert W. House. *Foundations and Principles of Music Education.* New York: McGraw-Hill Book Co., Inc., 1959. See Ch. 4.

Madison, Thurber H. (Chairman). *Perspectives in Music Education:* Source Book III. Washington, D.C.: Music Educators National Conference, 1966.

Meyer, Leonard B. *Music, the Arts and Ideas: Patterns and Predictions in Twentieth-Century Culture.* Chicago: The University of Chicago Press, 1967.

Phenix, Philip. *Realms of Meaning.* New York: McGraw-Hill, 1964. See Ch. 1.

Reimer, Bennett. *A Philosophy of Music Education.* Englewood Cliffs, N.J.: Prentice-Hall, Inc., 1970.

Schwadron, Abraham A. *Aesthetics: Dimensions for Music Education.* Washington, D.C.: Music Educators National Conference, 1967. See Ch. 2.

CHAPTER FOUR

MUSIC LEARNING AND TEACHING

You cannot teach a man anything; you can only help him find it within himself.

Galileo

This Chapter will present some of the principal tenets of learning theory, past and present. Music educators should understand the process of acquiring concepts, techniques, skills and affective qualities which result from students' learning experiences. Recent research stresses the interrelatedness of motor and mental growth in various stages of the learning process. The role of maturation, motivation and experience will be discussed in relationship to concept and skill development. It is obvious that the nature of music as an art form (Chapter II) and values (Chapter III) will also affect learning. It is hoped that this section of the book will form the basis for learning strategies provided by teachers and leaders in music education.

Definition

Learning is a process of behavior-modification. It denotes the way in which individuals come to know, understand and develop. It is an active process--one in which the learner is in continuous interaction with his learning environment. Consequently, the structure of the environment (provided by the teacher) becomes especially important since it is actually the vehicle for learning.

Learning in music is a multi-dimensional process. The theories of how individuals learn are complex and are rooted in several areas of psychology. When change occurs in learning, it alters the way individuals behave with regard to their

* concepts
* feelings
* values and judgments
* understanding and use of symbols
* skills
* habits

Each of the foregoing elements become products of a learning experience and is governed by psychological principles which are discussed in this chapter.

Triangular Structure Of Learning

Learning structure is based on an equilateral triangle in which the components of educational (psychological) theory, student needs and social setting play an equal part. When we say the "individual is learning from experience", it must be remembered that this involves *where* the individual lives and learns as well as *his own needs and drives* as a human being.

Figure 8

The Structure of Learning

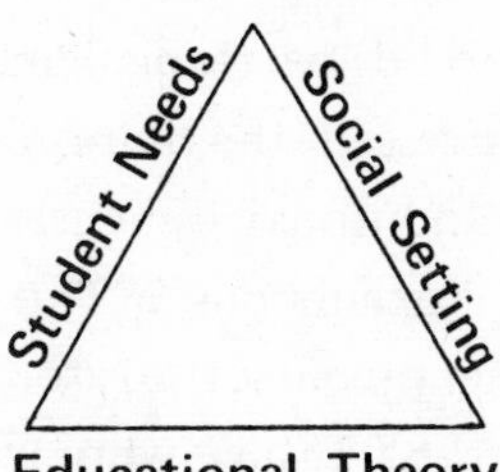

From Figure 8, we may deduce that the learning needs and conditions are many and diverse. It is obvious that although psychological laws of learning operate in the same general way, the socio-economic backgrounds, community-school settings, and attributes of individual learners all vary enormously. Thus, in learning educators must provide for:

* An enormous range of individual differences within a normal heterogeneous group of students.
* Diverse socio-economic and cultural differences among student populations.
* The need for identity and acceptance as an individual.
* Differences in maturation rates: physical, mental and emotional.
* Societal (i.e., peer group and adult) pressures.
* The need to succeed.

It will be noted in due course that the implication of meeting these needs is *how to truly individualize instruction.*

Historical Perspective

Jean Jacques Rousseau (1712-1778) advocated the notion that each child should be allowed total freedom until pubescence, at which time his formal education would begin. According to this naturalistic theory, the freedom to learn in non-structured ways permitted the child to become "self-actualized" and ready for the formal structure of the classroom.

Johann Pestalozzi (1746-1827), the famous Swiss educator, applied Rousseau's ideas of naturalism to a more structured concept of experimentation. He was perhaps the first educator to formulate what today would be recognized as "teaching method". The Pestalozzi theory stressed the importance of the psychology of learning, adding the additional dimensions of sense impression, learning "activity" and "excursions". The orderly progression of learning activity was the precursor of today's learning sequence.

Friedrich Froebel (1782-1853) who was a close associate of Pestalozzi introduced an additional dimension of learning into his experimental school at Blankenburg, Germany by including handwork, self-expression, and self-directed activities which were to be practiced within a community of learners.

The Victorian Era ushered in the "genetic-constitutional" theory of learning. This view espoused the notion that if the child turned out satisfactorily, it was primarily due to heredity and nature rather than to any scientific reason.

Johann Herbart (1776-1841) introduced learning as a science. This ushered in the beginning of the psychological school of learning in which prevalent theories were based upon experiments conducted with children. These ideas gained considerable momentum during the Nineteenth Century, and formed the basis of present-day psychological research in learning. The Herbartian theory stressed the continuum of preparation-apperception-application, resulting in the following five steps of learning:

* Preparation-apperception
* Presentation of new material
* Comparison-association
* Generalization
* Application

A great deal of similarity will be noted in this theory in comparison with the present day ideas of modern educators.

From mid-Nineteenth Century until the present, several other psychological theories of learning have influenced education, including those of:

* *Wundt* in Leipzig and *G. S. Hall* in the United States — Learning problems, memory, transfer of training.
* *E. L. Thornkike* — laws of readiness, exercise and effect.
* *Pavlov* in the USSR — conditioned response.
* *J. B. Watson* — behaviorism; stimulus-response or reaction psychology.
* *Gestaltists* — learning as a totality; the whole conditions the activities of the parts; insight develops through watching a phenomenon, applying or recalling related experience, and forming a complete mental image or concept.
* *Field theories* (G. Hartmann, R. Lundin et al) — insight

> results in adaptive adjustment,. problem-solving, or skill improvement; a neural or cortical organization is established as soon as the learner achieves his purposes providing a meaningful pattern of learning.

In reviewing early historical views of learning, the reader will note that their views were atomistic (single responses induced by specific stimuli) as opposed to pluralistic-holistic (many responses produced by a variety of complex stimuli) of the Gestalt and field proponents.[1] The latter stress learning which is possible only if students are approached from a "whole" experience. Learning to play an instrument, for example, requires several types of insight about the components of music (tone, duration, timbre, intensity), muscular skills, decoding the symbols of the musical score, and affective qualities involved in performance. *None of these may be learned in isolation.*

Contemporary Theories Of Learning

Piaget.

The ideas of the Swiss psychologist, Jean Piaget have been widely accepted in present-day education.[2] Piaget stressed both physical and mental readiness in a sensorimotor-mental developmental process. According to his theory of "expectancy-probability", Piaget claims that there are four stages in the child's development:

1. *Sensori-motor-preverbal stage* (birth to 3 years)
   Child learns from randomized behavior, repetition, and association.
2. *Pre-operational stage* (3-6 years)
   Child is influenced by irrelevant factors--does not yet distinguish possibility from necessity, nor does he respond to unequal relative proportions in an experiment.
3. *Concrete-operational stage* (7-10 years)
   Child separates that which is necessary from the simply possible--accepts multiple possibilities and develops notions of probability, possibility, and simple chance.
4. *Formal-operational stage* (beginning about age 11)

Child begins to master concept of probability--acquires abstract mental or conceptual abilities.

From the foregoing stages in Piaget's theories of educational development, it can be noted that there is a direct relationship of age to the complexity of learning task. By contrast with stimulus-response, association, and maturation theories of learning, Piaget stressed the notion of "equilibration"--the idea that learning is a developmental process. Children learn through trial and error, pleasurable activity, and success. Ideas and skills develop through a limited world of "one's self" and successful experiences with one's own environment. Unorganized ideas begin to assume meaning by association and reinforcement. Ultimately, the learner begins to assume control over his responses as he gains mastery of himself and becomes a social being in a world of other people. "Equilibration" takes place when the individual's ideas come into conflict with external forces. At this point, a counterforce (by means of educational processes) can be placed in motion to resolve the conflict. The harmonizing force of equilibration may be brought into play at given stages in the individual's development. It is important to remember that *experience is the key to learning.* The more the child experiences and the more meaningful the guidance provided to help him discover facts and relationships, the greater and more lasting will be his learning.

Gagné.

Learning, according to Robert M. Gagné, is hierarchal in nature. It involves a progression which begins with a series of three or four levels of motor learning, followed by additional levels of conceptualization, which in turn leads to problem-solving and critical judgment. Due to the complexity of this learning hierarchy, planning and instructional sequence become important elements for the music educator to remember.[3]

The steps in the process, according to Gagné are:

Signal-learning: reflexive response to repeated signal or stimulus.

Stimulus-response learning: (sometimes called "instrumental" learning) learning by "trial and error".

Motor-chaining: connection of a set of stimulus-response

learnings.

Verbal chaining or association: learning of chains of verbal associations.

Multiple-discrimination learning: learning to make different responses to objects and events or to distinguish among them.

Concept learning: learning to put objects or events into a group.

Learning of principles: learning to link concepts together to show relationships, as in generalizations and formulas.

Problem-solving: using principles to attain a goal and thereby learning a higher-order principle that changes the learner's capability.

Gagné's theory of learning is progressive and cumulative, as in a continuum. Pre-existing and prerequisite conditions which are both internalized and externalized (inside and outside the learner) are of equal importance to the educator. Consider how the beginning music students comes in contact with a musical experience. He may approach it as a:

* performer
* conductor
* composer
* listener

Although he may respond to musical stimuli and learns a great deal by S-R "trial and error", a truly *musical learning experience requires guided interaction* implying the need for the teacher's expertise. Behavior-modification in the Gagné model is thus dependent upon how learning is sequenced, as well as the amount, type and quality of the musical experience.

J. P. Guilford.

In his "structure of the intellect," Guilford suggests that intellect is composed of a variety of intersecting and related elements. By observing Figure 9, it will be noted that there are three modes or classes of abilities--*operation, product,* and *content.* The front face of the diagram illustrates cognitive abilities which represent figural, symbolic, semantic, and behavioral areas of knowing. Directly behind this cognitive layer are parallel structures for memory, productive-thinking, and evaluation. In each horizontal

Figure 9

Guilford - Structure of the Intellect Model

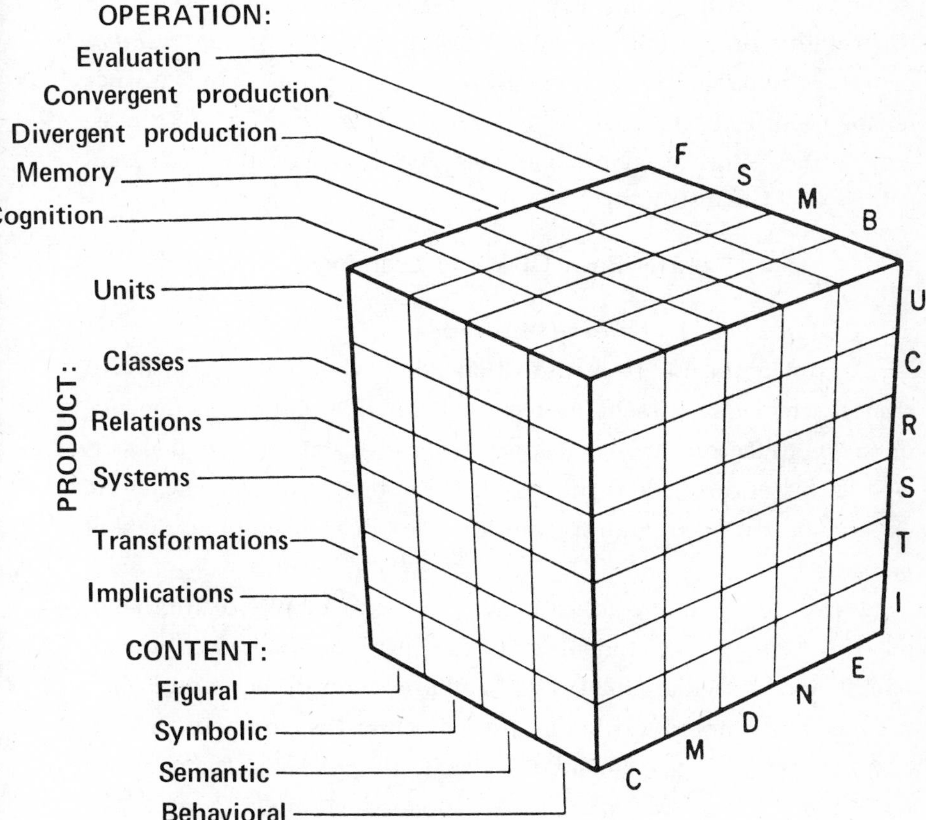

layer there are also products which are assumed to be common to all columns and tiers (note specific cognitive abilities such as knowledge of elements, classes, relations, systems and implications). Guilford claims that it is possible for more than one factor to be present in a given figural cell. An illustration would be when one cognizes auditory aspects of music in one cell, while in another cell two corresponding memory abilities are at work. The activities of the cells are interrelated.[5]

Piaget, Gagné and Guilford all contradict the notions of older schools of psychology which claimed that it was possible to measure, predict, and learn about single aspects of a music experience in isolation. In reality, contemporary theories of learning all stress the totality of learning in which the *individual learns by reacting to all components of a musical experience simultaneously.* Behavior modification results when conditions for learning--readiness, maturation, motivation--are enjoined by means of the intelligent guidance of the instructor.

The Basis Of Music Learning

Readiness, Maturation and Motivation

A student begins to learn at that point when he is receptive to stimuli which are present in a given learning situation. It depends upon such factors as the learner's physical state of readiness as well as his curiosity and motives. He is "ready to learn" when he experiences a need and/or use for the idea, technique or skill being presented.

Maturation, on the other hand, is a stage of physical development by which the student is sufficiently coordinated in motor, neural and muscular ability to handle a given psychomotor skill. As has been noted earlier in this chapter, the complex task of playing a musical instrument involves both intellectual and motor responses. Before the student can understand how to play 1st-valve Bb on the trumpet, he must be ready to apply motor and verbal chaining. If he is neither ready nor mature enough, no amount of prodding by an eager music instructor can accomplish the job for him. Maturation and learning are inseparable--if maturation is stressed as in traditional "growth and development" charts, the role of learning is minimized. By the same token, when psychological aspects of learning are stressed, problems of maturation occur.

Motivation is a drive, stimulus, impulse, or intention which causes individuals to act the way they do. A student has a great deal of natural curiosity. His response to a given learning situation depends upon such factors as involvement, the intensity and maturity of his drives, and the personal satisfactions he not only gains but perceives he has gained from the experience. Motivation may be relatively naive or it may involve an intensive pursuit of sophisticated personal goals.[6]

Learning may be internalized or externalized. Those forces which operate outside the individual--called *extrinsic motivation*---are variables with which the student is in a state of continuous interaction. Extrinsic forces are partly psychological and partly functional. Inevitably they tend to influence learning behavior, particularly if the stimulus is strong enough. This type of motivation frequently involves such extrinsic motivators as games, contests, uniforms, trips, and awards. They give tangible evidence of achievement. When not used to excess, extrinsic motivation is not undesirable since it may be helpful to fulfilling the need for self-image and personal achievement. It should be pointed out, however, that the cumulative effects of learning may be short-lived since *extrinsic factors do not center on the learning activity* and may set up a pattern of expectancy quite aside from what the instructor hoped to accomplish. Not infrequently, emphasis may be put on arbitrary levels of memorization and achievement in order to gain a given reward. Extrinsic motivation is best where peer group and social needs of individuals are met--worst where it is based on threat or promise of artificial reward.

The most effective type of motivation occurs within the individual when he is fulfilling real goals and discovers the satisfaction of achievement. This is called *intrinsic motivation.* This type of learning is concerned with factors which are an integral part of the educational experience. Intrinsic motivation develops when instructors expect students to assume a greater degree of responsibility for their own behavior. The classroom which emphasizes inquiry, discovery and problem-solving is thus self-actualizing for the student. In this frame-of-reference, each person becomes more self-motivated and self-goal oriented. Teaching strategies which stress *intrinsic qualities within the musical experience are the most effective for long-range, lasting results of learning.* In terms of music education, intrinsic motivation is achieved through a developmental program which places priority on the individual's own musical perception, imagery, thinking and feeling.

Teachers should be aware of high drop-out rates from musical organizations where there is little challenge in the material, tasks are too difficult or improperly developed, or undue pressures are present. Students need to have the feeling of success which comes from interests cultivated by the teacher. They need enough structure to succeed and opportunities for guided development which will help them discover and react to suitable musical activities. It should also be recognized that permanent changes in behavior result from felt needs arising from the learner and the degree of success which he derives from satisfying those needs. This in no way negates the role of the teacher as a guide and stimulator. Students recognize the maturity and competence of their teachers and will work to develop internal goals if they feel secure in personal esteem and worth. They accept criticism of their efforts if there is corresponding praise for trying. When a student knows what is expected and that he is making substantial progress toward a goal, his real education has begun. The lasting effect will, of course, result from personal satisfactions gained from the individual's interaction with music.

Perception

Perception denotes the consciousness or awareness of something. Learning begins at the level of perception, then is followed successively by stages of conceptualization-memorization, experimentation, practice, and ultimately mastery and application of the concept. The degree and mastery of the concept depends on the initial richness of the early perceptual experience as well as the kind and quality of succeeding experiences as the learner progresses through school. This thought is underscored by representing musical growth as a continuum proceeding through five discrete stages; namely, musical awareness, initiative, discrimination, insight and skill.[7] Perception of a musical experience is represented by musical experience is represented by musical awareness--the enjoyable exploration of musical sound at a level of conscious activity. If the learner is "engaged" by his initial contacts with music, he generates initiative or wants to progress further with the experience. Musical initiative thus is part of the process of inner or intrinsic motivation. As the learner is guided toward involvement in greater depth and meaning, he develops discrimination, insight and skill. How one first perceives music is thus of great importance. Hopefully it will engage the learner on his own grounds and put the wheels of teaching and learning in motion.

Discovery, Deductive and Inductive Learning

Inquiry and problem-solving are essential to learning. As an investigative-examining activity, inquiry engages the learner from the point of his perceptual experience. This is accomplished in one of three ways:

Discovery — self-actuating experiences which lead to personal interaction and discovery.

Deductive learning — working from a concept, skill or technique presented by the teacher to achieve a specific application (from the general to specific).

Inductive learning — solving problems to determine the concept (from the specific to the general).

The quality of problem-solving depends upon the opportunities which are provided by the instructor. Since our complex society requires individuals who can successfully cope with changing and sophisticated environments, skills and technologies, the challenge to today's music educator is enormous. Since music is not a "tool" skill, he must find ways to make music learning vital and meaningful. He must be imbued with the feeling that music exists not primarily to earn a living, but to live a life! The teacher also understands that due to the uniqueness of the music experience, his principal task is to select and arrange materials which will facilitate exploration, manipulation, experimentation, invention and discovery. . . all essential to the understanding of music. Motivation, curriculum and learning sequence are important in the development of insight, understanding and skill. The teacher must be willing to provide sufficient structure for learning to succeed--then, step out of the way and "let it happen". His role should become that of *leader, guide,* and *stimulator* rather than overseer-director. The key to discovery, deductive and inductive teaching is individualized instruction which will be discussed later in the book.

Concept Development

A concept is roughly a thought or an idea. As applied to music education, a concept indicates the residual effect of a concrete learning experience in music. If an individual grasps a concept, it indicates he understands its meaning. This involves a rather complex set of motor-mental processes (Piaget, Gagné et al) and it should be obvious that no two individuals arrive at the same concept in precisely the same way. Since perception, however, is essential in this process, we may generalize by saying that *concepts are acquired gradually through the basic senses* (sound, sight, touch, etc.) when they are in touch with real things. Thus, in music, our attention as teachers must be to help students direct themselves toward (or *center in*) the *actual musical experience itself.* Consequently, it becomes essential for the teacher to *analyze the music carefully* in order that the concept be derived from this source.

To grasp a concept, it may be necessary to provide a variety of musical settings and experiences which will allow children to *focus on* or *experience* the same type of concept which is drawn from this musical analysis.

Concepts may be:

Specific — limited to a given idea or purpose

General — an integration of specific concepts

Concrete — perceived at first hand

Abstract — remembered from previous experience and transferred to a new, sometimes related experience (this is the highest level of conceptual understanding).

Steps in Conceptualization (Concept-formation):

1. *Perception* — this is the first phase in teaching (the importance of *real* musical experience in which behavioral objectives are clear-cut).
2. *Conceptualization* — assembling and organizing bits of meaning into a conceptual whole. (The individual gradually puts the pieces of the experience together to achieve synthesis.)
3. *Application and transfer* — the individual becomes able to use his new understandings in a variety of settings to solve new problems.

An important step in the conceptualization process is that teachers must help students become aware of *musical ideas in musical settings* . . . that is to say, *the student must become involved in some form of music-making or music-experiencing, together with conceptualizing his experiences.* In this process, it is essential to help students sort out and classify in their minds such musical features as rhythmic combinations, tonal patterns, chord-harmonic relationships, comparative timbres, phrase and pattern structure, qualities of musical expression, similarities and differences in form. These understandings form the *conceptual objectives* which are one of the most important of the desired musical behaviors. Thus, the first step in deciding on appropriate musical behaviors (concepts) for a given group of students is to turn to an analysis of the music itself.

It must also be remembered that *continual exposure and reinforcement of concepts is essential to musical growth.* Once the educator has determined what conceptual learnings are desirable, realistic, and possible for his class to achieve, behavioral objectives--the learning expectancies of the students may be established. The precise manner in which this is done forms the basis for Chapter V.

Developing Meaning

Concepts acquire meaning only in terms of the experience of the learner. Thus, there must be a concept-referent by which the student can understand and utilize the knowledge which is presented to him. To understand how this works, examine the general process of referent-stimulus-percept shown in Figure 10.

Figure 10

CONCEPT AND ITS REFERENT

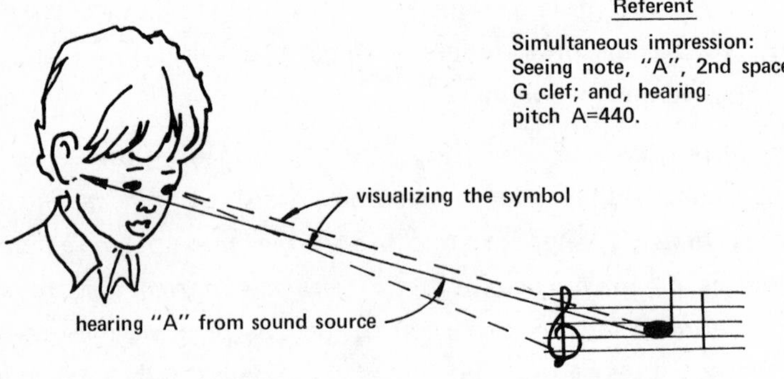

Referent: (single) seeing or hearing the note "A" (multiple-simultaneous) seeing and hearing the note "A"

Stimulus: the physical impression on the eyes and ears (receptors)

Percept: psycho-neural connection made which causes the brain to receive, process, and convey the meaning of the contact to the individual

Concept: when the connection between percept and experience has been so organized that it is understood by the individual

The first perception of the national symbol "A" is meaningless to a student, unless the referent also includes the musical pitch. The singer or instrumentalist also requires accompanying neural and physiological associations connected with the manner by which they produce the sound "A". Thus, the student sees, feels, and hears--going from referent to stimulus--he perceives and begins to comprehend as his experience is organized to make sense to him. It is at this stage that *meaning must be reinforced by practice* to establish the pattern and fix the learning.

If we were to substitute a picture of an object such as a person, place, or thing in the above figure, it would be easier to understand the process-but music adds a further dimension of complexity. The referent shown here is a *musical symbol*---thus it is *not* the real referent but rather the symbol for it. This is the reason that the learning of musical symbolism (music reading) should never be taught in isolation until students have sufficient experience to remember what sound the symbol represents. Consequently, children must have a great deal of experience in hearing and working with musical sound prior to practice and drill in music reading.

The general process of learning from referents is shown in Figure 11.

Figure 11

Learning from Concept-Referents

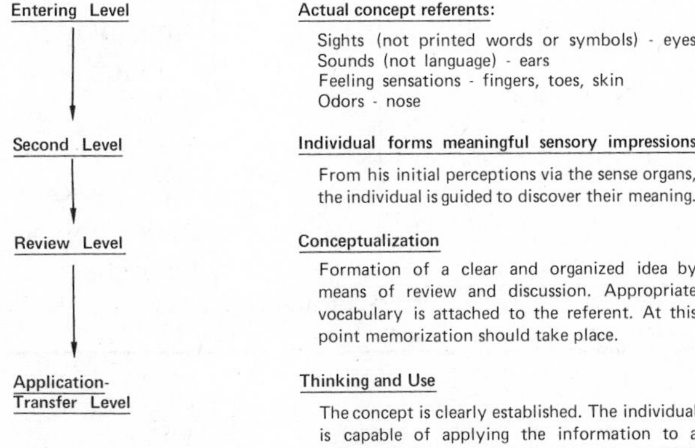

Entering Level
Actual concept referents:
Sights (not printed words or symbols) - eyes
Sounds (not language) - ears
Feeling sensations - fingers, toes, skin
Odors - nose
Second Level
Individual forms meaningful sensory impressions
From his initial perceptions via the sense organs, the individual is guided to discover their meaning.
Review Level
Conceptualization
Formation of a clear and organized idea by means of review and discussion. Appropriate vocabulary is attached to the referent. At this point memorization should take place.
Application-Transfer Level
Thinking and Use
The concept is clearly established. The individual is capable of applying the information to a variety of situations. He is also able to think abstractly about the concept.

Figure 12 illustrates how this process is applied to the learning of musical concepts.

Figure 12

Music Reading as Concept Development

(Read down)

Process	Music Media	Application
Decoding initial sensation or perception	**Structure of Music** 1. Elements 2. Activity media 3. Musical form 4. Expression	Analysis of the quality of sound the symbol represents.
Comprehension hypothesizing and problem-solving	↓	*Music vocabulary introduced. Concept understood
Utilization try-out and practice	↓	Reading music in order to perform (sing, play, conduct). Reading music to understand what others are performing (listening)

*Note: an accurate musical vocabulary is essential to music reading and concept development

Implications for teaching are several, particularly for young children and inexperienced music students in junior and senior high school.

* *First impressions are lasting* — the initial perception or mental set often overrides later associations (how often have we heard the expression, "If he could just have been started correctly!")
* *Associate pitches with visual clues* — initially, this may be in terms of "opposites"--high and low. Later it should incorporate more precise discriminations of "step, skip, or jump". Finally, exact pitches and intervals should be associated with musical symbols and vocabulary established.
* *Use musical instruments with melodic and harmonic sounds* — to establish accurate referents. Remember that the student who is allowed to manipulate (play) the sound on an instrument has a much more accurate association of pitch to symbol. (Does this "ring a bell" for vocal music students?)
* *Develop tonal relationships by providing opportunities to "connect" different pitches in a musical context.* Since musical tones used in melody are components of melodic structure, the tonal memory of students should be reinforced by repeated associations with aural-visual melodic fragments, motives and phrases.
* *Establish eye-ear durational concepts* — progress from simple perceptions of "long-short", "even-uneven", etc. to precise rhythmic durations and patterns.
* *Introduce the feeling of modality and key centers* by careful listening to chords and chord progressions and relating them to appropriate use in the music being experienced (autoharp, guitar, piano, singing in harmony, etc.).
* *When coordinated neuro-muscular actions are required as in performing (singing, playing, etc.) a psychomotor "set" should be established--the "feel" which accom-*

panies the sound referent. The degree of musical skill involved can be raised or lowered, depending on use and practice.

* *Symbolic concepts (sight reading of music) should be presented only when the students have experienced music sufficiently to recall its sound from previous experience.*
* *Habitual response (automatic reaction, as in remembering correct fingering patterns) occurs only after many replications of a given learning experience in which the students' responses may be repeated with little or no variation.* (Susie--why can't you remember to play the correct finger for Ab?!)
* *As concepts are being formed, the student is also learning the value of that experience for him*--thus, his sense of value of how his impressions affect him becomes part of the total concept-formation. This tends to influence his behavior toward that thing. This is *affective learning.*

The object of the teacher should be to facilitate concept-learning by providing the necessary experiences and conditions to produce the desired student behavior. From the foregoing, it should be obvious that in order to understand concepts, the student must be guided to experience music meaningfully. It also involves providing referential information at appropriate times. An important step in this process is helping the student become aware of musical elements and ideas and how they are expressed in a musical context. It is essential that he begin to sort out, classify and use such things as rhythm and tonal patterns, chord progressions and relationships, comparative timbres, phrase and pattern structure, qualities of musical expression, similarities in form, techniques for performing, and so on. These elements may be generalized and later brought forth to apply to successive experiences.

Creativity

Creativity deals with individual qualities which may be described as innovative, inventive or original in nature. As one aspect of its relationship to ideational behavior (concept-formation), creativity implies the manner in which the unique experiences and ideas of individuals are organized and expressed.

Fluency, flexibility and elaboration are all considered to be facets of creativity. Research has shown that individuals who are unusually creative are those who are:

* Capable of unusual abilities to think fluently
* Able to remember many things and recall them for later use
* Flexible, pliable, changeable (not habit-bound)
* Capable of inventing and elaborating in great detail from what they already know
* Willing to find a variety of solutions to the same problem
* Make up their own theories and postulates based on real or imagined experience

Elaboration is one aspect of creativity which is especially important in music and art. From psychologists' descriptions of artists and composers at work, Guilford reports that most persons involved in creative activity develop quite early a type of generalized scheme, motif or plan which, considered psychologically is a system. The system obtains clarity and detail with preliminary evaluations and revisions which may be either major or minor in nature. The elaboration is completed with whatever "touch-up" work the artist or composer deems necessary to perfect his work of art.[8]

The child who is never allowed to explore or use musical media on his own is never exposed to his potential for self-expression and creative development. It should be remembered that although every child cannot hope to be a creative genius, *each one is his own kind of musical inventor.* Teachers should encourage every child to experiment with music--to analyze, inquire, and solve his own problems in addition to those presented to him in the planned instructional sequence. There should also be a variety of teaching strategies to fit different learning situations--large group, small group, and individualized learning. Teachers should also try various ways of explaining musical concepts and skills and take care to stimulate and nourish self-expression and creative diversity. As we shall see in a later section of the book, there should also be a reorganization of the school in terms of more efficient use of time, space and personnel--one aspect of helping teachers (hence, also students) be more creative.

Summary

Learning is a process of behavior-modification. It is how individuals know, understand and use concepts, feelings, values, symbols, skills and habits. Learning is a process of complex change which is rooted in psychology. As its base, it is structured on educational theory, youth needs and social setting.

Historically, learning theory has progressed from earlier atomistic (singular) views which emphasized naturalism, memory, transfer of training, readiness-exercise-effect, and conditioned response to pluralistic-holistic theories currently predominant. Field and Gestalt learning emphasizes the totality of one's learning from a variety of stimuli simultaneously present. Piaget and Gagné stress the importance of maturity in relationship to sensorimotor and intellectual development. The latter author introduced the concept of sequential behavior modification through the cumulative effects of problem-solving. Another dimension of individual learning provides clues to the importance of related intellectual factors which are changeable both quantitatively and qualitatively (Guilford).

The bases of learning presented in this Chapter included motivation-maturation-readiness, perception, discovery-deductive-inductive learning, concept development, meaning, and creativity. Intrinsic learning provides a significant clue to self-motivation and individual developmental growth in music. Ideational learning in music stresses concept-development by means of perception, inquiry-problem-solving, and development of specific concepts from abstract generalizations (and vice versa). Discovery allows each student to find meanings and relationships on his own. Deductive learning stems from concepts presented by the teacher with inferences and applications deduced by the students (from the specific to the general); and, inductive learning reverses the process (from the general to the specific). Musical ideas and insights grow from total experiencing of music in feelingful, apperceptive ways. Creativity stresses uniqueness of individual musical expression. Fluency, flexibility and elaboration are all considered facets of creativity.

Topics For Discussion

1. How would you characterize musical growth in terms of current learning theory? What are its various stages? What type of musical experience appears essential to it?
2. Can you apply Piaget's or Gagne's theories to the learning of specific musical behaviors?
3. Discuss Guilford's "structure-of-the-intellect" model in terms of its implications for music symbolism and music reading. How would you relate this to "decoding" music symbols, presented later in the chapter?
4. Can you cite specific examples from your own experience of types of problem-solving and self-motivated activities which aided you or someone whom you know to acquire concepts?
5. How does maturation and experience affect musical growth and concept development?
6. List and discuss several extrinsic motivators which you feel to be valuable to learning. Under what conditions might these affect learning adversely?
7. What are some of the most important values which you have derived from your experience with music (intrinsic values derived from learning music in school)?
8. Select a given music activity and describe how it might be presented to a group of students who had never done this before. What part does learning sequence play in this process?
9. How can individuals be encouraged to discover facts and relationships in music (discovery, deductive and inductive learning)?
10. Describe some classroom conditions which would be conducive to creative development of students.

Suggested Readings

Guilford, J.P., *Intelligence, Creativity and Their Educational Implications.* San Diego, California: Robert R. Knapp, Publisher, 1968.

Gagne, Robert M., *The Conditions of Learning.* New York: Holt, Rinehart and Winston, Inc., 1965.

Leonhard, Charles and Robert W. House. *Foundations and Principles of Music Education,* 2nd Ed. New York: McGraw-Hill Book Company, Inc., 1972. See Ch. 5.

Mursell, James L. *Education for Musical Growth.* Boston: Ginn and Company, 1948.

__________ "Growth Processes in Music Education", *Basic Concepts in Music Education,* National Society for the Study of Education Fifty-seventh Yearbook, Part I. Chicago, Illinois: The Society, 1958.

Sidnell, Robert., *Building Instructional Programs in Music Education.* Englewood Cliffs, N.J.: Prentice-Hall, Inc., 1973. See Ch. 4.

Thorpe, Louis P., "Learning Theory and Music Teaching", *Basic Concepts in Music Education,* Fifty-seventh Yearbook of the National Society for the Study of Education, Part I. Chicago, Illinois: The University of Chicago Press, 1958.

CHAPTER FIVE

GOALS, CONCEPTS & OBJECTIVES IN MUSIC EDUCATION

Where there is no vision, the people perish.

Proverbs XXIX. 18

Goals, concepts and objectives are related aspects of planning for teaching. Whether for guiding individual educative actions of the classroom or for program planning and budgeting systems (PPBS -- later to be discussed), the distinctions are important to all music educators. The educator must first think in broad terms of those aspects of the music program which are held to be essential for learners through their school years. From these broad goals *(global objectives)* come the teacher's own long-term goals *(program objectives)* of what he/she hopes to accomplish in music for his/her own class for the school year. From these long-term goals, shorter goals will be developed by means of organizing into various educational "packages", which include classes, units, monthly or weekly learning segments, and finally -- *daily lesson plans* which utilize extremely short-term, very specific objectives, and procedures for implementing these objectives. At the level of the daily lesson plan, specific teaching strategies will be devised, generally thought of as *teaching procedures.*

All goals and objectives should be considered of and stated in terms of desired educational behaviors. Thus, what is being described here is a hierarchy of *behavioral objectives* which *contain instructions concerning the proposed level of performance expected of the learners as a result of a given educational experience.* Behavioral objectives place emphasis on observable (measurable) student growth -- the accent thus is placed on *content* and *what the student is reasonably expected to do with this content over a prescribed period of time,* such as a semester, month, or day. Social goals and broad, subjective areas of affective behavior may be important contributors to this process but are important only if they contribute to the student's use and understanding of what he is doing. Thus, it becomes important for the music educator to use action verbs such as (will) play, demonstrate, describe, compare, or choose, rather than more subjective words such as appreciate or like.

Long-range plans should include broad statements, such as:

The music program at XYZ School will assist each student to

* Become aware of musical sound and expression as an important artistic expression of man.
* Participate in a wide variety of musical experience, appropriate to his/her level of experience, understanding, and accomplishment.
* Demonstrate increasing skill, understanding and critical judgement in the use of the tools of music by which he/she may recreate the works of others or express himself/herself in musical ways.
* Understand representative musical literature of various forms, periods, and styles performed in a variety of idioms.

Conceptual Objectives

Concepts were defined in Chapter IV as thoughts or ideas which resulted from concrete learning experiences in music. It will also be remembered that continual exposure and reinforcement of concepts is essential to musical growth. The first step which should precede the statement of behavioral objectives is to state those concepts upon which the proposed learning experience is to be based. These become the *conceptual objectives,* which are applied primarily to cognition (knowing).

If we begin with an inspection of the music we wish to present to a given class, the first step is to analyze those aspects of the music which will lead to concept formation. The following are illustrations:

Elements of Music:

Concepts of Tonal Organization:

* Melody is formed by means of a series of musical tones (pitches) which may be described as *tonal movement.*
* The shape or contour of the melodic line results from successions of higher or lower tones which can be identified and remembered.
* Tonal movement may be described in terms of the way individual sounds in the melody are presented; such as, moving up, down, or by repeated tone.
* As individuals become more expert in recognizing intervals in the melody, tonal movement may be identified by the precise interval involved (such as primes, seconds, thirds, fourths, fifths, octaves, etc. -- or by half, whole-step, etc.).
* Musical scales are represented by the particular order of notes and the pattern of intervals involved in the tonal sequence. (These may be specifically described as major, minor, pentatonic, whole-tone, etc.).
* The tonal range of a given melody may be described as the *distance between its upper and lower limits.* The tessitura of a melody is its *average range* or, the range where most of its tones occur (Tessitura for singers is the average or *comfortable range* of the singer's voice.).
* Tones in a melody may form phrases, just as words form phrases or sentences. A phrase thus becomes a *musical thought or idea.* Songs may have several phrases.

* Phrases in a melodic line are sometimes repeated in a *sequence* which results from the repetition of the same melodic pattern or motif at a higher or lower pitch.
* Specific tones may be identified by precise pitches -- and are named by the letters A through G. Visual identification of these pitches is determined by their placement on the musical staff in relationship to the clef involved (F, G, C, etc.).
* Contemporary practice does not limit musical scales to 7 tones, but may include all 12 tones of the chromatic series. 12-tone technique may include such compositional practices as *retrograde, inversion, octave displacement, and canonic imitation.*
* Harmony results from the combination of two or more tones performed simultaneously. Harmony may be identified by the vertical organization of these tones on the musical staff.
* The characteristic sound of melodies results from a combination of tone and melodic rhythm.

Note: The above are basic concepts of tonal organization. A greater degree of sophistication would be expected as learners become more experienced, such as in specialized (i.e., choral and/or instrumental) classes or at secondary school levels.

Concepts of Rhythmic Organizations:

* Rhythm in music includes the following:
    - beat
    - sets of beats (2's, 3's)
    - stronger and weaker beats (accented beats, unaccented beats)
    - sets of beats grouped into measures (meter)
    - simple grouping of longer and shorter tones into rhythmic patterns (melody rhythm)
* Rhythm consists of both durational sounds and silences.
* Sets of beats (meter) move in 2's or 3's or multiples and combinations thereof (including simple quadruple and various compound meters).

* There is a regular grouping of accented beats and unaccented beats in symmetrical rhythm ($\frac{2}{4}$, $\frac{3}{4}$, $\frac{4}{4}$, $\frac{6}{8}$ etc.).
* Assymmetrical meters, such as those with 5, 7 and 11 beats in a measure, are distinguished by irregular patterns of accents of *both* two's and three's (/uu/u; /u/u/uu; etc.).
* The characteristic pattern of sound duration within a given melody is called *melody rhythm.*
* Polyrhythms are created when contrasting rhythmic groupings occur simultaneously. Polyrhythms and changing meters are interesting rhythmic devices used by many contemporary composers.
* Accents occurring on normally unaccented beats results in *syncopation.*
* Various types of meters, tempi and rhythm patterns are used in different forms of music.
* In a given composition, the tempo (speed of performance) may be changed for expressive purposes.

Concepts of Harmonic Organization:

* Two or more sounds created simultaneously are called *multiple sound.*
* When single tones of a melody are heard sequentially, this is called *melody.* When two or more tones are heard simultaneously, this is called *harmony.* Conventional harmony is created by a characteristic vertical arrangement of tones in intervals of 3rds, called *chords.*
* *Monophony* consists of a single, unaccompanied melody. *Homophony* results from a melody (usually the highest part) supported by chordal structure. *Polyphony* is characterized by music having two or more independent melodies or parts of relatively equal importance.
* Melodies may be accompanied by harmonizations created by other voices or instruments. A given melody may be harmonized in various ways.

* Chords may be inverted to place the root and other members of the chord in positions other than the conventional root, 3rd, 5th (etc.) placement. Thus, an *inversion* is created by placing a tone other than the root in the lowest voice of the chord.
* Chords may contain added tones for quality and variety.
* *Bitonality and Polytonality* result from chords or harmonizations in two or more keys being performed simultaneously. These devices are often found in contemporary music.
* In serial music, members of the "tone row" may also be played simultaneously. This device is called *a tone cluster.*

Concepts of Intensity and Timbre:

* The expressive effect of music is changed by means of *dynamics* (degrees of loud and soft) and *tempo* (speed of performance).
* The characteristic sound or tone color produced by various music sources (i.e., vocal, instrumental, electronic, etc.) is called *timbre.*
* Individual tones have characteristic shapes known as the *envelope.* Envelope may be programmed by a computer as in electronic music.

Concepts of Style:

* Not all music is played or sung in the same manner.
* The purpose of the music determines its character and how it should be performed (sung or played).
* *Articulation* describes the type of attack used to produce a given tone. This involves the relative degree of release and whether melodic tones are played in connected or detached fashion. The style of the composition dictates the correct articulation to be used in its performance.
* Various historical periods of music may be identified by their characteristic styles.

* The elements of music (tone, duration, timbre, intensity) may be used to describe a mood or an action or to suggest a story (as in program or descriptive music), or may be used simply in various expressive ways to vary the texture and style of music (as in absolute music).

Concepts of Form:

* Form in music results from the structure of its musical components. It is based upon the principle of repetition and contrast. *Unity* results from repeating musical patterns (melodic and/or rhythmic); *Variety* results from non-repetition. Contrast offers variety.
* The smallest musical segment (either melodic or rhythmic) is called a *motive.* Its fragmentary nature may be likened roughly to a word in spoken or written language. A *phrase* is a musical thought or idea resulting from several motives or a continuous pattern, punctuated by cadences. Phrases vary in length -- with conventional phrases being two or four measures in length. Phrases may be combined to produce a larger whole.
* Compositions may have two or more sections which offer variety. Phrases and/or sections may be identified by repetition or contrast as being the same, similar, or different according to the use of the melody and melody rhythm. Some of the characteristic designs include:

  Antecedent-consequent phrases (question-answer)

  Unary (A), Binary (A,B) or Ternary (A,B,A) simple song forms

  Rondo (A,B,A,C,A)

  Theme and Variations (A,A',A'',A''',A'''', etc.)

  Fugue (repetition of principal subjects in higher or lower pitch or in contrasting instruments)

  Sonata-allegro (classical symphony form -- exposition, development, recapitulation)

* Other types of form providing variety for contemporary composition include:

  Improvisation (freedom from conventional form)

  Aleatoric music ("chance" music--resulting from ways of producing music completely by "lot" or "chance".)

Concepts of Music Types and Performance Media:

* The characteristic sound of compositions results from the type of music and performance media utilized. These include:

  Folk music

  Composed music

  "Art" music

  Vocal music

  Instrumental music

  Electronic music

  "Pop" music

Concepts of Notation:

* Melodic contour can be pictured by a line drawing or other notations picturing the up-down, sequential movement of the melodic line.
* Notation of pitch on a staff also illustrates the contour of a melody.
* Melodies that move by intervals of a 2nd (step) are written from a line to a space to line on the staff.
* Melodies that move by 3rds are notated from line to line (skipping a space), or space to space (skipping a line) -- in each case, there is an intervening note which is omitted.
* Locating "one" or "do" identifies the tonal center of the song to which all other notes on the staff are related. In relative minor keys, "six" or "la" becomes the tonal center of the song.
* The top numeral of a meter (time) signature tells how many metric units are in the measure; the lower numeral indicates the kind of note that is the metric

unit. 8th, quarter, and half notes are commonly used as metric units.

* Durational values can be represented by various types notes (such as whole, half, quarter, eighth, sixteenth, etc.) and various divisions or combinations thereof. Rest symbols are used to indicate silences in the music of comparable duration.
* Clefs (such as F, G, and C) are used to indicate precise pitches on the musical staff.
* Other symbols (such as flats, sharps, dots, ties, slurs, repeat signs, etc.) may be used to indicate specific alterations in pitch, rhythm, articulation, mode of performance, etc.

It will be recognized that the foregoing concepts are not of equal difficulty. Therefore, music educators must be able to establish levels of difficulty appropriate for various levels of age and musical experience. This classification is known as a *taxonomy.* Such a taxonomy of concepts will help in specifying the precise objectives and learning experiences for a given group of learners -- as well as helping in the evaluation process as a result of the given learning. The taxonomy should be educationally and psychologically sound and should also make it possible for teachers and learners to use common vocabulary and musical principles with understanding and consistency.

According to Bloom and others, the taxonomy contains six major classes:[1]

1.00 Knowledge
2.00 Comprehension
3.00 Application
4.00 Analysis
5.00 Synthesis
6.00 Evaluation

Examples of the taxonomy, as applied to music education, may be found in a recent publication of the music committee of the California Association for Supervision and Curriculum Development.[2] By using the taxonomy to classify musical concepts, primary children might find that a concept which expresses the idea that "The contour of the music in this song results from up-down-same tones which sound and look like a hill" may be appropriate (1.0 Knowledge). Successively more mature and experienced students may, however, work with progressively higher levels of the same concept. For example: "This melody has characteristic motives and phrases which may be identified as the same, almost the same, or different" (2.0 Comprehension); "The harmonic structure of this song is based on I, and V_7 chords, which may be played on the autoharp" (3.0 Application); "The specific intervals used in this song range from primes, to 2nds, 3rds, and 5ths -- each may be properly identified." (4.0 Analysis); "The notational devices and symbols used in this melody may be applied to a new and unknown song." (5.0 Synthesis); and, "The melodic materials used in this composition will provide resources for the student to compose, perform, and evaluate the results of his musical efforts in parallel idioms. (6.0 Evaluation).

Concepts about music also involve the way in which it is performed (musical activity media), how it is constructed (musical structures), and its style and expressive elements. The combination of these musical elements comprise what is known as *concept clusters.* Thus, it is possible to identify tone as a specific element of music, but a *concept cluster dealing with music as a total experience involves tone in combination with duration, timbre and intensity.* To fully experience music, it is necessary to consider how it is produced, structured and expressed -- which is known as a concept cluster or synthesis of all the components of a musical experience.

Statements which illustrate the idea of concept clusters include the following:[3]

* Music is a combination of sounds and silences which are used to express the thoughts and feelings of composers.
* Musical sound involves the key elements of tone, duration, timbre and intensity which can be produced in a variety of ways.

* Musical styles are influenced by the various historical practices in music expression.
* Notation used in music is the symbolism used to communicate musical ideas from composer to performer to listener.

Figure 13 illustrates how concept clusters may be applied to the development of the "musical individual".

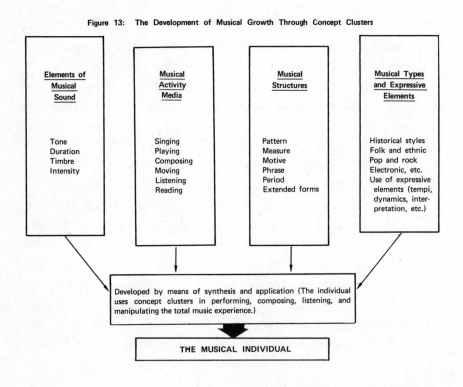

Figure 13: The Development of Musical Growth Through Concept Clusters

Elements of Musical Sound	Musical Activity Media	Musical Structures	Musical Types and Expressive Elements
Tone Duration Timbre Intensity	Singing Playing Composing Moving Listening Reading	Pattern Measure Motive Phrase Period Extended forms	Historical styles Folk and ethnic Pop and rock Electronic, etc. Use of expressive elements (tempi, dynamics, interpretation, etc.)

↓

Developed by means of synthesis and application (The individual uses concept clusters in performing, composing, listening, and manipulating the total music experience.)

↓

THE MUSICAL INDIVIDUAL

Behavioral Objectives

Behavioral objectives are those behaviors which the teacher expects the student to demonstrate in grasping a concept, skill or technique. Behavioral objectives apply to *cognitive, psychomotor, affective,* and *critical judgement* domains of musical learning. As noted in the previous section, it is important *first to state the concept, then the desired behavior.* Behavioral objectives may vary for the same concept, since the teacher should be looking for a variety of ways to present the same idea in a new setting to achieve the various levels of conceptualization (see Chapter IV). They will also vary in level, according to the age, maturity, experience and individual differences of students.

To state the process involved, the teacher should first examine the music from which the cognitive objectives are to be derived (concepts) -- then proceeds to state the behavioral objectives in terms of specific skills and competencies applied to these concepts. The difference in objectives for teacher and student is that teaching objectives tell what the instructor intends to teach whereas student objectives (i.e., behavioral) describe what it is that the student will learn as a result of the application of teaching procedures. Both types of objectives deal with *intent* but the focus in dealing with instruction should be on behavioral objectives which should be thought of as *expected changes in behavior* which are attainable by by most[4] of the students working at a given level or area of learning. This also involves a careful analysis of levels of difficulty required in the process of producing a given concept, skill, or technique. The manner of stating the objective should indicate what is to be learned, how it will be learned, and indicate some means of evaluating the effectiveness of the learning experience.

Well-stated behavioral objectives should state the *conditions* (how, where, when), *what the student will be doing,* and his *expected level of performance* in completing the musical experience. This requires that verbs be as specific as possible -- and that the statement be carefully phrased to provide the necessary description.

Terms Which Are Imprecise and Overly-General:

The following partial list of terms are too general and should be avoided in writing behavioral objectives:

Do
Enjoy
Believe
Appreciate
Know
Understand
Examine
Develop

Terms Which are More Specific:

The following verbs are more specific, hence, they are better suited to use in writing behavioral objectives:

Compare
Contrast
Alphabetize
Arrange
Compose
Conduct
Describe
Clap/tap
Match
Sing
Improvise
Dance
Play
Articulate
Identify and read (as in music)
Locate
Orchestrate
Tape (as in electronic music)

General Considerations in Selecting the Learning Activity:

The most important general considerations in writing behavioral objectives are:[5]

1. The primary goal of any learning activity is positive *behavior modification.*

2. Behavior modification is accomplished by changing the student's *concepts, actions, feelings and judgements.*
3. Change is effected by means of *personal interaction with the learning activity.*
4. Permanence (retention) of learning is accomplished by *fixing habits and motor skills which accompany the concept being learned.*
5. Musical symbols stand for specific musical concepts and should always be *introduced by means of the musical sound or activity which they represent.*

Examples of Behavioral Objectives in Music:

The following examples illustrate ways of writing behavioral objectives in music:

* After learning the song, "Joy to the World", in which step-bells were introduced to show the descending scale-wise motive beginning the opening phrase, students of the 1st grade will be able to identify the melodic direction of succeeding portions of the song by using corresponding hand levels with 70% accuracy.
* After reviewing the score to "Old MacDonald Had A Farm" in which note values were identified, students of the 3rd grade class will be able to identify and clap the note values of "Skip to My Lou", and will further use correct vocabulary to name quarter, eighth, and sixteenth notes in the latter with 75% accuracy.
* Given an unfamiliar piece of music, the above 3rd graders will be able to tap or clap the rhythm of the melody with 75% accuracy.
* After listening to an unfamiliar selection of music, a 5th grade class will be able to name 3 out of 5 of the predominant solo instruments with 80% accuracy; after three hearings, they will also be able to identify form as ______________________________ .

A higher degree of performance expectancy would be illustrated by the following:

* After four weeks of instruction in a beginning instru-

ments class the students will demonstrate the correct fingering for the written C major scale with 90% accuracy.

* Upon completion of six weeks of the voice class, students will be able to demonstrate correct posture and breathing and utilize these in singing a simple melodic line, with 80% accuracy.
* Given an opportunity to use the materials of the media center on an individual basis as part of the humanities-arts class, high school students will select and use appropriate reference materials in preparing listening reports.

To write the appropriate behavior for a specified music activity, music educators must be able to:

* Identify the expected terminal behavior by name (teaching objective).
* State the conditions under which the behavior will operate.
* Use the appropriate verb to describe what will be done.
* Give the expected performance level which indicates *how well* the student is expected to perform as a result of a given learning experience.

Remember -- the general rule in applying an area of music learning to one of the behavioral domains is indicated by the type of action expressed in the behavior.

The Cognitive Domain - has to do with recognizing or knowing.

Example:

(After working with the music specialist and classroom teacher for one semester in second grade music - - -)

Given an example of a song with two contrasting phrases - - - the student *will identify* with 75 percent accuracy each phrase as "same" or "different" from a listening example.

The Psycho-motor Domain - has to do with a form of action in responding, acting, or performing.

Example:

Given a semester's work in a junior high school beginning

instruments class - - -

the student will play with 75 percent accuracy the correct fingerings for the major scales of ______, ______, and ______.

The Affective Domain - has to do with accepting, valuing, or choosing.

Example:

(After 6 weeks of playing autoharp accompaniments in a general music class - - -)

Given a new (easy) folk song using I and V^7 harmonizations - - -

the student *will choose* I and V^7 chords to accompany the song with 80% accuracy.

The Critical Judgment Domain - has to do with receiving, choosing, and preferring.

Example:

Given a year's study in a high school instrumental performance group in which interpretation and musicianship have been stressed - - -

the student will select the best performances in a competition-festival and give reasons for his preferences in musical terms.

Behavioral Objectives in the Psychomotor Domain:

Skills in listening (the student will be able to hear and identify - - -)

High and low pitches; repeated tones; melody contour

Varying intensity in sound (dynamics)

Fast and slow (tempi)

Different tone colors (timbre)

Characteristic melody rhythms

Phrases which are identical, almost identical, and different

Metric groupings of 2's and 3's

Specific intervals of a given scale form

Multiple sounds, including chordal structure

Characteristic musical forms

Skills in singing (. . .will be able to. . .)

Sing with correct tone (commensurate with age and experience)

Sing with correct tone production (relaxed, easy, supported breath)

Sing with good enunciation and diction

Sing melodies with increasing accuracy in terms of pitch and rhythm (independently of teacher and/ or recording)

Develop a singing range consistent with age, experience, and physical capacity

Sing with increasing expression and artistry (phrasing, tempo, dynamics, color and mood)

Skills in bodily movement and rhythms (will be able to - - -)

Express feelings and ideas in movement

Respond physically (bodily or with instruments) to melody rhythm

Interpret music freely and creatively with bodily movement which is appropriate to the characteristics of the music

Contour melodies with their hands

Tap the pulse of the music correctly

Skills in Playing instruments (will be able to - - -)

Play simple pitched and non-pitched instruments to represent or accompany songs learned in class

Improvise original melodies and rhythms

Compose in a variety of styles

Select and use various instruments with a growing understanding of appropriateness of sound and tone color

Play "real" instruments (i.e., band and orchestra) of their choice with increasing skill and musicality as a result of class music instruction

Skills in using musical notation (will be able to - - -)

Understand how music is a visual representation of how music sounds

Use various forms of "intermediate" notation (i.e., "blank" notation, contours, butcher-paper compositions) to represent sounds they can perform

Use charts, flannelboards, chalkboard, etc. for more precise applications of notation; such as identifying phrases, motives, intervals, and reading simple melodic or rhythmic patterns

Read and use (as in sing, play, or compose) various precise symbols of notation; including, melody, rhythm, key, meter, marks of expression and performance.

Behavioral Objectives in the Affective Domain (having to do with one's feelings about music):

The student will give increasing evidence of:

Pleasure in participating in music (singing, playing, rhythms, etc.)

Greater attentiveness while listening

Gradual preference for some activities in music

Desire to use music in informal (non-structured) situations--including at home and in the community

An increasing appreciation of the performance of others

Behavioral Objectives in the Critical Judgment Domain (having to do with use, valuing, and forming independent judgments):

The individual will give increasing evidence of:

Selectivity

A high level of response to music

Preferential judgments and valuing

The ability to conceptualize valuing and critical judgments

Note: At this level of behavior, the *sine qua non* of musical experience should be reached. Thus, critical judgment behaviors should include *how the individual responds to values, and organizes musical experience in meaningful ways for himself.*

Model For Writing Lesson Plans

In addition to conceptual and behavioral objectives, lesson plans should list the necessary activities, materials and procedures required to complete the lesson. Music educators should understand that learning will be as good as the quality of planning involved. From what has been said in the previous chapter about the importance of learning sequence, it should be obvious that sequencing of daily learning experiences (the step-by-step procedures of the lesson plan) are exceptionally important. This sequence should contain four steps; namely, (a) an introduction (possibly also review of previously learned material); (b) the new problem or activity for the day; (c) application and transfer to a related problem; and, (d) evaluation, summary and conclusion. A highly critical aspect of this sequence will be a decision as to the relative amount of time required by each activity of the lesson.

First Grade Lesson Plan:

ABC School   Miss Smithson, Room 4   Time Allotment: 20 minutes

Objectives:

Conceptual:

Music has two basic ways of moving--up-down in melody, and long-short in rhythm. The songs used in this lesson illustrate scale-wise movement (up) and contrasting walking, running, and holding notes in rhythm.

Behavioral:

Given an opportunity to learn a song with a 5-note ascending scale pattern (repeated), the children will identify its upward movement by using hand levels; some will play the pattern on the step-bells. (Another song will provide an opportunity to distinguish long-short rhythm patterns. After seeing the chart showing stepping, running, and holding rhythms, the children will learn a song and identify where they hear-feel these patterns in the music.)

Materials:

Charts, step-bells, drum rhythm sticks, teacher's music books.

Activities:

Singing, chart-notation identification, dramatizing rhythm, playing step-bells.

Procedure:

Introduction & Review:

Review familiar song, "If You're Happy and You Know It." (clap your hands, snap your fingers, tap your toe) Question: "How did we move to this music?" Mention that there are also other ways of moving to music.

New Problem:

Question: "Have you ever had to have someone call you

to get up in the morning?" Introduce and Teach New Song, "Five Angels," p. 46, *Making Music Your Own, Teachers Edition I* (Silver Burdett Co., 1964). Chart: We've been singing about *getting up.* Does anyone hear (or see) something in this song that is also *getting up? (or going up?)* This is called *stepping up in melody.* Application: Invite 5 different children to play melodic pattern on step bells as class sings. (If time--dramatize what each angel is doing.)

Transfer:

There is also another way of stepping in music. (show chart) Question: "What 3 ways of stepping do you see on this chart?" (Walk, run, hold--perhaps tip-toe) Called *stepping in rhythm.* "We're going to learn a new song which uses all 3 ways of stepping in rhythm." Teach song: "Hey Betty Martin," p. 10, *Making Music Your Own, I.* Question: "What's different about a tip-toe? (contrast with Walk) Invite different children to walk to the rhythm (or have entire class walk in place at their seats).

Evaluation, Summary and Conclusion:

Question: "What 2 ways of stepping did we learn today?" *(stepping in melody, stepping in rhythm)* "What was different about these two ways of stepping?" Sing review song of children's choice.

Third Grade Lesson Plan:

DEF School Mr. Rogers, Room 8 Time Allotment: 25 minutes

Objectives:

Conceptual:

The grouping of underlying pulses by measures of 2, 3, and 4 beats is called *metric beat.* The metric beat may be identified by the upper figure in the time signature, and may be heard by placing the strong beat (accent) on the first beat of each measure. The melody rhythm *(rhythm pattern)* is characterized by the relative duration of the notes in the melody.

Behavioral:

Given an opportunity to identify the 3 terms *metric beat, accent, and melody rhythm,* the students will apply this to a known song by clapping all three. They will then apply the information to a new song.

Materials:

Charts, autoharp (for pitch reference), drum, 2 rhythm sticks, 1 pair maracas, *Exploring Music, Book 3* (Holt, Rinehart, Winston)

Activities:

Singing; chart-notation and term identification; clapping metric beats, accents, melody rhythm; identifying meter from the upper number of time signatures, playing 3 rhythm instruments.

Procedure:

Introduction and Review:

Review familiar song, "Skip to My Lou"

New Problem:

Question: "What ways do you know that music moves?" Introduce Chart. Today, we will find 3 specific ways related to the beat of music--*metric beat, accent, melody rhythm* (define). Let's try these (do examples from chart) Introduce Chart 2 (rhythmic notation for "London Bridge") Can anyone identify this song? (You may recognize it as "London Bridge") Discuss why it is difficult to recognize music without the tune. Introduce new song, "Michael, Row Your Boat Ashore," EM3, p. 91. After learning the song, identify its metric beat, accent, melody rhythm (clap)! If time, add the following instruments to emphasize:

DRUM - accent

STICKS - metric beat

MARACAS - melody rhythm

Transfer (and application):

Using pp. 8 (2's), 20 (4's), and 27 (3's) in the students' books, identify from the time signature the metric beat of each song. Teach new song, "Love Somebody," EM3,

p. 116. Identify and clap metric beat, accent. Question: "Can you discover where these melody patterns are found?" (Teacher claps "Johnny, Johnny, here I come"-line 1 and "Find me very quickly, here I come" -line 4. Question: "This song has an interesting melody rhythm--can anyone tell me whether most of this melody rhythm is longer or shorter than the metric beat? (shorter) Is it even or uneven? (even)--We call this dividing the beat." Repeat song for emphasis, practicing new information by clapping (divide class for metric beat, accent, melody rhythm).

Evaluation, Summary and Conclusion:

"What did we learn about the 3 new terms today?" "If we learn a new song tomorrow, how should we go about doing each (metric beat, accent, melody rhythm) to help learn the song?" Conclude with a familiar song of the children's choice.

Junior High School General Music Lesson Plan:

Jetstar Jr. High Miss Rosemead, A-1, Music Bldg. Time: 45 minutes

Objectives:

Conceptual:

Unary, variations, and fugue forms in music are all represented by one principal theme.

Behavioral:

Given an opportunity to review a familiar canon and listen to appropriate recorded examples, the students will correctly describe the principal uses of a single theme in unary, variations, and fugue examples. They will also sing canons and rounds to illustrate imitation in music.

Materials:

Recordings:

"Wild Horseman," Bowmar Orchestral Lib. BOL-64

"Little Fugue in G Minor" Adv. in Music 6-1

"Pop Goes the Weasel" Adv. in Music 4-1

Music Book:

Discovering Music Together, Book 8 (Follett)

Activities:

Singing, listening, term identification (vocabulary words: unary, canonical imitation, variations, fugue).

Procedure:

Introduction and Review:

Review "Dona Nobis Pacem," p. 117. After singing this canon, discuss its melodic qualities, pointing out the imitative concept in canonical imitation (rounds and canons).

New Problem:

We have other ways in which composers use single themes. Play "Wild Horseman," by Schumann. Listen and discuss. What happens on successive repetitions of the theme (minor changes in dynamics and a few alterations in melody)?

Transfer and Application:

What would happen if a composer took a familiar theme and decided to vary it upon successive repetitions? (Theme and variations) In what ways could the building blocks of music (tone, duration, timbre and intensity) be changed to provide interest and variety to a single theme; (list on chalkboard) Play "Variations on the Theme, 'Pop Goes the Weasel' " by Calliet. Discuss how this composer varied the music.

Additional Transfer:

Define fugue. Have class develop a fugue in rhythm--notate on chalkboard (1st-clap; 2nd-tap; 3rd feet; 4th-pencils) Learn by rote the theme to "Little Fugue in G Minor" by Bach--then listen.

1st hearing - give basic clues to watch

Repeated hearings(s) - Discover how many times subject reappears (what instrument?) What is surprise at end of composition? (tonic MAJOR chord)

Evaluation, Summary and Conclusion:

Briefly review (questions) what was learned. Assign committees for tomorrow--problem: find other melodies which are essentially single themes and discover how the composer has treated them. Be prepared to report to class. Conclude by singing review song, "Music Alone Shall Live," p. 25

Branching and Enrichment:

Discover (books) how artists and writers have treated single themes.

Junior High School Instrumental Music Lesson Plan

Jetstar Jr. High Mr. Ross, A-2, Music Bldg. Time: 45 minutes

Objectives:

Conceptual:

Lesson ______ introduces a new problem of divided beats and uneven rhythm in simple quadruple meter$^{4}_{4}$. The regular metric beat may be divided into notes of even or uneven duration.

Conceptual: Behavioral:

(Select one or more, as appropriate to the lesson)

1. The students will tap, then play an even succession of quarter notes with 75% accuracy on the reference pitch of concert Bb.
2. After explanation of equal divisions of the beat
   ♩ = ♫

   the students will demonstrate the ability to count the metric beat ($^{4}_{4}$) while tapping with 70% accuracy the equal eight note divisions.
   ♫ ♫ ♫ ♫
3. (Based upon the assumption that 1 and 2 have been completed) The students will demonstrate the ability to play alternating quarter and eighth note rhythm patterns on the reference pitch with 80% accuracy.
   ♩ ♫ ♩ ♫
4. After explanation of even-uneven rhythm equivalents, the students will be able to clap the following patterns with 75% accuracy.
   ♩‿♫ = ♩. ♪
5. The students will be confronted with a new problem of even and uneven rhythm patterns and will be able

to clap and/or perform on their given instrument correctly 5 out of 7 given examples.

Materials:

Instruments, chalkboard, *First Division Band Course, Book 2* (Belwin-Mills Publishing Corp., 1968)

Activities:

Warm-up, review, playing, identifying and applying new concept.

Procedure:

Introduction and Review:

(Order of rehearsal-lesson is on board) Remind group what is to be covered during the day. Listen-tune-adjust. Warm up on unison Bb concert scale, using various rhythms and articulations. Check intonation on leading tones. Review "Frere Jacques" p. 4, checking articulations. Refer to various note (rhythm) divisions in this (half, quarter, eighth).

New Problem:

Check notation on blackboard (see behavioral objectives). Discuss and clap equivalencies for dotted quarter-eighth. Play. Introduce p. 3, "College Song." First apply rhythm patterns to each note of the Bb concert scale. Then play patterns a through d, indicated in this lesson. Clap uneven rhythm of the song, by reading its melody rhythm at sight. Now, try playing entire song. Correct as necessary to reinforce.

Transfer and Application:

Continue this rhythm problem by learning new scale of F-major. (Ask where the altered note occurs--Bb). Look at new song, "Goin' Home March" to discover whether it is even or uneven (why?) How would the rhythm equivalents for this song be written?

Evaluation, Summary and Conclusion:

Assign: Practice on "College Song" and learn "Goin' Home March" by first writing out the equivalents in quarter notes as we did with eighth notes in today's lesson. Review "Man on the Flying Trapeze" p. 2 Check for $\frac{3}{4}$ meter, articulation, and dynamic level (mf).

Summary

Goals, concepts and objectives are related aspects of planning for teaching. Broad goals (global objectives) apply equally to all areas of the music curriculum and generally indicate those attitudes, skills, appreciations, knowledge and habits which the instructor feels to be essential to *all learners* in music. From these broad goals, program objectives are derived which describe what the instructor hopes to accomplish in a given class during the year or semester. Shorter goals, called objectives, will apply to segments of the program, such as monthly, weekly, and daily plans for instruction.

Concepts are those thoughts of ideas which the instructor wishes to put across to the students. They are *derived from the music itself.* Conceptual objectives involve tonal organization, rhythmic organization, harmonic organization, intensity and timbre, style, form, music types and performance media, and notation. Concepts are classified according to levels of difficulty--called a taxonomy. Such a taxonomy is used in preparing behavioral objectives.

Behavioral objectives are those behaviors which the teacher expects the student(s) to demonstrate in grasping a concept, skill or technique. Well-stated objectives state the conditions, what the student will be doing, and his expected level of performance in completing a given musical experience. Precise terms and verb forms are desirable in writing behavioral objectives. Behavioral objectives apply to cognitive, psychomotor, affective, and critical judgment domains of musical learning.

Lesson plans provide the means for short-term (daily) planning. They should include conceptual and behavioral objectives, time limitations, materials, activities, and step-by-step procedures for carrying out the teaching strategy. Procedures are essential to conceptualizing (teacher) the learning sequence and should have four parts; namely, (a) an introduction and review; (b) the new problem or activity for the day; (c) application and transfer to a new or related problem; and, (d) evaluation, summary and conclusion.

Several sample objectives and lesson plans were included in this Chapter.

Topics For Discussion

1. Write a list of broad (global) goals which you feel are essential to all students at the ___________ school level. Which of these lead to or are dependent to a degree on other levels of education?
2. Write a set of program objectives for each of the classes you now teach (or hope to teach in the near future). Be sure to include each domain of learning in these objectives.
3. Interview a "status" leader in education (music coordinator, principal, assistant superintendent for instruction, curriculum coordinator, etc.) and ascertain what he/she feels to be the most important goals for the music program in general. If courses of study are available, check these for program objectives and be prepared to discuss in terms of this chapter's suggestions.
4. Select a piece of music for a beginning or intermediate music group (any level). Analyze this music in terms of its principal concepts. List a minimum of 4 concepts which you feel illustrate its musical organization (tonal, rhythmic, harmonic), intensity and timbre, style, form, music types and performance media, and/or notation.
5. Write conceptual and behavioral objectives for No. 4.
6. Write a sample lesson plan incorporating the ideas presented in this chapter. Use other formats, if you wish, but be sure to include all four sections of the plan.

Suggested Readings

Arizona Department of Education. *Identifying and Developing Musical Behaviors: a Design for Learning (K-6).* Phoenix, Arizona: Arizona State Department of Education, 1973. The "Concept/Competency Bank" suggests the process of synthesis by which the child applies learned musical knowledge to existing literature and to his own compositions.

Bergethon, Bjornar and Eunice Boardman. *Musical Growth in the Elementary School, Second Edition.* New York: Holt, Rinehart and Winston, Inc., 1970. See preface and appendix.

Bloom, Benjamin S. (Ed) *Taxonomy of Educational Objectives. I: Cognitive Domain.* New York: David McKay, Inc., 1956. The pioneer reference source in this field.

Colwell, Ricahrd. *The Evaluation of Music Teaching and Learning.* Englewood Cliffs, New Jersey: Prentice-Hall, Inc., 1970.

California State Department of Education. *Music Framework for California Public Schools, Kindergarten Through Grade Twelve.* Sacramento, California: California State Department of Education, 1971. A definitive work on the various domains of learning in music.

Krathwohl, David R., Benjamin S. Bloom and Bertram B. Masia. *Taxonomy of Educational Goals. Handbook II: Affective Domain,* New York: David McKay Co., Inc., 1969 (1964).

Landon, Joseph W. *How to Write Learning Activity Packages for Music Education.* Costa Mesa, California: Educational Media Press, 1973. Part II of the author's book has been extracted in part for this chapter, but should be read in its entirety for further perspectives in writing objectives.

Livingston, James A., Michael D. Poland, and Ronald E. Simmons. *Accountability and Objectives for Music Education.* Costa Mesa, California: Educational Media Press, 1972. A Concise, informative guide which gives practical insight into writing performance objectives.

Mager, Robert F. *Preparing Instructional Objectives.* Belmont, California: Fearon Publishers, 1962. See Ch. 3, 4, 5 and 6.

PART TWO

frontiers of educational structure — (curriculum)

CHAPTER SIX

THE MUSIC CURRICULUM

The things taught in schools and colleges are not an education, but the means of education.

Emerson

A knowledge of curriculum and curriculum development is one of the most important goals of leadership. The effective music educator must understand not only his art but also how it is effected in organized education. The central theme of curriculum should deal with *content* and the *improvement of instruction in music.*

In Part I, we dealt with such matters as the basic qualities of leadership, the nature of music, values and valuing, music learning and teaching, and goals, concepts and objectives in music education. These are the *Foundations of Music Education.* In Part II, we will discuss *Frontiers of Educational Structure*, beginning with this Chapter which deals with the content of music education in the schools.

Curriculum Defined

Broadly defined, curriculum refers to all the educative experiences which the individual is exposed to -- in or out of school. Although it is obvious from this frame-of-reference that there are many non-curricular experiences which affect learners greatly, for the purpose of this book, we will define curriculum to be *all the organized learning experiences provided by the school in an educational setting.* This includes *content, method, and resources.*

Present-day education stresses the importance of providing learners with a greater freedom of choice, more personalized and individualized instruction, and participation, where appropriate, in its development and organization. Indeed, the development of curriculum is such an important matter which touches the lives of teacher and learner alike, curriculum processes should involve all persons who are affected by curriculum -- teacher, administrator, parent, student, and lay person. More will be said concerning the participation process in Chapter VII.

Communication between those involved, particularly teacher and student, school and community has become increasingly important to meet changing conditions of our times. Reform in content and structure has brought about many new developments in all educational fields, even in those disciplines which in the past have been taught only in a very orthodox manner. In general, there has been a growing realization in educational circles that a rapidly changing culture demands greater *individual adaptability* for personal as well as societal reasons.

Any examination of curriculum, both present and past, should begin by challenging certain tenets which at various times have governed the content of school curricula. These include the notions that (a) education should be a transmission of accumulated knowledge; (b) a free society requires little if any planning and educational matters should be left to the individual; (c) traditional modes of human behavior are eternally valid and unchanging; (d) hard work is good for people -- hence, education should be difficult and distasteful; (e) careers develop along planned lines; and, (f) childhood and adolescence are primarily preparation for adulthood rather than stages of developmental growth.[1] These ideas should be evaluated in terms of present-day knowledge of curriculum, learning processes, and social institutions.

Conceptual Framework

In order that we may give appropriate consideration to situational factors in contemporary education, it is important to accept the premise that schools and learners are *part of our society.* They cannot operate in a total vacuum, but rather are affected by the dynamics of interaction between individuals in a complex society. It will be remembered from Chapter IV that curriculum (the "structure of learning") is based on three equal elements; namely, (a) youth needs, (b) educational theory, and, (c) the social setting. In addition to these broad considerations, music educators must have a greater understanding of:

* man as a species
* the nature of intellectual growth
* the processes of education; and
* the forces of society which cause us to redefine how we shall educate a new generation

In a world of changing conditions and where the accumulated knowledge and technology even in a single field is enormous, individualization of learning is increasingly important. Educators should discover and utilize all possible techniques by which students may explore, invent, discover and develop tools of inquiry related to the given field of investigation -- including music. Strategies for individualization will be covered later in this book -- but music educators must be aware that both curriculum and methodology should be adaptable to a variety of instructional and learning needs.

Tangentially, schools of the 70's are being called upon to help in the elimination of poverty, providing economic opportunity, achieving racial equality, eradicating delinquency, and retraining workers displaced by automation and industry. Small wonder that the curriculum finds itself being bent in so many directions!

The concept principle in this Chapter is that formal learning is organized in terms of what we know as the school's curriculum. This emphasizes the notion that the specific function of curriculum is to provide a coordinating structure for the necessary elements of time, space, material, personnel, equipment, and so forth. In essence, *the curriculum provides a structured environment for learning arranged in sequentially developed, behaviorally-oriented ways.*

It has been stressed that curriculum includes all the experiences by which the student learns -- specifically, those organized learning activities which constitute the school's regular educational program. This includes all sequential experiences, courses, and contributing media which are brought to bear on the act of teaching and learning. The accumulation of wisdom, ideas, experience, and process-expertise of all persons who are involved in the teaching-learning act also are essential elements of curriculum. Curricular sequence implies *planned organization* by which skills, concepts, understandings and appreciations are acquired and mastered.

Unruh and Leeper suggest that curriculum should be comprised of interrelated learning experiences which are designed to fulfill three major purposes; namely, (a) the personal development of the individual; (b) his continued learning (i.e., the continuity of educational experience); and, (c) how organized experience relates to him.[2]

Curriculum content should be organized in such a way that its substance and learning processes are derived from appropriate behavioral objectives. From an analysis and diagnosis of the nature of subject matter and learners, a prescription must be formulated as a means of achieving the various domains of learning, as was noted in Chapter V. This prescription must recognize individual learning needs, since to be effective, curriculum must have a variety of ways of activating children and involving them in the learning process. The curriculum, thus, should have several tracks which lead to the same learning goal.[3]

Some authors contend that learning is a 24-hour-a-day process and that "extra-curricular" or "non-curricular" experiences are also rich learning experiences. Other authorities contend that the curriculum consists of *all the experiences which the school deliberately sets up* -- and any learning which results from this should not be considered "extra". From this notion has come the term "co-curricular", which is used to describe events planned or under the auspices of the school but which take place outside the normal activities of the school day, including those of an off-campus nature.

Viewed in its largest dimension, curriculum is more than learning facts and skills; it is a program of living. In such an enlarged definition of curriculum, the school becomes responsible for guiding *all* aspects of the educational growth of students while they are under its jurisdiction, and experiences in *all planned aspects are considered to be curriculum content.* This concept supports the recent view of schools as year - 'round, twenty-four hour learning centers.

Historical Influences

Historically, curriculum has always been influenced by major social trends. According to Gwyn and Chase, the development of curriculum in the United States has been dominated by the influences of five major period motives; namely, (1) the religious motive (1635-1770); (2) the political motive (1770-1860); (c) the utilitarian motive (1860-1920); (d) the mass education motive (1920 to the present); and, (e) the motive for excellence in education (1957 to the present).[4] Although the religious motive was inoperative for many years after its period of significance, it has reemerged today as one of the major factors influencing education. In addition, the political motive remains dominant in some areas of the country, particularly with reference to the teaching of the tenets of Americanism and our historical heritage. Mass education and utilitarian factors also continue to be important, since our society, perhaps more than at any previous time, is now attempting to cope with equal opportunities for youth to become effective, contributing members of our country. In 1957, the dawn of the Age of Sputnik revealed a new concern for excellence. The effectiveness of this curricular goal will depend in large part on how schools help individual learners to respond to their environment to become both technically competent for survival and educated qualitatively for living a life.

Recent trends and influences which affect the curriculum are:

1. Spectacular advances in space-age technology and communication
2. Urbanization of population, both in the United States and abroad
3. Legislation which affects schools and school curricula
4. Extension of leisure time into most segments of American

society

5. The desire to equalize educational opportunity, regardless of race, sex or socio-economic status
6. The interdependence and specialization of modern society
7. A growing concern with general education
8. An awareness of educational influences from abroad
9. Public attitudes concerning education (particularly those of a negative nature directed toward non-support of fiscal issues)
10. Automation and computer-assisted programs in business and education
11. Outside support for education from federal, corporate and private foundations
12. Conflicts in beliefs concerning the "public good" versus individual concepts of morality, values, etc.
13. Restive attitudes of youth based on conflicting value systems
14. Abortive, anarchial, and illegal efforts to "get at" the establishment by destroying property and disrupting schools
15. Psychological research which emphasizes the importance of the self-concept
16. A growing understanding of the importance of multi-tracked and individualized instruction
17. Applied research in theoretical aspects of learning which emphasizes the importance of developmental processes in cognitive, affective, psychomotor and critical judgement areas of behavior.
18. Recognition of the importance of providing students with opportunities for *making choices* and of accepting the consequences and responsibility for these choices.

Makers Of Curriculum

In general, all persons affected by curriculum should share in its development. Since organized education is responsible for all formal aspects of learning, curriculum development, therefore should fall chiefly within the purview of schools and school personnel.

If curriculum is to be totally effective in individual behavior-modification, its development must include the expertise of many persons in the planning stages. Since inputs at appropriate levels from parents, interested lay persons, and students should be part of the curriculum schema, the teacher is the key figure in curriculum development. This requires new and higher levels of professional competence as a part of the pre-service and in-service training of all music educators if they are to meet this responsibility effectively. In addition, as other persons outside the "normal" instructional framework (classroom) are included in the various processes of planning and development, this will require additional competence in eliciting and synthesizing a variety of inputs by means of the dynamics of group and personal interaction.

A Variety of Roles and Levels of Professional Competence are involved in curriculum development. Each of these is related and interdependent, according to the requirements of the educational structure and learning involved. For example, some of the typical roles would include the following persons:

* Discipline specialists who work with content aspects of the learning program to serve as resource personnel (this may include music specialists, consultants, etc.)
* Other specialists who work with on-going, continuing aspects of the program (guidance counselors, media technicians, independent study coordinators, directors of exploratory and special programs, specialists from family and community agencies, etc.)
* Consultants from universities and colleges who provide information, special techniques and resources -- or who assist with structural and/or in-service phases of curriculum development.
* Classroom teachers and teacher teams who are responsible for planning specific components of the curriculum and team assignments of those involved; for feedback systems by which evaluative devices and other information may be used in curriculum revision.
* "Other" educational leaders who will help to provide

leadership in planning, policy making, and interpreting school programs and needs to the community (this will include principals, music coordinators, curriculum directors, superintendents, etc.)

There has been considerable discussion in recent times about the lack of relevancy in school curricula. Those who work with curricular processes should be aware of some of the problems of relevancy having to do with (a) faulty educational goals (emphasis on extrinsic factors); (b) improper emphasis; (c) incomplete and out-of-date subject matter; (d) improper teaching procedures; (e) instruction centered on subject matter rather than behavioral objectives which stress what students can reasonably be expected to do in a given time as a result of a learning experience; (f) insufficient (or no) attention to individualized learning; (g) failure to include contemporary trends and ideas which are valid and pertinent to the learning experience; and, (h) failure to understand needs of cultural diversity, particularly those of culturally deprived students.

Education for minority and ethnic groups in inner city schools also presents a frontal area with great challenge to curriculum makers and music educators. Relevancy for a large number of persons within such groups may in large part be determined by whether the music educator understands the full implications of the *what, why, and how* of curriculum and instruction and how the real learning needs of these people are incorporated in these things. Individualization of learning and drastic changes in content may be one key to involvement and self-motivation.

It is painfully true that one aspect of the problem of curricular relevancy centers in the lack of concern for personal and community aspirations and with such intangibles as individual values and self-concepts.[5] Gardner suggests that if apathy, tradition, or oppression are removed as lifestyle determinants, human ambitions rise greatly.[6] Unfortunately, however, too many educators and schools are observed to move with glacial speed in recognizing and satisfying any intrinsic individual ambitions.

Hopefully, leaders in music education will place high priority on making curriculum vital and relevant to a majority of students in the schools in the decade of the Seventies.

Implications For Music Education

The challenge for music education for the Age of the Seventies is essentially, "How can the other eighty-five percent be reached?" While it is generally recognized that schools in the United States have achieved a norm of performance excellence generally unequaled in other areas of the world, it is tragic that they have on the other hand failed generally to meet the artistic and aesthetic learning needs of the majority of students.[7] Part of this problem stems from the fact that historically American schools have rejected the notion that public education exists to provide a conservatory-type training for individual solo performers. Hence, we have turned to group performance as the unique mode of musical expression which seemed to be compatible with mass education, thereby rejecting other possible dimensions by which individuals could experience music. The only other alternative which appeared possible was to offer group instruction for non-performers, usually *about* rather than directly *involved with music making.* Such experiences were usually conceived in sterile, traditional, and unimaginative terms or courses such as "general music" or "music appreciation". In fact, many dealt with theory for non-performers, thereby denying such learners *any valid connection with the substance of music itself.*

This dichotomy should be circumvented by considering another range of alternatives having to do with *other types of music experiencing,* and *other modes of instruction* in addition to large group performance.

The following illustrate recent developments in music curricula which have great promise and are catching on in educational circles:

The Contemporary Music Project. Experiments in musical creativity sponsored by the Contemporary Music Project have provided an exciting answer to the dilemma. Documentation of these programs reveals several successful pilot programs which were based on providing elementary and junior high school students with ways of using the tools of contemporary music to develop their own musical ideas. These projects successfully demonstrated that musical potentials of young learners (both elementary and secondary) could be reached effectively through experimental techniques by using Twentieth Century compositional idioms, and in developing musical resources through rhythmics, singing, improvisation, and composition.[8]

Manhattanville Music Curriculum Program.

Another very successful innovative program in music education was developed in the Mid-1960's at Manhattanville College, Purchase, New York. Under the specially funded program, the Manhattanville Music Curriculum Program worked with fifteen school districts throughout the country to develop promising music curricula. While the greatest number of these were at the senior high school level, several were geared to elementary and junior high school instruction. All made use of individualized instruction. The MMCP strategy was based on individual involvement, personal discovery and creative exploration, with the teacher playing the role of guide-resource person and stimulator of creative thinking. In addition to group efforts aimed at composing, performing, evaluating, conducting, and listening, MMPC stressed individual and small group research and creative exploration, student recitals, oral reports, listening, guest recitals, and skill development.

Physical requirements for the MMCP demanded work areas which allowed the student a great deal of freedom. These included the music lab, stations for listening, skill practice and strategy work, use of carrels, practice rooms and the like. Scheduling for the MMCP utilized greater flexibility than in traditional patterns, since it called for only a portion of time to be spent in large group activity; the remainder being divided between small group and individual work.

Some of the MMCP projects included activities designed to:

1. Involve young children in composing for voices and instruments.
2. Utilize unique visual devices in place of traditional notation, where the latter was a deterrent to creative effort.
3. Use performing organizations as laboratory groups for

exploring musical structure.

4. Begin the study of music with contemporary idioms, using traditional means only when it seems useful to help solve some particular problem of musical experimentation.
5. Approach all music as a means for analysis (this analysis increasing in complexity according to the age and experience of the learners.)[9]

Electronic Music Composition

Original student compositions utilizing the medium of electronically produced sound is another recent adaptation of extending the music curriculum to a wider spectrum of learners. Virtually all the major textbook publishers are including such strategies in the music books for upper elementary, junior and senior high school and the educational publications all display advertisements describing a fairly wide range of medium to high-price hardware. Fortunately for most music educators and classroom teachers, very exciting electronic music strategies may be accomplished with a minimum of equipment, some of which is readily available in the average school.

In a sixth grade classroom of a nearby school, the writer recently observed an electronic composition "being born" under the guidance of a sixth grade teacher and the visiting music specialist. The previous week, the children had all gathered sounds by means of tape recorders from household and playground sources. These were made into three-foot tape loops for playing on open-reel tape recorders. The day of the composition arrived and, under the direction of the specialist, an electronic composition by Milton Babbit was played and discussed. Using the "building blocks" of tone, duration, timbre, and intensity, small committees of six then planned one-minute compositions utilizing the tape loops (all thirty were available to each committee).

When the strategy had been fully discussed, appropriate tape loops were selected and orchestrated. Then a conductor was chosen by the children. The conductor helped the committee chart the orchestration. Finally, when all were ready, each committee explained their orchestration and prepared to play it for the class. The playing was done in the following fashion -- six tape recorders were at the front of the room; five for playing the tape loops, one for recording the sounds from all five to make a master tape of the composition. The loops were placed on the five recorders in such a way that they could be played continuously by the student-player -- only the volume control was to be activated at the instant the particular sound from a given recorder was desired. This provided five separate instruments -- the five tape loops being played on the five different tape recorders -- each a separate kind of electronic sound. "White noise" was provided on one loop by a simple sound generator. At a given signal from the student conductor, the groups played their compositions of one-minute, raising or lowering the volume control to enter, combine, or delete the sound, as desired. The result, which had been taped on the master tape recorder, was then played back for all to evaluate. A significant aspect of the observed learning was that the children were given appropriate musical and electronic vocabulary and could apply this to the evaulation and discussion. This demonstrated a high level of musical experiencing and corresponding conceptual ability with reference to the activity involved. Small wonder that this exciting experience rubbed off on more traditional forms of musical experience as well!

Folk, Pop and Rock Music in the School Curriculum

It is fortunate that music educators are now beginning to recognize that musical idioms formerly felt to be slightly "less than respectable" may present many legitimate educational and musical experiences in the classroom. Folk, pop and rock music as part of the school curriculum are creating new interests in many forms of music among learners who were not previously involved in the traditional music program. Guitar classes have sprung up like wildfire throughout the schools of the country, reaching children whose needs have not been met by the traditional fare of orchestral instruments classes, and have at the same time unfolded a new potential for this very fine instrument. In many humanities-arts classes students have begun to perceive musical elements and expressional qualities in pop and rock music, and to find hitherto unexplored relationships with historically significant music of other eras. The potentials of pop, rock, and jazz are finding additional applications by means of "quest" (i.e., "mini") courses and in stage bands--the latter now becoming an accepted part of the American high school curricula. It would also be a rare school indeed which did not have a variety of "co-curricular" and "extra-curricular" pop and rock student instrumental and vocal groups.

Growing enrollments in traditional music courses resulting from participation in such activities as those described in the foregoing should demonstrate to the forward-looking music educator that there are many legitimate and viable uses of folk, pop and rock music which will make for a better-rounded, more inclusive music curriculum. At the same time, progressive leaders in music education will find that these activities, if done in balance with the *total music curriculum* can contribute to greater support and more interest by the students as a whole in the progress of fine music performance groups sponsored by the school.

Promising Research In Music Curriculum

General Fields of Music Education:

One of the recent fields of education is that of early childhood education, from approximately 3½ to 5 years. Barbara Andress and others have incorporated considerable research in their very excellent book, *Music in Early Childhood,* which should be read by every leader in music education.[10] Other definitive research on conceptual, affective, vocal, motor, and early instrumental development as applied to children in the elementary school is also reported by Marilyn P. Zimmerman.[11] The latter is especially important to those who are interested in applying such ideas as the theories of Piaget to musical experiences in the school curriculum. It is especially significant to note the longitudinal study by Petzold which revealed that the most promising development in auditory perception occurs between ages six and seven but reaches a plateau by age eight. Other clues obtained from the Zimmerman review of research reveal overwhelming support for the emphasis on early musical experience, preferably with the aid of music specialists *who understand the nature of musical experience.* Visual clues must be supported and associated with musical sounds in a musical context, wide intervals used in early pitch discrimination, phrases and motives sung and reinforced instrumentally, and musical elements studied both in isolation and in context to overcome the tendency to listen only to one aspect of the music.

The research in general fields of music education includes the following:

* Collections of excellent representative music of the major historical periods, through the contemporary era, used to broaden the insights of elementary school children (Julliard Research Project, 1967).
* Leonard B. Meyer's theory of "expectation" used to identify behaviors and to structure listening according to such elements as imitation, motives, thematic uses of melody, dissonance and consonance, forms, etc. in teaching fifth graders (Colwell, University of Illinois).
* Redefining the aims and re-structuring the junior high and senior high school general music class in order to focus on musical structures and aesthetic experience associated with "absolute expressionism" (Reimer, Case Western Reserve University, 1967.)
* A study of the development of musicality and aesthetic judgments of adolescents through performance (Kyme and others, University of California, Berkeley, 1967).
* An in-depth study of a limited number of representative compositions at the high school level to develop intrinsic musicality (Wendrich, Yale University).
* The use of special overhead transparencies and taped music to heighten musical perception (Glenn, University of Iowa).
* Definitive research in aesthetic education (Barkan, Ohio State University).
* Use of programmed instructional devices for students and classroom teachers (La Bach, Kent State University;

Hargiss, University of Kansas).

* A study of child-centered music activities in junior high school--emphasizing the understanding of concepts and practices through visual analysis, creative and improvisatory activities (Fitzpatrick, University of Iowa, 1968).
* Research concerning various adaptations and techniques from abroad, including the programs of Dalcroze, Kodaly, Orff, and Suzuki.[12]

Specialized Fields in Music Education:

Under the auspices of the Music Educators National Conference and the Council for Research in Music Education, a number of recent publications have appeared which relate research in specialized fields of music education. MENC, in particular, has published a series of monograph-bulletins entitled, *From Research to the Music Classroom.* Two of the latter, entitled *Teaching Performing Groups* and *Teaching Instrumental Music* deal precisely with summaries of research concerning performance groups. These materials are invaluable resources for leaders in music education.[13]

Selected findings from the research in specialized fields of music education indicate the following:

* Improving and extending junior high school orchestra repertory through degrees of technical challenge (Moore, Lincoln, Nebraska, 1967).
* Compositional analysis for better performance by specialized music performing groups (Trotter and McManus, University of Oregon).
* Choral participation has a potential for achieving musical goals other than performance, as illustrated in a seven-point outline of content (Maharg, University of Illinois, 1968).
* The study of music theory and literature can be incorporated successfully into rehearsals without lowering the performance level of the group (Coleman, University of Kansas, 1966; and, Linton, USOE Research Project #6-8220).

* Studies in learning and motivation reveal that these depend partly on outside (extrinsic) forces and partly on the individual's psychological and functional characteristics (Hamacheck, NEA, 1968).
* A study of the dynamics of rehearsal activities reveals that directors of public school instrumental groups are not aware of group forces and do not use them to enhance the social and psychological setting of group rehearsals (Van Sickle, Ohio State University, 1965).
* Delayed auditory feedback regarding sight-reading resulted in poorer performance then from simultaneous feedback (Havlicek, University of Kansas, 1968).
* Junior high school students can succeed in instrumental performance without prior work on preinstrumental instruments (Manor, *Journal of Educational Psychology*, Vol. 41, 1950), although more recent studies showed considerably greater performance on the part of elementary students who had participated in preinstrumental instruments (Tietze, University of Iowa, 1958).

In addition to the foregoing, Ernst and Gary list a variety of devices by which more traditionally oriented music classes may reach a wider spectrum of learning needs.[14] Some of the more promising practices reported by these authors include such ideas as structuring the performance class repertoire to be more representative of all periods and styles; relating performance material to the society and historical period which produced it; using problem-solving and analysis to study musical elements, styles, accoustical principles, etc.; composing, arranging, transcribing music for the performance group; studying ways musical ideas are used in composition; observing and comparing characteristics of large ensemble, chamber music, and solo works; observing characteristics of musical expression in relationship to other art forms; hearing and analyzing the works of artist performers, and others.

Recent Practices and Trends

Some major influences in education which have specific implications for improving the quality of programs in music education include the:

1. Expansion of the range of musical offerings of the school to meet the needs of all students rather than exclusively those of high motivation and interest.
2. Development of music philosophy, curriculum, and method based on current research and practice in other fields of education.
3. Selection of content to make students aware of the wide range of musical learnings which are significant to mankind.
4. Development of a conceptual framework for music by means of musical experiencing, use of appropriate vocabulary, musical terminology, and descriptive verbalization to use in reference to what the student hears and/or performs.
5. Concern for (and use of) contemporary influences in music.
6. Programs of music education which are student-oriented and based on individual discovery, inquiry, and problem-solving (in a musical context).
7. Self-directed activities of students which utilize all appropriate forms of individualized instruction.
8. Musical developments from abroad which make use of such contributions as those of Dalcroze, Orff, Kodaly, and Suzuki to provide additional meaning and insight.
9. Performance which stresses the same processes of intrinsic learning as do other areas and disciplines. Under this system, there is a de-emphasis on rote learning and technical training which is unrelated to the primary focus on musical experience.
10. Ungraded and multi-graded classes; levels of accomplishment rather than grade levels are stressed (continuous progress design).
11. Humanistic and aesthetic qualities of music where appropriately related to studies in other areas (humanities, fine arts, allied arts courses).
12. Improvement both in scope and quality of music pro-

grams, at all levels, stressing over-all educational and aesthetic values of music experience--with corresponding de-emphasis on limited, "extra-musical" activities (such as contests and athletic events).

13. Use of differentiated staffs to provide various levels of expertise in working with students.
14. Flexible design and use of school plants and schedules.
15. Extension of music programs beyond the customary limits of formal schooling to include pre-school, nursery school, adult education, recreation, university-level extended day and extension programs, etc.
16. Vertical coordination between all levels of music education, elementary through college, with opportunities for learners to participate in a variety of general and specialized music programs and courses throughout the entire formal learning spectrum.
17. Use of "mini" or "quest" courses to meet short-term or singular music interests of students.
18. Individual progress of students is met in a variety of ways, including flexible scheduling, individual pursuits, accelerated programs, independent study, and other special interest activities--in addition to regular music activities of the school curriculum.
19. Ways of releasing creative abilities of all students (Contemporary Music Project, Manhattanville Music Curriculum Program, etc.)
20. Teaching of limited concepts and skills by means of Learning Activity Packages (LAPS, Unipacs, Mini-units, etc.)
21. Use of artist-teachers, composers-in-residence, resident artist performers.[15]
22. Team teaching by which outstanding competencies of each teacher are utilized to the fullest.
23. Research programs designed to discover more effective curricular programs and teaching techniques in music.
24. Improved teacher pre-service and in-service training (which

we will call "developing repertoire potential" in a later section of this book) which stresses the overall general and music education of the professional staff, rather than the traditional limited training of bandmasters, orchestra and choral directors, theory teachers, and so on.

25. Education which is becoming more dependent upon large support systems, especially those concerned with instructional resources, TV, information storage and retrieval, multimedia instructional packages, and systems which bring the environment of the subject to the learner on something like a time-reality basis.
26. Extension of the school year beyond the traditional nine or ten month period to year-'round operation.
27. Use of multiple texts rather than uniform books for each child.
28. Flexible assignments of teachers and administrators to make full use of teaching potentials in all facets of expertise, teaching, and leadership. Concomitant development of more flexible music specialists, including consultants and resource persons either to schools or school districts.
29. Transportation packets by which students are transported to nearby professional performances. In addition to those events scheduled in conventional theaters and concert halls, transportation packets make possible performances and musical events in museums, homes, churches, lecture halls, outdoor arenas, etc. Extensive preparation and follow-up in schools prepares students to participate as knowledgeable, sophisticated audiences.

Summary

Contemporary education stresses greater freedom of choice, personal and individualized instruction, and active participation in all processes of education. Although general guidelines concerning characteristics of growth are helpful, schools should discover and cultivate the unique potential of each child. To achieve this goal, schools must provide adequate diversity of curricula and method to accommodate the needs of the wide variety of individuals in our society.

The music educator should understand that curriculum is viewed as all planned educative experiences designed to further the personal development of individual learners in a school setting. Recent literature suggests the focus on early childhood and continuing education (including year-'round schools) as dimensions of such learning. Curriculum has been influenced by social developments and trends, more recently those which underscore how individuals respond effectively to their environment, think for themselves, and become effective, contributing members of society. All persons affected by curriculum and learning should play a role in curriculum development. However, teachers, discipline specialists, and consultants will be those most actively involved.

Topics For Discussion

1. Can you cite illustrations of curriculum influences which are "throw backs" to trends and influences of earlier historical periods still in evidence? In what way have these enhanced or retarded the development of ideas to meet current conditions and needs?
2. In what way have the various philosophical positions noted in Ch. 3 affected curriculum development in the school systems of this country?
3. Make a brief survey in a neighboring school district to discover ways in which they have begun to up-date various curricula in music and other subjects. List those which you feel to be promising.
4. To what degree do you feel that persons outside the regular instructional staff should influence curricular decisions (lay persons, parents, students, etc.)? Is there any evidence of community pressure groups of which you are aware exerting informal or overt pressure to change curriculum?
5. Discuss how some of the recent trends and influences have affected music and general curricula. Do any of these present more problems than others?
6. Outline some of the ways in which you feel music educators should update curricula to meet youth and inner city needs in learning situations.
7. Make a list of noncommercial educational agencies (non-school or higher education) in your community. Present some of the ways in which their resources may be utilized in school curriculum.
8. There have been many comments on the effectiveness of educational or public TV (Sesame Street, the Electric Company, etc.) on children's learning. Can you give examples of television programs which enhance and/or undermine the effectiveness of the school curriculum?
9. Are there any aspects of contemporary music idioms (including folk, pop and rock) that you feel may be too difficult or inappropriate to use in the regular school curriculum? What criteria were used in "screening out" those felt to be unsuitable?

10. Should school credit be given to students for participation in student activities? Outside music study? Attendance at programs or in musical activities of other schools? Defend your position.

Suggested Readings

Andress, Barbara L., et al. *Music in Early Childhood.* Washington, D.C.: Music Educators National Conference, 1973. Useful in planning music for the 3½-5 year olds.

Bessom, Malcolm E., Alphonse M. Tatarunis and Samuel L. Forcucci. *Teaching Music in Today's Secondary Schools.* New York: Holt, Rinehart and Winston, Inc., 1974. See Ch. 2.

Conner, Forrest E. and William J. Ellena. *Curriculum Handbook for School Administrators.* Washington, D.C.: The American Association of School Administrators, 1967. An overview of curriculum develops in various curriculum fields to assist school administrators in becoming aware of trends and emerging concepts in the organization and application of knowledge. Includes music, fine arts, and representative other curricular fields.

Ernst, Karl D. and Charles L. Gary (Ed) *Music in General Education.* Washington, D.C.: Music Educators National Conference, 1965.

Goodlad, John I., *School, Curriculum, and the Individual.* Waltham, Mass: Blaisdell Publishing Co., 1966. This provacative and stimulating book deserves a complete reading.

Gwynn, J. Minor and John B. Chase, Jr., *Curriculum Principles and Social Trends, Fourth Edition.* New York: The MacMillan Co., 1969.

Kansas State Department of Education. *You Can Build a Comprehensive Music Curriculum.* Topeka, Kansas: The Department, 1972. An excellent guide to music education in this state which is designed on lines of the Contemporary Music Project and the Manhattanville Music Curriculum Program.

Klotman, Robert H., *The School Music Administrator and Supervisor: Catalysts for Change in Music Education.* Englewood Cliffs, New Jersey: Prentice-Hall, Inc., 1973. See Ch. 4.

Landon, Joseph W., "Music--the Uncommon Denominator in Secondary Education," *Journal of Secondary Education* (February, 1965), 57.

Michaelis, John U., Ruth H. Grossman, and Lloyd F. Scott. *New Designs for the Elementary School Curriculum.* New York: McGraw-Hill Book Co., 1967. See Ch. 1, 2 and 12.

CHAPTER SEVEN

FRAMEWORK FOR MUSIC EDUCATION: DEVELOPMENT, ORGANIZATION AND EVALUATION

> **Since the time available for non-remunerative pursuits is likely to increase, it is necessary that we examine immediately the imbalances in the curriculum. In spite of an assumed "culture explosion", we continue in the schools to neglect art, music, drama, dance, sculpture, and, in fact, almost everything that smacks of being non-utilitarian. Ironically, we may discover not long after 1980 that, in the 1960's and 1970's we had an upsidedown curriculum, with what was considered then to be of most worth proving to be of little value to masses of people. Let us at least hedge our bets by assuring a reasonable balance among the several realms of human inquiry.**
>
> **John I. Goodlad**

An "Open" Systems Approach To Music Curricula

During the past two decades or so, many public and private enterprises in the United States have incorporated a new structural approach in their organizations. By a variety of sophisticated and unsophisticated means, these endeavors have sought to find greater productivity and output. With the advent of systemic changes in organizations, there has come a new look at both *function* (organization) and *system* (product). Although the technology of engineering, business, industry and science is applicable to many enterprises, a "closed" system is less desirable than an "open" one, since education deals with human beings rather than machines. Consequently, what will be described here should be considered to be an "open" humanistic system for developing, organizing and evaluating music curricula.

Any system of curriculum essentially is a description of how the enterprise is organized--herein for the *improvement of learning in music education.* While it is hoped that the system itself will be adaptable to a wider array of management information and phenomena, some of which may involve retrieval and other technological assists, the principal ingredient of the system which will be described in the Chapter is the *human element in curriculum development and instructional implementation.* What we shall speak of, therefore, is both a framework of curriculum (music content areas), plus an array of human talent to achieve individual humanized learning--on the part of music education leaders, music specialists, administrators, teachers, and others concerned.

In describing our "open" system which will apply to the music curriculum, it is proposed that we deal principally with the ingredients of level (elementary or secondary), learning theory, global, program and instructional objectives, content, courses and the sequence of learning activities, media-materials-facilities, and, evaluation.

In Chapter VI, the curriculum was defined as "all planned educative experiences designed to further the personal development of individual learners". In the systems approach, curriculum becomes one application of a system, inasmuch as it becomes an attempt to organize all learning components to accomplish stated objectives. Basically, it is an additive approach, attempting to arrange sequentially-ordered tasks in an inquiry-problem-solving orientation to provide insightful music experiencing and conceptual development for the learners involved. Since the final product, however, is dependent upon *specific learning applications,* it will be up to those most directly concerned with teaching-learning--namely, the teachers themselves--to make the final adaptation of this curriculum system.

The Music Education Program

Development.

Any system of curriculum has two principal phases in its organization--(a) the developmental or planning phase, and, (b) the implementation or action phase. In the development or planning phase, it is customary to consider a sequence of possible actions on the part of curriculum workers. The first of these involves a comprehensive survey of the nature of the school-community--its characteristics, aspirations, contributing personnel, and resources. Educational leaders should develop procedures for making such a survey, one of which is illustrated in Figure 14, "A Survey of Community Needs in Music". Information from this survey should be summarized, made into a community music "profile" and used by the developers of curriculum to indicate the level of cultural aspiration or need revealed by the various component resources. This may serve as a beginning point and may be referred to while the music program is being considered and planned.

The next step is the clarification of the posture of the school and its personnel regarding education. A general statement of aim and areas of interest, those of primary concern, etc. will be helpful at this point. Next should come a statement of purpose for the music program as a whole (global objectives), followed by the identification of specific courses and/or sequences of learning activity in which curriculum needs are to be applied.

The following are steps in the planning-developmental stage of curriculum:

1. Stating which area of the program is to receive the emphasis
2. Assembling a steering committee to make preliminary decisions
3. Deciding on the tentative structure, content, types of experiences (courses, programs, etc.) and resources which will be necessary
4. Designating task force work groups which will have a responsibility for various segments of the development.
5. Planning topics and sequences for presenting the content

Figure 14

A Survey of Community Needs in Music

Note: Surveyor should note types of establishments, organized activities, number, personnel, and other pertinent statistics under each category--together with annotations concerning function, resources, and other pertinent data, where available.

I. Church Music
   A. Church organization (choirs, membership, number of paid directors, salaries, soloists, libraries, etc.)
   B. Church schools
   C. Equipment

II. Radio and Television
   A. Broadcast and telecast (number and type of stations, hours, amount of music programming, number of professional music employees)
   B. Educational radio and TV (those devoted in large part or exclusively to non-commercial education, including those programming music, number of hours, etc.)
   C. Libraries and musical equipment

III. Concerts and Entertainments
   A. No. of separate artist-concert series (no. and type)
   B. Total attendance for each series
   C. No. of individual impresarios
   D. No. of sponsoring organizations
   E. Average price of series and single admission
   F. No. and type of youth concerts provided

IV. Public and Private School Music Program
   A. No. of schools (list by elementary, junior high, senior high, college)
   B. No. of music personnel (total, full and part-time, by school)
   C. No. of individual music courses (general, instrumental, vocal, theory, "special")
   D. No. of students concentrating or majoring in music at high school level
   E. No. of graduates who attend college. No. majoring in music
   F. Annual budget for music (personnel, equipment, operating)
   G. No. of students taking private lessons
   H. Distribution of awards or ratings achieved in festivals during past three years.
   I. General attitude of administration toward music (good, fair, poor)
   J. No. of students active in community music activities.
   K. No. of students attending student concerts annually
   L. Curriculum (Is music required of all elementary students? Minutes per week? Junior High? Minutes per week? Performing organizations--number of those enrolled. General studies in music--enrollments.
   M. No. of school music programs per year? Type? Attendance?

V. Public Incidental Music
   A. Service clubs (total, number using music, those having community singing)
   B. Theaters (no. and type scheduling music programs)
   C. Restaurants (no. having some form of live music)
   D. Miscellaneous (community music festivals, etc.)

VI. Music Stores and Music Manufacturing Institutions
   A. No. and whether individual or a department in a large store
   B. No. music manufacturing institutions (those making instruments, publishing music, etc.
   C. No. of piano tuners, instrument repairmen, salesmen having music training.
   D. No. of records sold annually (percentage of "serious" music)--sheet music sales, gross sales
   E. No. pianos, other instruments rented, sold annually
   F. No. organs, "major instruments" (requiring large financial outlay, some form of permanent installation) sold annually.

VII. Private music teachers
   A. No. of private schools or conservatories of music
   B. No. of schools in which music plays a major role in curriculum (such as Montessori, etc.)
   C. No. of voice, piano, instrument, theory teachers
   D. Average compensation of private teachers
   E. Is there a professional guild, union, or organization primarily devoted to private music teachers' welfare?

VIII. Professional Musicians
   A. No. of union members earning all or part of income from music. Non-union.
   B. No. of instrumental, vocal, "pop" combo groups using professional personnel.

IX. College Music Programs
   A. No. music students, music majors, institutions, teachers
   B. No. concerts annually. Annual budget
   C. Library, listening facilities, etc. open to public

X. Community Music
   A. Is there a community music or fine-arts council?
   B. Is there a recreation department music program? No. and type of courses. Personnel, salaries
   C. Public library music: is there a music librarian, books on music and musicians,

   C. Public library music: is there a music librarian, no. of copies of orchestrations, sheet music, books on music and musicians, recordings, annual budget, sponsored exhibits and/ or music programs.
   D. Use of Muzak or other "canned" music in community.

XI. Music in Industry
   A. No. firms, hospitals using music for recreation, therapy, etc.
   B. No. industry music directors

of the curriculum; deciding on appropriate teaching processes and instructional resources.

6. Deciding on alternate strategies, by which the content may be individualized to fit the needs of various students and teachers.
7. Placing units, topics, sequences in an appropriate outline format, together with suggested resources and materials pertinent to the learning situation; providing evaluative devices for assessing the effectiveness of instruction (pre and post-tests, where necessary).
8. Preparing teachers' guides, bibliographies, additional student resource material, etc.
9. Trying out the new curriculum proposal in a pilot or trial program. Revising, re-evaluating, adopting for use.
10. Presenting the curriculum material to all personnel concerned by means of in-service meetings; making further revisions.

The implementation phase of curriculum development comes at the point of refinement and further development. This begins approximately at Point #10 in the foregoing list, and is characterized by massive in-service education programs designed to involve *all* teaching personnel and others of the professional staff who are affected by the specific curriculum concerned. Although the two phases are coordinate and interdependent, this last phase concentrates on the *how* rather than the *what* aspect of what is to be taught. Consequently, a wide array of personnel and material resources are brought to bear to develop in-depth expertise in the teaching act. Outside consultants, college and university experts, media and textbook resource personnel, and others may be invited as appropriate to participate in introducing, demonstrating, working with teachers, training inexperienced personnel, and evaluating various phases of the new curriculum. Their efforts are combined to form a "cybernetic loop"--or feedback system, by which the curriculum is always open-ended and subject to modification.

It should be obvious that the system just described for curriculum development must be modified to *accommodate the size of the developmental enterprise.* This may apply to a single classroom or a single school. Whereas "task forces" may then describe one or two individuals (chiefly the teachers concerned), the process which proceeds from decisions concerning overall structure, to courses and experiences, to units and topics, to teaching strategies, to securing resources, to trial, evaluation, and revision--all these are valid for *any type* of curriculum development.

Organization.

A preliminary approach to the discussion of the nature of the developmental design for curriculum should begin with an analysis of the types of systems involved.

Concrete System — types or sets of learning experiences

Subsystem — refers to curriculum (all learning experiences provided for students)

Bisystems — all components of the subsystem

Traditionally organized courses of study are arranged around a specific course or grade level, whereas a system has to do with types or sets of learning experience. The Manhattanville Music Curriculum Program "spiral curriculum" in which the larger elements of music--pitch, rhythm, timbre, dynamics, and form--are considered the principal types or "sets" of musical experience is an example of this concept.

Subsystems in traditional curriculum refers to grade levels--herein the subsystem may be used to organize and classify certain vertical dimensions of content and learning experience. For example, each of the five MMCP learning experiences may be experienced at various levels of expertise and comprehension, regardless of grade level.

Bisystems are related to the total system by both vertical and horizontal elements of level and/or content. They are located where a vertical and horizontal subsystem intersect (See Figure 15). In traditional practice, this could refer to ninth grade girls chorus, 4th grade general classroom music, high school intermediate orchestra, and so on.

Bisystems are further subdivided into learning packages (units or smaller PACS) for the teaching of more limited or single concepts. Each of the learning packages is conceived in terms of a set of behavioral objectives (limited) and procedures (also limited). These may have to do with how to utilize the tape recorder in making sound tape loops (essentially a LAP) or larger units, such as how to play the guitar, and so on.

Figure 15

A CONCRETE SYSTEM OF CURRICULUM DESIGN IN MUSIC

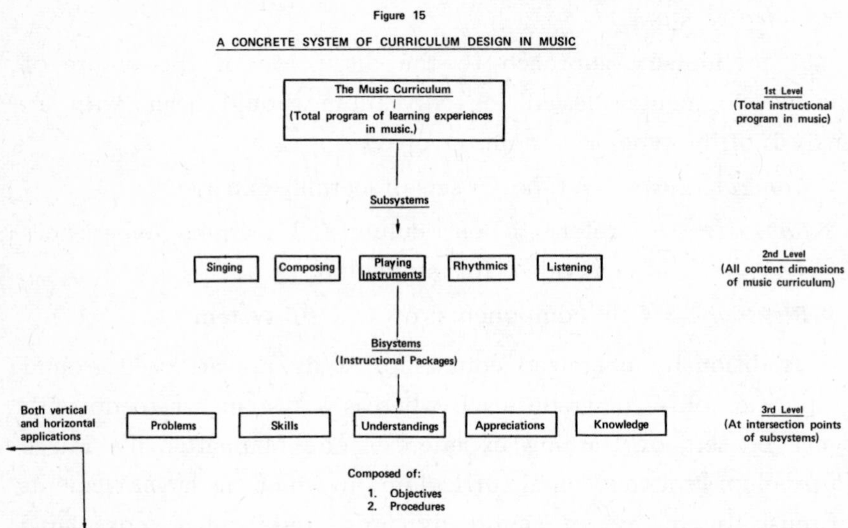

Principles of Organization

In most new programs of curriculum organization, a direct analysis of the essentials of the discipline leads to a desired pattern of instruction on which the system is based. In this approach, curriculum is organized to place primary consideration on the *desired concepts and central ideas to be derived from the discipline itself,* rather than "persistent needs" of students, social settings, community needs, etc., although from what has been said previously these matters, these influences also affect *how to approach the curriculum.* Michaelis and others suggest three principles by which such an approach should be made.

1. Determine the scope of instruction (key concepts, ideas, processes, generalizations).
2. Determine the sequence of instruction (logical-psychological order found through tryout of subsystems or bisystems in in the classroom which reveal effectiveness of plan for cumulative learning of key ideas, methods of inquiry, skills, attitudes, etc.).
3. Determine required units of instruction or bisystems by which attainment of objectives may be realized (optional or supplementary learning activities may be required).

Other considerations must include whether programs are to be considered *pre-disciplinary* (preparational experiences for the main content area itself); *single-disciplinary* (involving concepts, ideas, principles which center on the content of the particular field); or, *multidisciplinary* (cutting across content areas of more than one field).

All organizational approaches must consider teaching strategies techniques for evaluating the system.

Developments in music and the arts in general are important in any consideration of a balanced aesthetic curriculum. These experiences should be available continuously for as many learners as may wish to take advantage of them throughout all levels of education. Bush and Allen emphasize that all students should have continuous, rigorous study in breadth and depth in all of the basic subject matter fields (visual-performing-practical arts, languages, natural sciences, mathematics, physical education and health, social sciences, and guidance).[2]

Michaelis and others group the components of the "balanced" curriculum under four principal areas of learning activity, each of which is related in terms of teaching strategy. These include:[3]

> *Problem-solving areas:* those which are related to the acquisition of understandings and development of requisite thinking and data-handling skills (especially in fields of health education, social science, mathematics, and science).
>
> *Skill development areas:* those related to attainment of specific skills (athletic, computational, foreign language, etc.).

Creative expression areas: those related to development of "divergent" expressive abilities (music, visual arts, oral expression, etc.).

Analytical and appreciative response areas: those related to evaluative criteria for use by the student as a consumer (music, art, literature, dance, and various expressive experiences).

While music and the related arts have enjoyed fairly well-established positions in the curricula of elementary schools in this country, curricular experiences in music in secondary schools is another matter. Secondary education has concentrated its efforts largely on elective programs in music which reach but a small percentage of students in grades seven through twelve. Feyereisen and others feel this to be particularly regrettable and stress the importance of music and the arts by suggesting that education should ". . .cultivate in the society as a whole an understanding and appreciation of the arts." These writers also point out that music and art educators recommend that all students of the secondary level be given an opportunity to take courses in the arts.[4]

Some encouragement may be taken from reports from the U.S. Office of Education's Arts and Humanities Program which in 1966 alone reported support of some forty-six educational research projects in art, forty-eight in music, eighteen in theater and dance, four in the arts in general, and eleven in the humanities.[5] The only regrettable aspect of this report is that the percentage of music-arts-humanities projects is still very low in comparison to the vast number in the sciences and recently has almost dried up in terms of both governmental and private foundation support. Previously reported programs by the Contemporary Music Project, Manhattanville Music Curriculum Program and the Yale Music Curriculum Development Project in literature and materials for the high school have each demonstrated promise, providing these starts are adopted on a wider scale throughout the United States by music educators, administrators, and school districts in order to provide greater balance and quality in total curriculum systems.

A Total Program For Music Education

The music program may be organized either by traditional or "systems-experience" approach. Since most music educators are more familiar with the traditional method--organization in terms of grade levels and courses--let us first inspect this method.

Traditional program of music education.

In order that the needs of a wide spectrum of learners be considered, the "Total School Music Curriculum" (See Figure 16) includes two areas; namely, Music in General Education and Music in "Special" Education. The former consists not just of courses for students with low interest, skill and motivation, but rather includes all those experiences in music which are designed to fulfill "breadth" requirements in the discipline. Music in "special education" is designed to represent performance and other applied aspects of the program.

System-experience program of music education.

A systems-experience approach to the total music program is a newer approach which involves an outline of all learning experiences in music, rather than specific courses, grade levels, etc. expressed in conventional curricula. Thus, we may approach the development of such avenues of experience as:

Analytical-critical listening
Performing
Composing
Conducting

The systems approach to curriculum does not, however, eliminate the need for another organizational approach at the level of by-systems in terms of packaging experiences for the convenience of the institutional (i.e., school) structure. Figures 17-19 indicate how this may be done at various levels. Since many differences in interests, backgrounds, experience, and motivations of students and ways of making music highly individualized have been stressed throughout this book, it should be apparent that there must be *many tracks of experiencing music curricula.* In order to reach a range of learning needs, it is advocated that the school, at all levels, develop an appropriate organization of experiences, courses, learning packages, etc. Aspects of continuous progress, non-gradedness, and so on can

Figure 16

THE TOTAL SCHOOL MUSIC CURRICULUM

Level	MUSIC IN GENERAL EDUCATION	By Whom and How Long Taught?	MUSIC IN "SPECIAL" EDUCATION	By Whom and How Long Taught?
ELEMENTARY SCHOOL Early Childhood (K-1)	**Classroom Music** Basic experiences in: singing, listening, bodily movement, playing simple instruments (pitched and non-pitched), creative expression and music reading. Large-small group and individual act.	Classroom teacher (15-20 min. daily). Music Specialist assistance assigned or "on call".		
Later Childhood (4-6)	**Classroom Music** Basic experiences in music expanded to fit the needs of older children, including harmonic experience and wider use of simple instruments. Exploratory classes in keyboard, orchestral instruments, guitar, recorder and "quest" activitios of short-term nature.	Music Specialist and classroom teacher (20-30 minutes daily)	**Instr. & Choral** Class lessons in orchestral instr. School instr. ensemb. and choruses Area and city-wide orchestras & chor.	**Instrumental** "Traveling" instr. music teacher (30 min. once or twice weekly) **Choral** Resident teacher or trav. specialist (30-40 min. 1 week)
Early Adolescence JUNIOR HIGH SCHOOL (Normally gr. 7-9)	**Exploratory Music or Allied Arts Class** Greater refinement in use of the basic experiences, generally centering around topics such as: Music and Man, the "Now Music," Music and Art, Theory, Instrumental Music, Music and our History, the Human Voice, Folk and Pop Music, Music of Great Composers, etc. **Special Activities for General Students** Guitar classes, keyboard for "non-musicians", non-selective chorus, and short-term "quest" activities in music.	Instrumental, choral or general music teacher (1 period or module daily--approximately 40-45 minutes each)	**Instrumental** Class lessons in homogeneous groups (strings or winds) Band (intermediate and advanced) **Choral** Boys chorus, girls chorus, mixed choir "special" vocal groups	Instrumental music teacher, approx. 1 period or module daily (40-45 min.) Choral-general mus. teacher, approx. 1 period or module daily (40-45 min.)
Late Adolescence SENIOR HIGH SCHOOL (Normally gr. 10-12)	**Humanities, Allied Arts, Survey of Music** A study of the artistic contributions of music and musicians throughout the ages--with emphasis on its influence in contemporary life. **Theory (or Harmony) I, II** Music Theory and Harmony **Special Activities for General Students** May include guitar, keyboard (piano and organ), folk & pop music, Hi-Fi, plus short-term "quest" activities in music.	Humanities-arts team, or any comb. of instructors, (incl. music teacher) Choral or Instr. music teacher or specialist in gen. music & theory (1 period or "mod" daily 40-55 min.)	**Instrumental** Intermediate Orch. Intermediate Band (or Prop Band) Concert Orchestra Stage Band **Vocal-Choral** Beg. Voice, or Cho. Boys or Girls Cho. Mixed Cho., A cappella Vocal Ensemble	Instrumental mus. teacher (1 period or mod. daily (50-55 min. each) Vocal-Choral music teacher (1 period or mod. daily (50-55 min. each)

Figure 17

A Program of Music Education in the Elementary School

E xperiences designed to develop the curriculum concept spiral, in the areas of: 6	The Development of Musicality through:	Experiences for All Students	Students of High Interest	Gifted – Talented
	Performing:	Recreational instr. Singing Conducting Playing Simple Instruments Creating and composing Reading	Group lessons; instrumental Ensembles; vocal, instrumental: orchestra, band, chorus, small ensembles Opportunities to extend other interests to self-generated activities in performance, listening, rhythms, composing	Individual development voice, instruments, conducting, composing, dance, etc.
1. Tone (pitch) 2. Duration (rhythm) 3. Color (timbre) 4. Intensity (dynamics) 5. Form	Listening:	Music of various types & styles Vocal, instrumental, mixed Ethnic music		
	Rhythmic Activities:	Moving to music Creative, spontaneous Patterned, formal Ethnic dances		Opportunities to work as teacher aides in music classes and/or with individual students
	Composing:	Free ideas in music Experimental, electronic, etc. Vocal, instrumental, combined Composing with various notational & modal systems		

Figure 18

A Program of Music Education in the Junior High School

The Development of Musicality Through:	Experiences for All Students	Students of High Interest	Gifted-Talented Students
Performing:	*Interest courses in: Chorus (general); Guitar class; Exploratory piano; Basic musianship; Instrumental classes Singing, playing, conducting, rhythmics as part of a survey class	Instrumental classes Beginning band, orchestra Band, Choir, Orchestra	Solo study as a vocalist or instrumentalist Small advanced ensembles. Advanced band, choir, orchestra Independent study projects Serving as an aide in performance and other activities
Listening:	Independent listening in music resource centers →	→	→
	Group listening, as a member of music survey or humanities-arts class →	Listening clubs → Listening related to area of special interest	→ Development of personal listening collections
Rhythmic Activities:	Various forms of dance activities socially or as member of music class	Interpretive, creative, patterned rhythmics as member of music or P.E. class	Group or solo opportunities in dance and eurhythmics
Composing:	Free ideas in music Experimental, electronic, other composition as member of survey or humanities-arts class	Development of individual talents in Musical composition	Lessons and/or other activities designed to develop individual compositional interests and talents
Short-term "choice" Activities:	General exploratory "mini" or "quest" courses	"Quest" courses in areas of high interest and talent →	→
	Music assemblies	→	→
	Field trips, performances, concerts	→	→

*Interest courses should cover a wide range of activities, including music experiences in contemporary musical influences, such as "The 'Now' Music," "General Performance Activities for Non-music Majors," etc.

Figure 19

A Program of Music Education in the Senior High School

The Development of Musicality Through:	Experiences for All Students	Students of High Interest	Gifted-Talented Students
Performing:	Interest courses in: Class voice, chorus Class instruments Exploratory piano Guitar Folk and Contemporary music Singing, playing, conducting, etc. as part of a survey or allied arts class Basic musicianship	Instrumental classes Voice classes Piano, organ classes Band, choir, orchestra Ensembles Stage band Music productions	Solo study as a vocalist or instrumentalist Advanced ensembles (madrigal choir, chamber singers, instrumental & vocal duets, trios, quartets, chamber orch, etc.) Advanced Choir, A Capella Choir, Symphonic Band, Symphony Orchestra, stage band
Listening:	Independent listening in music resource centers Group listening, as a member of music survey or humanities-allied arts class	→ → Music Lit. & analysis Listening clubs & seminars Listening related to area of special interest Development of personal listening collections →	Serving as a teaching aide in other high school and pre-h.s. music classes. Highly developed areas of independent
Rhythmic Activities:	General dance activities	Marching band, drill team → Interpretive, creative, patterned rhythmics and dance, individually or in special dance classes →	Lessons and/or solo dance opportunities
Composing:	Development of compositional ideas as member of survey or allied arts	Basic theory and harmony → Contemporary music (incl. electronic music) lab. → Arranging →	Lessons in theory-comp.
Short-term "choice" Activities:	General exploratory "mini" or "quest" courses Music assemblies Field trips, performances, concerts	"Quest" courses in areas of high interest and talent → Preparation of "performance packages"	Independent study-research

become integral parts of such organizations. Consequently, the curriculum in the Systems-Experience approach will be aimed at three levels of students; (a) all students, (b) students of high interest, and, (c) gifted-talented students.

"Special" Curricular Opportunities.

Opportunities to experience artist performances and to pursue short-term interests in music should be provided for all children at various levels of learning. All subsystems (courses, etc.) should therefore include supplementary activities in which students may participate in field trips, trips to museums, concerts, electronic music laboratories, trips to colleges, universities, concerts, exhibits, clinics, demonstrations, etc. In addition, paraprofessionals and artists should visit the school to demonstrate, concertize, provide clinics, give lectures, and so on. Highly motivated and gifted students should have further opportunities to see, hear, and work as directly as possible with artists, paraprofessionals, and musical groups which supplement the regular school musical offerings. "Mini" and "Quest" courses at all levels of interest, in various fields of music and allied arts should be provided to care for short-term (from one day to a week or longer) learning and experiential needs of students. The latter may be suggested by faculty or generated from interests and expressed desires of the students themselves.

Organizational Plans

In the previous chapter on the music curriculum, it will be remembered that it was advocated that all persons involved in teaching and learning share in developmental processes of the instructional program. While this should involve persons in addition to the professional staff, the burden of the program development (the general systems level of curriculum) must fall heavily on leadership personnel; music coordinators, consultants, department chairmen, resource teachers, and other music specialists who have access to or who have opportunities to lend their expertise to larger applications of the system, as opposed to those with more limited instructional responsibilities.. At this level (subsystems), music courses and the special activity packages will rely heavily on the teachers involved, since these learning experiences are most closely allied with the day-to-day instruction in the classroom.

At this point, a word should be said about some of the patterns of school organization and ways in which personnel typically are involved with students.

Horizontal Organization.

The two most common modes of horizontal school organization are (a) the self-contained classroom, usually limited to elementary grades, but occasionally found in some intermediate school structures and (b) departmental organization at the secondary school level where teachers are assigned to such courses as seventh grade English, social studies, general music, ninth grade girls' chorus, etc. Advocates of the horizontal plan, particularly at the elementary level, feel that teachers in this system have the advantage of knowing children better and that they therefore can take care of learning needs of children more advantageously than in other plans. Departmental specialists (who may assist classroom teachers) are also felt to have highly specialized knowledge from which students may benefit and grow in greater intellectual depth. Critics point out that the horizontal plan in reality lacks depth and breadth and that many learning experiences tend to be fragmented, unrelated, and lacking in significant meaning. The horizontal organization also is best geared to traditional scheduling of time, space, personnel, and learning resources. For these reasons, it is felt that if applied in the "pure" sense, horizontal organizations are the least flexible of the arrangements for students.

Recent Organizational Plans.

There are several recent modes of organizing instructional personnel resources, the most common of which are: (a) team teaching; (b) cooperative-differentiated staffing and, (c) independent study-research under the guidance of appropriate teaching staff. In team teaching, two or more instructors representing various teaching orientations and/or strengths provide additional expertise and responsibility for learning activities in a particular course. Differentiated staff arrangements involve a hierarchy of instructional and instructionally-related roles, including both certificated and non-certificated personnel. Typically this may include a master teacher, assistant teachers, instructor's aides or assistants, clerks, paraprofessionals, media technicians, and the like. The success of this arrangement is dependent upon a careful delineation of roles in which the unique contributions of each is clarified. The master teacher is, of course, the key to such an arrangement, since by training and experience this person is in a position to offer educational leadership for the total educational enterprise. However, without the support of assistants, aides, and others, including wherever appropriate those from the central office and/or community, differentiated staffing is not possible. Independent study-research develops from individual learning needs of students and may involve, at a given moment, any member of the instructional team, certificated or non-certificated. Depending on level, this type of learning may assume the form of (a) discovery-type activities; (b) assigned work; (c) contracts; (d) learning activity packages (LAPS); (e) free and non-structured research pursuits; and, (f) independent study supervised by instructors or aides.

Resource Characteristics of "New Look" Schools.

"New look" schools, whether characterized as "open" or "modified open" have certain special characteristics which should be noted here. These characteristics include:

* Flexibility of programs and schedules
* Diversity of offerings
* New techniques and media for learning
* Quality programs
* Several tracks to learning
* Appropriate facilities which are designed for varied types of instruction, variations in use, and aesthetic effect.[6]

Evaluation

The music curriculum should always be evaluated in terms of the original goals and objectives established. Chapter V illustrated how objectives should be conceived and written. Evaluation, thus, will involve gathering and interpreting data concerning the degree to which the stated objectives of the music curriculum have been met. Evaluation is also both continuous and terminal. Since planning is both long and short-term in nature, not only must music educators have a means of assessing the success of courses and experiences upon their conclusion, but there must be continual evaluation and feed-back of short-term objectives in the day-to-day teaching activities of the classroom.

Evaluation may be both observed and measured. The former has to do with observable progress which students demonstrate in meeting instructional objectives, as well as ways by which students use music in a variety of in or out-of-school situations on a skill and/or valuing basis. Anecdotal records, performance tryouts or challenges, quality and accuracy of information used in discussion, results of practice and/or independent study projects, and the degree of change or use of music in school or out-of-school music activities are part of observed or informal evaluation.

Measured evaluation may be accomplished by means of norm-referenced or criterion referenced evaluative devices. Music tests of of achievement which have nationally standardized norms (such as the Aliferis, Colwell, Gordon or Oregon tests are all examples) provide a means of evaluation both as pre and post-tests. Teacher-made devices may be more specifically applied to criteria however, since they may deal directly with the behavioral objectives of the course. All such measures should be both reliable (tests with accuracy and consistency) and valid (tests what it is supposed to measure). Rating scales for performance, verbal and paper-and-pencil tests, check-lists, student logs, attitude scales, adjudicator ratings (as in festivals), completed contracts, and self-evaluation instruments are examples of measurable evaluation.

PPBS (Program Planning and Budgeting Systems) place emphasis on systematic evaluation. The success of any plan of curriculum evaluation will be determined by the quality and validity of the goals and objectives for the music program and the means by which they are achieved. Leaders in music education must therefore be competent to assess the appropriateness of content and sequence in terms of the stated objectives of the program and should be ready to change or modify any elements in the system which do not produce desired educational results.

Summary

An "open systems" approach to curriculum is another approach to development and organization of the school program which involves at the first (or primary) level, the total music curriculum, followed by appropriate subsystems which include all forms of packaging (experiences and/or courses) and other forms of sequentially-ordered learning.

Curriculum organization involves the various phases of development, organization and implementation. Typically, development may be initiated from a survey of community music needs. This is followed by formulating objectives of the program, deciding on structure, topics, courses, units, etc., and is then implemented in trial and final adoption stages, from which reorganization and restructuring from the application of evaluative criteria may be accomplished.

The music curriculum may be organized either on a traditional (courses and grade levels) or systems-experience (areas of learning--listening, performing, composing, conducting) basis. The systems-experience approach emphasizes behavioral objectives in the cognitive, psychomotor, affective and critical judgment domains of learning and the development of musicality by means of appropriate musical experience. Figures presented in this Chapter apply to (a) experiences for all students, (b) students of high interest, and (c) the gifted-talented students.

The organization of resources for teaching indicated both horizontal and recent instructional alignments. Team-teaching, differentiated staffing, and independent study-research were advocated in addition to more diverse and flexible school characteristics for fulfilling individual learning potentials in contemporary education.

Evaluation, which may be either observed or measured should always be based on educational goals and program objectives. Norm-referenced devices provide measurement according to national standards. Criterion-referenced evaluation provides greater flexibility of adaptation by instructors to fit behavioral objectives of learning. PPBS provides a systematic approach to determining the quality and validity of the learning experience.

Topics For Discussion

1. Using Figure 14 as your guide, conduct a survey of a nearby community. Summarize that community's "music profile" and implications for the music curriculum in its schools.

2. Discuss your interpretation of Figure 15, "A Concrete System of Curriculum Design in Music." Do you feel the systems approach could work in a traditional school, and if so, under what conditions?

3. From your research, reading, or practical knowledge, can you cite examples of special programs in music education which have been sponsored wholly or in part by governmental or private foundation agencies.

4. Discuss how the various domains of learning (cognitive, affective, psychomotor, critical judgment) can be applied to specific courses and/or music learning activities.

5. Compare the "traditional" total music curriculum shown in Figure 16 with the school district where you attended as a student. How is it similar or different?

6. In what ways may the "spiral" (MMCP) of developing music concepts be applied to given courses (see Figures 17, 18, or 19)? Choose one or more courses for "all" students and for those of "high interest" or the "gifted-talented."

7. Is it possible to modify the "horizontal" organizational plan as an effective intermediate step to restructuring the school along more contemporary lines?

8. Select a course in which you are most interested (band, chorus, orchestra, allied arts, general music, theory, etc.) and discuss how you would propose to organize the music curriculum by making use of the differentiated staff concept.

9. Can you think of several ways of illustrating the idea of independent-study-research in a given class?

Suggested Readings

California State Department of Education. *Music Framework for California Public Schools, Kindergarten through Grade Twelve.* Sacramento, California: The Department, 1970.

Feyereisen, Kathryn, A. John Fiorino, and Arlene T. Nowak. *Supervision and Curriculum Renewal: A Systems Approach.* New York: Appleton-Century-Crofts, 1970. See Section II, "Curriculum Renewal."

House, Robert W. *Administration in Music Education.* Englewood Cliffs, N.J.: Prentice-Hall, Inc., 1973. See Ch. 3.

Jones, J. James, C. Jackson Salisbury, and Ralph L. Spencer. *Secondary School Administration.* New York: McGraw-Hill Book Co., 1969. Contemporary influences in leadership and curriculum at the secondary level.

Kohut, Daniel L. *Instrumental Music Pedagogy.* Englewood Cliffs, N.J.: Prentice-Hall, Inc., 1973. An excellent source book for all instrumental music educators.

Kuhn, Wolfgang E. *Instrumental Music, Second Edition.* Boston: Allyn and Bacon, Inc., 1970. See Ch. 4.

Michaelis, John U., Ruth H. Grossman and Lloyd F. Scott. *New Designs for the Elementary School Curriculum.* New York: McGraw-Hill Book Co., 1967. An excellent source book for curriculum in the "new mode." See Ch. 1, 2 and 12.

Roe, Paul F. *Choral Music Education.* Englewood Cliffs, N.J.: Prentice-Hall, Inc., 1970. Authoritative book on voice production and choral music education.

Sidnell, Robert. *Building Instructional Programs in Music Education.* Englewood Cliffs, N.J.: Prentice-Hall, Inc., 1973. See Ch. 1 and 2.

CHAPTER EIGHT

INDIVIDUALIZED INSTRUCTION

The arts play a radically different role in the open classroom than in the traditional school. Painting, sculpture, music, dance, crafts--these are not frills to be indulged in . . . they are the business of education as much as reading, writing, math, or science.

Charles E. Silberman

Background

Until recently it was felt that schools could operate most efficiently in the area of mass education and should deal primarily with group instruction, leaving only incidental opportunities for individual learning. The interpretation of growth characteristics tended to emphasize general characteristics rather than individual differences of learners. The difficulty with this approach is that although individual differences appear even in early childhood education, these differences tend to widen with maturation. Hence, schools which have stressed mass or large-group instruction to provide for general growth characteristics often inhibit rather than provide opportunities for optimum growth which capitalize on individual learning rates.

If humans are viewed in group dimensions, one is impressed with commonalities which appear to be shared by all members. Yet, on second inspection, it is quite apparent that these commonalities are overriden by startling differences between individuals. The social process of formal education tends to homogenize these differences and to help the individual identify with his kind in terms of how he/she can contribute to his/her society. In so doing, however, some of the exciting and necessary possibilities for the development of individual potential are thwarted. In the long run, society will benefit not only from the fulfillment of group functions, but more particularly from helping individuals develop their unique characteristics and potentials by which the benefits to society and themselves are released.

The individualization of instruction is not new in the United States--it dates back easily to the Nineteenth Century. The so-called "Pueblo Plan" was one of the first of record. More recently in the 1920's and 1930's, several laboratory-type schools for self-instruction were devised. At the same time, the mental testing movement of Binet and Terman was providing additional impetus by suggesting individual learning tasks for diverse populations. B. F. Skinner invented crude teaching machines in the early 1950's which provided still another track of individualization by programming textbooks into simple teaching devices which allowed students to proceed at their own learning rates. Research in learning theory rapidly accelerated after 1957, leading to wholesale reforms and far more sophisticated applications of individualized learning.

The Committee for Economic Development in 1968 espoused the importance of individualized instruction, geared to the interests, learning rates, and unique abilities of learners. The CED also suggested that various methods must be adopted in order to achieve this goal and suggested replacing what they felt to be indefensible and educationally unproductive traditional forms of instruction. It was further suggested that schools adopt differentiated staffing, and outlined a program in which master teachers, assistant teachers, aides, interns, media technicians and the like were teamed to provide more effective teaching and the deployment of human skills to provide new curricula and teaching strategies.[1]

The five most important guidelines for individualizing instruction are:

* Providing the individual with the opportunity to proceed through content materials at his own pace.
* Working at times which are more convenient to the learner (and, often tangentially, to the instruction).
* Gearing the beginning point of his instruction to previous experience rather than starting "at the beginning" of a given course, experience, or skill.
* Removing inhibitions regarding developing a small number of easily indentifiable skills or concepts.
* Utilizing a larger range of instructional media, from which the learner is also free to choose.

The most important types of individualized instruction include:

1. Independent study options provided by scheduled time for all or most of the students.
2. Programmed independent study by which individual learning needs are met in a variety of ways, including concept development, skill reinforcement, remedial work, etc.
3. Learning Activity Packages (LAPS) which provide greater flexibility than strictly programmed material (see following section of the Chapter).
4. "Contracts" in which students and teachers agree upon student-identified instructional goals (also to follow).
5. Independent study seminars in which individuals meet to share the results of their reading, research, creative efforts, etc.
6. Small Group Music Strategies (SGMS) in which "task forces" of students work on common problems, then share the results with the class.
7. Computer-assisted instruction in which students have opportunities to solve unique problems or to gather information (these may also be in the form of LAPS).
8. Task-related study which is geared to particular career interests. Sometimes performed in conjunction with

community agencies.

9. "Quest" courses (sometimes called "mini-courses") to meet short-term or special learning interest needs of students. These are frequently self-generated and self-directed.
10. Non-graded (continuous progress design) schools which allow students to progress at their own learning rates.

The underlying principle of individualized instruction is that of developing and releasing the human potential of each student. Although learning sequence is an established factor in curriculum, "mosaic" learning, which actually proceeds from established "islands" of learning experience by means of informal participation is often more natural, involving, and personal to the student. Both sequential and mosaic learning are important to individual development, however, but the latter occurs almost exclusively as learners pursue somewhat unrelated, independent courses.

Implications For Educational Organization

If education for the development of human potential is our goal, the question arises whether public schools which have long organized almost exclusively for mass education can now begin to individualize instruction. It is certain that modifications must be made to meet the needs of students, but again, we must ask how these changes are possible within present school organizations without financially prohibitive wholesale revamping of structures and personnel. Fortunately, there is rather common agreement that not only are many changes now possible but that they can be no more costly than traditional planning--even with some changes in curricula and up-dating physical facilities. At the same time, it is desirable if music educators and administrators begin to plan for the future in terms of better designed plants and instructional programs. Some of these have been indicated in general in chapters on curricula, and will be discussed also later in terms of specific designs for music rooms, facilities, and so on.

In general, the implications for organizing to meet individualized instruction goals are fourfold: (a) program expectations, (b) curriculum, (c) method, and, (d) physical facilities. Facilities must include areas for group activity as well as places where students may work by themselves. Although this may be achieved in a variety of ways even in traditional buildings, new facilities are conceived as being more open, to accommodate even larger group pursuits than in the past, while at the same time providing many areas and centers where individuals and small groups may work with materials, ideas, and so on. Seminar areas, study carrels, discipline-resource and media centers (i.e., music resource rooms) are now becoming quite common in such facilities.

Expectations for students should also transcend traditional "grade norms" which tend to restrict and measure each person in the same way, but which actually tend to limit or inhibit success to a large degree. Rather than being faced with repeated failure resulting from rigid grade and promotional standards, the concept of individualization provides each student with "accomplishment goals" which are characteristic of each person. Continuous progress design (non-graded) schools allow each student to advance at his own rate, some taking longer for certain tasks, others a shorter period of time. Such continuous progress is applied to differences which exist between children in their ability to work with different subject-matter sequences. Expectancies are stated in terms of *each learner's ability to work with a particular discipline area.* Grades, therefore, reflect the completion of individualized tasks rather than arbitrary norms of success or failure.

What has been said previously concerning curriculum and method which is based upon behavioral goals can also apply to individualized instruction, provided that such objectives consider individual as well as group learning expectancies. A school curriculum which is designed to reveal continuing threads--perceptions, conceptual development, generalizations, abstractions, and so on, by means of inquiry-problem-solving should relate fundamental processes and principles to instructional content, internally, as well as between subject matter areas. Individual experimentation and musical experiencing can be packaged, as we shall soon see, to reinforce and amplify group learning. Content and method should stress varying (situational) goals as well as those of the program if they are to meet the wide variety of educational applications.

Procedures for Individualizing Music Education

One effective way of meeting the need for individualization is the use of a "modified open classroom." This is not primarily a place, but rather a psychological and social condition that stresses the partnership of teacher and students in learning activities. In this situation, the primary task of the teacher is to select and provide materials that will allow students to explore, manipulate, experiment, invent, and discover—processes that are essential for the understanding of music. In a modified open classroom, the teacher must be willing to assume the role of guide and stimulator rather than that of director. And, where a classroom teacher and a music specialist work with the same group of children, both must be aware of this different role and act accordingly.

Two alternative and complementary techniques that can be used in the modified open classroom are *small-group music strategies (SGMS)* and individualized music activities. Small-group music strategies are accomplished by dividing the class into appropriate "task forces" to solve problems and work on a variety of music techniques. Instructions concerning the nature of the activity are generally given verbally by the teacher. Depending on the nature of the task, alternative methods for accomplishing the SGMS may be suggested; however, groups may decide on other modes of working, depending on their expertise and prior exposure to the music concept. The learning may be deductive (working from a concept, skill, or technique presented in class to achieve a specific application) or inductive (solving problems to determine the concept). Although a great deal of individualization is possible and members of the group benefit from their interaction, SGMS are not as personalized as other one-to-one individual pursuits.

Small-group music strategies can be used to help children relate their exploration of sound and music-making to concepts and activities introduced to the entire class. Both the music specialist and the classroom teacher should remember to provide sufficient structure to help the children succeed—then get out of the way. To prepare children for successful small-group music strategies, it will be necessary to provide instructions concerning:

1. the nature of the task
2. ways to begin and complete the problem
3. time limitations
4. what will be expected in reporting the final results of the project to the class.

Leaders may be selected by the group itself, although teachers, aides, and other available adults may be used as consultants. Groups should be expected to complete their small-group music strategy within a reasonable amount of time (always specified), ranging from a few minutes to (occasionally) several days, depending on the maturity of the children and the nature of the problem. At the conclusion, each group should report on what was accomplished in the manner that seems most appropriate.

The teacher may then pose open-ended questions that help students freely verbalize on inherent aspects of their music experience, as opposed to qualitative judgments such as "Did you like it?" or "Which was best?" It is important that children focus on the common ingredients of any music, such as tone, duration, timbre, intensity, form, and expression. The teacher could ask questions like these:

"What did you hear?"

"Were there any new sounds, or was this similar to something you have heard before?"

"Did you encounter any problems? Do you think there might be other ways to accomplish what you did?"

"How would you describe the effect in your own words?"

Figure 20 is a small-group music strategy that illustrates a way of exploring and notating sound that can be adapted to nearly any level, from primary grades through junior high school.

At any time during a given instructional sequence, students may be encouraged to explore sound and music-making media as individuals. These activities may be scheduled, or they may occur during informal, nonscheduled times in the school day. There are at

Figure 20
Small-Group Strategy

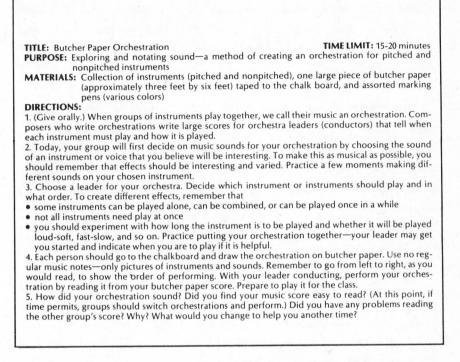

TITLE: Butcher Paper Orchestration **TIME LIMIT:** 15-20 minutes

PURPOSE: Exploring and notating sound—a method of creating an orchestration for pitched and nonpitched instruments

MATERIALS: Collection of instruments (pitched and nonpitched), one large piece of butcher paper (approximately three feet by six feet) taped to the chalk board, and assorted marking pens (various colors)

DIRECTIONS:

1. (Give orally.) When groups of instruments play together, we call their music an orchestration. Composers who write orchestrations write large scores for orchestra leaders (conductors) that tell when each instrument must play and how it is played.
2. Today, your group will first decide on music sounds for your orchestration by choosing the sound of an instrument or voice that you believe will be interesting. To make this as musical as possible, you should remember that effects should be interesting and varied. Practice a few moments making different sounds on your chosen instrument.
3. Choose a leader for your orchestra. Decide which instrument or instruments should play and in what order. To create different effects, remember that
   - some instruments can be played alone, can be combined, or can be played once in a while
   - not all instruments need play at once
   - you should experiment with how long the instrument is to be played and whether it will be played loud-soft, fast-slow, and so on. Practice putting your orchestration together—your leader may get you started and indicate when you are to play if it is helpful.
4. Each person should go to the chalkboard and draw the orchestration on butcher paper. Use no regular music notes—only pictures of instruments and sounds. Remember to go from left to right, as you would read, to show the order of performing. With your leader conducting, perform your orchestration by reading it from your butcher paper score. Prepare to play it for the class.
5. How did your orchestration sound? Did you find your music score easy to read? (At this point, if time permits, groups should switch orchestrations and perform.) Did you have any problems reading the other group's score? Why? What would you change to help you another time?

least four basic types of individualized music activities:

Conventional or "star" activities—a technique that allows highly interested and motivated students to pursue special talents on their own. For example, a student may practice an instrument or voice individually, or as a member of a duet, trio, or small ensemble. Where possible, "star" activities (such as descants, bell ostinatos, harmonized parts, and piano, Autoharp, or guitar accompaniments) should be integrated into the work of the class as a whole so that all children will benefit.

Quest activities—individualized music activities of the student's choice. This technique allows complete discovery-oriented learning by means of individual interaction and involvement with a variety of music media. No structure is necessary for quest activities.

Contracts—lists of activities provided by the teacher from which each child selects activities and options (including those of an out-of-school nature) that he agrees to complete. With this plan, it is necessary for the student and teacher to agree on the activities, resources, learning mode, and terminal assessment. The time selected for completion of the contract will vary, but it must be terminated within given limits, usually no longer than a quarter or a semester.

Learning activity packages (LAPS)—self-learning, self-pacing activities that the teacher provides for a student to pursue on his own. LAPs must be in written or taped form. They are generally geared to completion within a relatively short time span, usually ranging from a few minutes to an available period or time module.

Of these individualized techniques, the last three are by far the most flexible and adaptable to all types of schools—traditional, transitional ("modified"), or open. Whether small-group strategy or individualized activity, each is concerned with the exploration of musical sound by individuals acting as performers, composers, conductors, or critical listeners. Each type of activity must be tailored to the needs of specific classes—hence, the cooperation of classroom teacher and music specialist is essential to their success.

The "packaging" of music experiences is a relatively new technique. One example of this form of individualized learning activity, the learning activity packages (LAPs), are sets of teacher-prepared materials that help a student acquire a concept, a skill, or a technique. Although many LAPs can be written effectively by almost anyone familiar with the scope and content of the desired activity (including classroom teachers, aides, paraprofessionals, and student teachers), the special expertise of the music specialist makes him the one who should design the LAPs that explore music in depth.

LAPs are designed so that the student paces himself and does the learning by himself; therefore, they must contain built-in directions and methods for student assessment. Because LAPs are ideally suited to individual needs and learning rates, these packages must provide diversified content and allow for varying performance levels, ranging from remedial activities to experiences that are appropriate for advanced and gifted students.

LAPs may be used:

* to introduce a learning sequence or a new concept, skill or technique

* to speed progress
* to allow for additional practice of a skill or for work in greater detail on the same or a related concept or topic
* to pursue a student-planned activity (sometimes called "branching") on the same or a related topic.

The subject matter that can be included in LAPs is virtually limitless. They may cover such topics as introducing a new instrument; learning to construct or work with melody or rhythm patterns; decoding music symbols (music reading); composing music by various techniques; performing experiments with music sounds; learning a new technique for playing an instrument; listening analytically and critically to unfamiliar music; introducing alternative methods of achieving the same result; and researching a given topic in music.

Figure 21
Lap—Composition (Octave Displacement)

CONCEPT: Octave displacement, as a compositional technique, provides interest and variety. **TIME LIMIT:** 20-25 minutes.
MATERIAL: Set of resonator bells, one mallet, a plastic cover, a china marking pencil (optional: a recording of "Greetings Prelude" by Igor Stravinsky)
INSTRUCTIONS:
1. Twentieth-century composers often change music in interesting ways. One technique used is called OCTAVE DISPLACEMENT. To refresh your memory, an octave is an interval of eight notes. When you start counting from any letter of the scale, the eighth note will have the same letter; therefore, notes with the same letter are higher or lower than the original by eight notes, or an octave.
2. Use your bells to play the following octaves:

F F E E B♭ B♭ G G

3. In familiar music, notes occur in an expected order. However, if you DISPLACE the note by moving it an octave up or down, this is called OCTAVE DISPLACEMENT. Play "Jingle Bells" the usual way—then try it with some of its notes displaced.

4. You will now try writing a new octave displacement version of "The Man on the Flying Trapeze." First try playing the original version—then write and play your own.

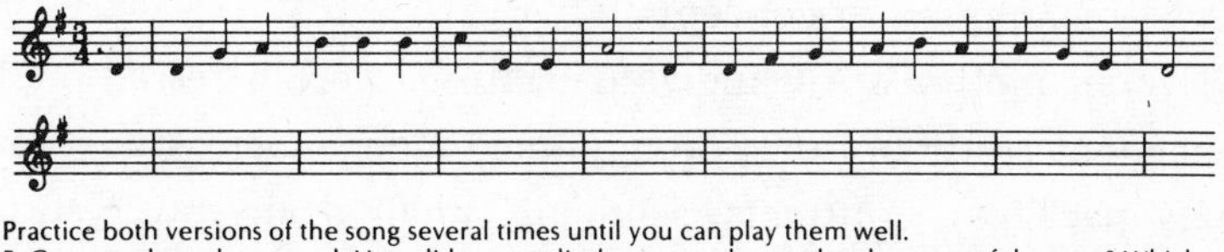

Practice both versions of the song several times until you can play them well.
5. Compare how they sound. How did octave displacement change the character of the tune? Which do you prefer? If time permits, listen to the recording of "Greetings Prelude" by Igor Stravinsky to see how this famous composer used octave displacement to change the sound of "Happy Birthday."

Figure 21 shows one method for constructing a LAP. Since modifications can be made both in procedure and in wording to accomodate the needs of specific individuals within a given class, this LAP can appeal to a wide range of upper elementary and junior high school students. Teachers will find LAPS to be an exciting and creative addition to any music program. When encouraged to use them, students will broaden their knowledge about music and expand their musical horizons.

Summary

The needs of students are many and diverse. Although individuals have many commonalities, the differences in learners require music educators to consider how to meet their learning needs on an individual as well as group basis. We know, for example that:

* There is a wide range of individual differences in students.
* There are diverse socio-economic and cultural differences in student populations.
* There is a need for identity and acceptance which stems from being treated as an individual rather than a member of a group.
* Students need to be active participants in learning activities.
* There is a dislike of a purely academic approach--individualization helps learners find ways of gearing learning to their own interest, experience, and skill and at their own pace.
* Students may succeed more readily when they can enter a learning sequence at their own "beginning point."
* By individualizing instruction, a wider range of experience and utilization of media is possible.
* Students frequently succeed more readily when working on their own and can readily learn easily identifiable skills, techniques, or concepts.

Several methods of individualization were stressed including independent study options, programmed independent study, learning activity packages, contracts, seminars, small group music strategies, computer-assisted instruction, task-related study, "quest" courses, and non-graded (continuous progress) activities. This requires organizing in terms of (a) program expectations, (b) curriculum,

(c) method, and, (d) physical facilities. In general, this requires more flexibility in terms both of teaching and space utilization.

Two methods for individualization were presented in this Chapter; Small Group Music Strategies (SGMS)--"task force" activities which assist small groups of learners to pursue music experiences independently of the teacher; and, Learning Activity Packages (LAPS)--sets of teacher-prepared materials by which an individual student may pursue a single activity, concept, or skill. The latter are self-teaching, self-pacing, but, unlike programmed materials, allow the student opportunities to pursue in depth, concentrate on perfecting an idea or skill--or, may permit him to branch into related or "quest" activities of his/her own choice.

Topics For Discussion

1. Can you cite evidence of ways in which schools in your community are incorporating some of the ideas for updating and individualizing teaching in their music curriculum?
2. Select a given age or grade level. Make a list of the most common general characteristics of these learners. Make a second list of the ways in which individuals of this group are individually different from their classmates. (If possible, base this on direct observation of a regular group of students in a nearby school.)
3. We know that there are wide differences between individuals in any given heterogenous school population with regard to learning rates in such subject areas as reading, computational skills, and so on. Discuss the range of music backgrounds, interests, skills, etc. in a normal group of persons (not the members of a select performance ensemble). How would you go about meeting these different backgrounds and needs if you had some type of "consumer" course in music? Consider those of high and low interest and motivation, as well as the "average" students in the group.
4. Select a performance group (band, chorus, orchestra, etc.) with which you are familiar. List and discuss all the possible ways of individualizing instruction for this group which you feel to be appropriate.
5. List and discuss the most appropriate activities in music for
   (a) large group
   (b) small group music strategies
   (c) independent, individualized activity
6. Design a Small Group Music Strategy (SGMS) and a Learning Activity Package (LAP) for a music class of your choice. Be sure to follow the format and instructions in this Chapter. If possible, administer each of these to a group of students to determine whether they work. Make revisions where necessary as a result of this.

Suggested Readings

Dunn, Rita and Kenneth Dunn. *Practical Approaches to Individualizing Instruction: Contracts and Other Effective Strategies.* West Nyack, New York: Parker Publishing Co., 1972.

Landon, Joseph W. *How To Write Learning Activity Packages for Music Education.* Costa Mesa, Calif. Educational Media Press, 1973. This entire publication is devoted to the LAP concept. Divided into three parts: (1) The Nature and Purpose of LAPS, (2) Goals, Concepts and Objectives Used In Writing LAPS, (3) Procedure for Writing LAPS In Music.

__________ *Individualized Music Activities Packet.* Fullerton, Ca.: California State University, Fullerton, 1973. This publication contains approaches to small group music strategies.

__________ "Music In Britain's Informal Classrooms; What Does It Suggest For American Education?" *Music Educators Journal.* (Vol. 59, No. 9, May 1973) pp. 49-51.

__________ "Strategies for Opening the Traditional Classroom." *Music Educators Journal.* (Vol. 60, No. 8, April 1974) pp. 64-69.

O'Brien, James P. "Packaging the One-Concept Music Period," *Music Educators Journal.* (Vol. 60, No. 1, September 1973) pp. 41-43.

Petrequin, Gaynor. *Individualizing Learning Through Modular-Flexible Programming.* New York: McGraw-Hill, Inc., 1968.

Silverman, Charles E. *The Open Classroom Reader.* New York: Vintage Books, 1973.

CHAPTER NINE

RESOURCES FOR SPECIAL LEARNING NEEDS

> The core of a developmental program of music education should be a sequence of vital musical experiences, activities, endeavors, and learnings, including performance in many media musical composition, ample and diversified listening, reading books and articles about music, discussing music, musical doings outside school. This sequence should begin in the nursery school or the kindergarten, and continue on through the grades into secondary school. Its prevailing purpose should be to promote all-round musical growth, to bring music home to large numbers of pupils, to make them musically responsive, sensitive and discriminating persons.
>
> James L. Mursell

The purpose of this Chapter will be to acquaint the reader with a range of activities which are peripheral or outside the normal music program of the classroom, yet which have to do with its effectiveness and ultimate impact. If we view curriculum in the broad sense as a totality of learning experiences, these activities are curricular. Some, however, are not music activities under the direct sponsorship of educational institutions (as in recreation, therapy, and industry), yet they are all educational in the sense that they provide opportunities for music experiencing and learning--and are thus subject to the influence and leadership of persons in music education. Other activities are directly related to school curricula, such as school resource centers, music for the disadvantaged, exceptional, and gifted.

Perhaps at no prior time in the history of music education in this country has learning been as diversified as at the present. The demands on schools are many, seeking to push learning beyond the normal boundaries of the four walls of the classroom to encompass many other activities both in and out of school. In approaching the question of how to make music education a more vital, personal force in the lives of individuals, the community itself also is viewed as a laboratory for learning. With "all-around musical growth" as its central purpose, music education is becoming concerned not only with in-school applications, but the additional possibilities of experiencing music in recreation, industry, therapy, and life-long learning. Music educators are also becoming increasingly aware that the needs of the disadvantaged, gifted and exceptional child are part of the ideal which seeks to bring music to learners at all levels.

The essential theme of this Chapter is that public education should prescribe no fixed beginning, restricted application, nor arbitrarily imposed terminal point if its central purpose is to assist all persons to grow in musically responsive ways. Hopefully, this goal will also include a variety of adaptations for learning needs which are essential to make education self-motivated, self-directed, and self-fulfilling.

School Resource Centers

The modern school emphasizes the need for independent study, individual investigation, research and creativity, and opportunities to work in a variety of ways on one's own initiative to extend group experiences which are common to the classroom. In order to do this, there is a need to provide classroom areas, carrels, and resource centers which are readily available to all students. Teachers must also encourage open-endedness in classroom presentations which will allow students to seek alternative and supplementary answers, solve specific learning problems, reinforce parts of the presentation needing further practice, create new adaptations of concepts and materials, secure additional information, and so on. If the individual's growth is viewed in the context of continuous progress design, it is obvious that this will involve different rates of speed in accomplishing learning tasks in different subject areas; different sets of skills; different applications of knowledge. It becomes vital then that provision be made for individual work in resource areas and centers, not all of which needs to be during class hours. By using resource centers, students frequently develop a greater concern for their work and improved study habits.

The most common of the resource centers for individualizing instruction include the following:

* classroom study centers
* classroom study carrels
* individual instruction centers
* discipline and/or area resource centers
* library and/or media resource centers
* computer-assisted instruction centers

Classroom study centers are found frequently in elementary classrooms and are simply centers provided by the teacher for use by the teacher for use by individuals and small groups apart from the normal learning activities of the total group. They consist of materials provided for individual perusal which will stimulate interest and activity or illuminate some phase of the work of the class. Examples may include such things as musical instruments for exploration and creative activities, LAPS prepared by the teacher for the children's use, science-music projects, book displays on music and musicians, books to read for information and pleasure, and listening center materials.

Classroom study carrels are an obvious adaptation of conventional library carrels. These require no structural changes in classrooms, but should provide some means of semi-isolation for individual students. Cardboard partitions added to library or calssroom tables may be effectively devised to do this. Occasionally, a couch or easy chair in a corner of the room will accomplish the same purpose. Carrels should be available for student use throughout the day and are readily adaptable to all levels of the school--elementary through senior high school.

Individual instruction centers should be contiguous to the classroom and adaptable to both individual and small group learning activities. Typically these may include a variety of listening and programmed music activities (including LAPS) for self-directed activities of students. There should be provision for use of listening materials (cassettes, cartridges, tapes, records) for review and supplementary study of such matters as music fundamentals, music listening examples, and practice. There should also be some of the following available: musical instruments, microfilm readers, programmed study devices, tape recorders for recording individual practice, film strip and film-loop projectors for viewing packaged musical concept materials, reproducing and multiple copy machines for reproducing scores and other materials, musical instruments, music scores, and so on.

Discipline and/or area resource centers are similar to individual instruction centers, but have the added advantage of being staffed (all or part of the day) by aides, assistants, media technicians, and instructors who serve as resource persons to help students in individual inquiries and creative endeavors. Customarily, such centers are located adjacent to or in close proximity to the discipline(s) which they serve, thereby serving both student and instructional staff needs. Since these centers are usually more complete and may serve several students at one time, ordinarily only one such area is provided. In addition to some of the resource-hardware previously listed, these centers may contain small electronic music-compositional devices; TV cameras, taping machines and projectors for preparation of class lessons, microteaching, viewing, etc.; music-writers; overhead projectors and transparency-producing equipment; phonograph record, tapes, and cartridge libraries; music books and scores; and a variety of materials for creating, performing and recording music.

Library resource centers are actually applications of the concept of the traditional school library, expanded to include all possible resource materials, including reference materials, books, periodicals, leaflets, sample curriculum materials and packets, microfilms and readers, computer-assisted retrieval systems for securing a variety of information on and off-campus, recording and tape libraries, film and filmstrip libraries, study prints, pictures and models, and other materials for individual inquiry and growth. Typically, such centers would contain conventional library tables, open-stack access areas for all books and periodicals, carrels and seminar rooms, microfilm and film projection rooms, TV viewing rooms, multiple listening centers (plug-ins may also be installed at conventional tables located throughout the main portion of the room which are operated on student request from a central control room), well-stocked work areas for the preparation of special reports and investigations, exhibit spaces for exhibiting rare scores, instruments, new books, etc. In short, the library resource center provides for a wide range of individual learning needs of the entire school. In small schools, this may take the place of discipline and area centers; in larger schools it would serve to supplement these facilities.

Computer-assisted instruction centers generally, due to cost and other practical factors, are located in a central school source or in a nearby university or college where the service is leased to the district. The installation of terminals or sub-stations located throughout the school makes recent adaptations of computer-assisted instruction more accessible to a wider range of instructors and students.

Computer-assisted instruction has a wide variety of uses. For example, it may be used for information storage and retrieval and sound synthesis and musical composition. It may also be programmed for sophisticated LAPS, in which the computer "answers" the student, checks his replies, suggests remedial and branching activities, and "awards him a grade." Frequently, they are used in conjunction with other mechanical devices, such as projectors and listening units.

One unique capability of computer-assisted instruction is the ability to make "real" time decisions regarding the material to be presented. For example, it is possible to program the computer to make immediate decisions about the sequence and difficulty of stimuli to be presented based on student response, and in addition to make such decisions based on certain characteristics of the students themselves. The computer also is capable of providing for drill, practice, tutoring, testing, simulation, problem-solving, games, or learner control. An interesting example of this is related by Hullfish and Pottebaum who suggest how the computer may be used for a musical game, based on the capability of "conditional branching," in which student and machine alternate responses in a heuristic approach toward concept learning. In this game, students are asked to think of a scale (major, minor, or modal), following which the computer asks whether the scale has a minor seventh interval between the keynote and the seventh step. If the student answers in the affirmative, the computer next asks if the scale has a minor sixth between the keynote and the sixth step--if not, it is identified as the Mixolydian mode.[1]

It may be noted that if students have been working with only one keynote in a game such as the foregoing, the program may be changed to force them to use others--and, as mistakes occur, the post-test suggests further changes in the game program. Thus, computer-assisted instruction has many advantages over "hard-cover" programmed material, including such aspects as repeating rules of a game after the player is asked if he would like to play again, changing the sequence of events by replacing one statement, adding questions and answers, and even completely restructuring programs to provide the student with an entirely different sequence of instructional events based on his previous responses.

Other applications of computer technology which are applicable to individualizing instruction include computation-analysis-diagnosis of specific learning problems; daily demand schedules (see section on scheduling); and obtaining documents and musical scores from remote locations for study, analysis, and performance. In addition, instructors may use computers as aids in testing and in prescribing instructional strategies. So great has the need for computer assisted instruction become in modern education that many training programs have now become available at the high school and college levels.

Electronic laboratories for music learning provide another resource. The technological revolution in education has produced a variety of hardware which has begun to change our notion of the role of machines in certain learning processes. Although most children daily experience more media in their living environment than at school, the typical classroom has now begun to use many of these promising devices.

Some of the new applications in music education include electronic piano and guitar classrooms with teaching consoles and individual headsets for individual learning (some of these utilize cassette tape recorders, slide projectors, and message lights to aid beginners); video cassettes for viewer-controlled programing, permitting maximum flexibility and instant retrieval of still pictures, motion picture sequences, or video-taped excerpts; video discs which may be operated to automatically repeat different video sequences; quadrasonic reproduction and playback of music through four-channel amplifiers and receivers; tape-loop and video-loop concept learning packages; and centralized audio/video distribution centers which provide building-wide or campus-wide applications of multimedia storage and retrieval systems.

Community Resource Centers

Community resource centers available for use by students and school personnel are similar in type but are more highly specialized than those found in individual schools. In addition, while some are adaptable to educational needs, their adaptability depends upon special arrangements. An illustration of this is found in industrial and private organization computer installations which may be incredibly advanced and sophisticated, yet specifically related to the nature of the organization's work. Thus, educational usage depends on special contracts and availability of personnel who understand the specificity of learning needs and who can set up specially designed programs to accommodate these needs.

Some of the more common community resource centers include: (a) public libraries (often having trained music librarians and highly specialized music resources of all types); (b) museums and exhibits; (c) community art centers; (d) radio and TV music libraries; (e) foundations and commercial enterprises devoted to music production and merchandising; (f) artist-concert offices; (g) private libraries and music collections; (h) university and college music libraries and resource centers; and (i) traveling exhibits and collections which are available to the community.

Music for the Disadvantaged

One of the problems of attempting to meet the needs of young students in mass education is that society, like individual learners, is a complex and varied structure. Kaplan stresses that while music education has dealt with many of the learning activities of students in the most minute detail, it has largely ignored the psychology of the youth culture.[2] This was stressed in Chapter Six of this book in terms of folk, pop and rock music. The music educator must indeed be better attuned to differing needs and values than those represented by middle-class culture, for in large part, the success of the program to reach and sustain any sort of viable music program and to have any substantial impact on future participation in music will depend on how well the needs of disadvantaged learners are met.

Disadvantaged students are those who for reasons of economic, social, physical or cultural deprivation, broken or handicapped homes, racial minority backgrounds or similar "atypical" reasons are not considered to be part of the mainstream of educational life. Depending on the school's constituency, a given school may find that the atypical are actually the typical. Schools in disadvantaged social areas obviously are not like those in affluent communities. Unless feelings of inadequacy, mistrust, and lack of understanding of students in the disadvantaged category can be coped with successfully by educators, they tend to regress educationally and adopt attitudes concerning schooling and related matters which affect their entire life span.

Recent evidence obtained in a study of the musical achievements of culturally deprived children at the elementary level supports the assumption that conditions of cultural deprivation are related to musical achievement in much the same way they are to other areas of school achievement. These findings were significant and constant at each grade level.[3]

Achievement among disadvantaged students is also related to one's self-concept in relation to others, which is frequently distorted and preemptive of effectual learning. Brookover and others found that the functional limits of one's ability are in part set by one's self-conception of the ability to achieve academically as well as in other areas. This self-concept of ability is acquired in interaction with significant others (such as normative patterns of the social group, role expectations held by significant others, learning of the individual--which are internalized and become part of the person's conception of himself). Thus, if a child perceives that he is unable to learn, this self-concept of his ability becomes the functionally limiting factor of his ability becomes the functionally limiting factor of his school achievement.[4]

If schools are oriented to individual learning needs of these students, there would be:

1. No early classification of students on the basis of assumption and measurements.
2. Programs which are developed to organize the resources of the community, family, and school to enhance the expectations and the self-concept of all students.
3. Changes in educational programs which are usually offered students from culturally disadvantaged segments of society and for retarded learners.

Particularly in the bario or inner city, more efficient lines of communication must be established to bring parents, community persons, students, and educators together. A general understanding of the culture and values of the community on the part of teachers and educational leaders is absolutely essential in this process. Schools having a large percentage of students for whom English is a second language should also hire personnel who can converse readily in the language of greatest use. For this reason, ethnic minorities should be included in large numbers at all levels of the teaching and administra-staff of disadvantaged school-communities.

Generally speaking, the same process of experiencing music in musical ways holds true for disadvantaged students. However, because these students come from widely divergent backgrounds, music educators must adopt a variety of means to make music experiences particularly meaningful to these individuals. Several suggestions are made by Nye and Nye who suggest, among other things, that music educators and teachers working with the disadvantaged be exceptionally well prepared and selected.[5] These authors feel that it is advisable to devise ways of working with parents in the music program of the school. Although disadvantaged children should be involved much as other learners in exploration, inquiry, problem-solving, analyzing, observing, hypothesizing, conceptualizing, and generalizing, this should at first be at a very elementary level.

It must be remembered that disadvantaged students need to master basic social skills in many cases, which gradually will help them cope with a rather "foreign" environment--and that in a short time, success in working with others will help them achieve and relate to learning conditions much as any learner would. Gradually and consistently, the standards, goals and mode of working are adjusted and elevated to a higher and more challenging level. A variety of modes of working and divergent materials should be provided for the program. Anecdotal records, student self-analysis, and other evaluative tools must be adopted which not only provide necessary data on the effectiveness of instruction but which will help build the students' self-concept, incentives and motivation to learn. The author is personally acquainted with a young music educator who is the only non-black in an inner city school in the mid-West. Finding that the "methods" of his University and the teaching materials available did not work, he re-wrote "the book." His highly unusual approach to teaching and exciting arrangements, plus a "common sense" approach to human values has not only been effective, but he is now faced with huge, excited student populations!

Music For Exceptional Students

The term exceptional is applied to students who are disadvantaged by reason of intellectual resources, brain-damage, physical disability, partial hearing or deafness, partial sightedness or blindness, and emotional disturbances--all of whom are considered, however, to be educable (as opposed to those who are "institutionalized").

Whereas the term "exceptional" implies a degree of difference, these learners have much in common with their more "normal" classmates. Children, in particular, are intrigued by and have a love of sound and beauty in various forms. With the exception of those with intellectual limitations or brain damage, these learners too are "normal" in every way except that of their particular disability. Many have deep and abiding interests in music and the arts and some have specific talents for music performance which should be aided in every conceivable way.

A variety of special programs have been devised at all levels to provide for the learning needs of exceptional students. This individual has need not only for the special activities in music which bring him satisfaction, but he wants desperately to do the things that other students do. Music to him can mean a needed outlet for self-expression, a social, or therapeutic force. While some efforts can be judged on the basis of successful musical and conceptual performance, the effectiveness of programs for exceptional children must be judged in terms of other behaviors. Such questions as the following may be asked:[6]

1. Has there been improvement in muscular strength or coordination?
2. Has there been improvement in speech?
3. Is the pupil successfully fitting into the group?
4. Is he doing his part according to his abilities?

An important factor on the part of instructors and educational leaders is the understanding of the backgrounds and capabilities of each student together with a corresponding knowledge of those facets of the music program which are specifically applicable for their learning needs. Several of these applications are suggested by Cole (1965)[7] and Coleman and others (1964)[8] in materials specifically devoted to a discussion of music needs for various categories of handicapped students. In suggesting activities appropriate for children of elementary school age, these authors are agreed on the desirability of utilizing rhythmic experiences with most categories of exceptional children--those with visual, aural, orthopedic, emotional, and retardation handicaps. Those with physical disabilities also can learn to play with great enjoyment and satisfaction such instruments as the autoharp, large drum, song bells, song flute, ukulele, guitar, keyboard and simple rhythm instruments with only slight modifications in procedure to provide for the type and degree of disability. Aurally handicapped children also respond well to rhythms, and can often feel pulsation or use hearing devices to aid in using instruments and to a degree for participating in listening activities. Educable and trainable mentally retarded children respond to most musical experiences, but especially enjoy rhythms and rhythm instruments. All groups may profit from appropriate listening activities.

Sur and Schuller (1966) in recommending activities appropriate for handicapped teen-agers feel that many may profit from participation in regular secondary school performance activities.[9] These authors cite examples of students who take part in chorus, composition, class piano, guitar and similar activities for which they are best suited. An interesting recent adaption is the development of braille music for partially-sighted or blind students. Individual work areas and resource centers which were mentioned previously in this chapter provide an excellent means for meeting individual needs of these students.

Music For The Gifted

The term "gifted" applies to students with measurable IQ's ranging from approximately 115 to 200. The customary designations with which we will be concerned are the classifications of moderately gifted with IQ ranges from 120 to 137 and highly gifted, with ranges above 137.[10]

There has been a tendency to accept "giftedness" as a capacity which applies somewhat equally to all abilities of children, thereby ignoring obvious individual differences which apply to all children. For example, a student with a high IQ may demonstrate high verbal ability and low mathematical ability--another may exhibit reverse characteristics--while a third child may have both high verbal and computational skills, yet be low in musical or artistic abilities. It is possible, by the same token, that students may be extremely gifted musically but make undistinguished records in some academic pursuits.

Since typical intelligence tests, however, measure abilities associated with verbalization, teachers and educational leaders must use other criteria in evaluating degrees of giftedness in music and in the music and the arts. Observation and anecdotal records, therefore are essential to the process of identification.

The gifted child may include from 20 to 30 per cent of a given typical school population sample, based on nationwide norms. The highly gifted probably will be limited to only 1 or 2 per cent. These children are usually a delight to work with, since they easily master concepts and require little direction from the teacher. They also tend to be self-directed and self-motivated. Sometimes the gifted child will display characteristics of non-conformity, will be antisocial, or will insist on doing this "his way." Teachers should avoid penalizing this child and should instead attempt to channel his efforts into creative, constructive endeavors which will not only be useful to him as an individual, but will help him adjust to his peer group as a social person.

Musical experiences which will benefit the gifted child in developing appropriate attitudinal as well as conceptual abilities are particularly important in early years. This is one reason for the increasing use of music specialists who are well acquainted with the needs of very young students in early childhood education. Thomas and Crescimbeni speak of the importance of guiding potentials of gifted children and in providing them with exciting and challenging tasks before they become frustrated from a lack of success or understanding.[11] This applies equally to non-academic areas, and in some cases is more important in music and the arts than in other fields.

It is important that the classroom program be a good one, for if so, potentially bright students will accept the challenges presented and will begin to make rapid strides to develop abilities and to assume leadership roles. In music, this will involve nurturing the spirit of independent inquiry, providing profuse opportunities for direct experiencing of music, and avoiding stress placed on prescriptive skills and imitation. Certainly these children have no need for dull, repetitive tasks and rote learning!

One device which is helpful in working with gifted children is the use of open-ended questions designed to stimulate thought processes. For example, such questions as the following may be used: "What did you hear?" "Is it a familiar sound?" "Can you describe it in your own terms?" "Is there another way of doing it?" "Can you think of a way to use ______________ (insert a term such as diminution, augmentation, retrograde, displaced octave, different texture or color, serialism, etc.) to change the melody?" Older students may also be interested and challenged by LAPS, computer-assisted learning, electronic music, and working out particularly challenging technical problems in performance.[12]

The highly individualized experimental programs of the Contemporary Music Project[13] and the Manhattanville Music Curriculum Program[14] lend themselves particularly well to working with gifted students at all grade or school levels. The strategies suggested by these projects were observed by the writer in recent visits to observe innovative curricula in CMP, MMCP and NASSP[15] model schools having particularly promising music programs. Additional suggestions are made by both Marsh[16] and Sur and Schuller.[17]

Some of the tests which are used in identifying gifted students include:

Tests to measure creativity

J. P. Guilford-type tests

Verbal abilities and reading tests

Durrell-Sullivan Reading Capacity and Achievement Test - Grades 2-6

Gates Primary, Advanced, and Basic Reading Tests - from Grade 1 through 8

Iowa Silent Reading Test - Grades 4-13

Traxler High School Reading Test - Grades 11, 12

General Aptitude and ability tests

Tests in general areas of the curriculum, including language, mathematics, science, abstract reasoning, spatial relationships, spelling, etc. These include:

The Differential Aptitude Test Battery - Psychological Corporation

Chicago Test of Primary Mental Abilities - Science Research Associates

Interest Inventories

Tests which indicate field of interest, breadth of interest

vocational preferences, etc. Including:

What I like - California Test Bureau

Kuder Preference Inventory

Strong Vocational Interest Blank

Tests of Musical Aptitude

Some of the most recent include:

Bentley Measures of Musical Abilities (1966) - Children ages 7-12 Wing Standardised Tests of Musical Intelligence - 1961 - ages 8 through adult

Colwell Music Aptitude Test - 1966 - elementary through senior high

Gaston Test of Musicality - grades 4-12 - 1957

Kwalwasser Music Talent Test; Forms A and B - 1953 - Form A: 7-adult; Form B 4-6

Gordon Musical Aptitude Profile - 1965 - Grades 4-12

Tests of Musical Achievement

Aliferis Music Achievement Test - 1954 - Music theory, college level, tape

Beach Music Test - 1939 - Grades 7-12, musical elements

Knuth Achievement Tests in Music - 1966 - from grades 3 through 12 (different forms)-includes tape--notation associated with auditory stimuli

Jones Music Recognition Test - 1949 - in two parts; Part I for elementary and junior high school; Part II-senior high school and college

Farnum Music Notation Test - 1953 - Grades 7-9 - with recording

Farnum String Scale - 1969 - grading chart furnished for violin

Colwell Elementary Music Achievement Tests - 1965 - Grades 4-12 - with L.P. recording

Tests of Performance and Appreciation

Contest-festival

Observed performance, auditions, challenge

Watkins-Farnum Performance Scale (band instruments) - 1962

Oregon Music Discrimination Tests

Measurements of motor skills and other traits

"Other" Tests of Standardized Achievement

California Achievement Tests - Grades 1-9
Iowa Test of Basic Skills - Grades 3-9
Sequential Tests of Educational Progress - Grades 4-14
SRA Achievement Tests - Grades 2-9
Stanford Achievement Tests - Grades 1-9

Progress Charts, Cumulative Data, Annecdotal Records, Etc.
(Teacher constructed)

The needs of the gifted may be met in a variety of ways. In many schools there are special classes for the gifted planned with special needs and enrichment opportunities in mind. In some cases, notably in New York City (High School of Music and Art) there are schools for children with special gifts and abilities. Smaller schools often meet group needs through part-time special classes for gifted learners. One example of the latter is the Colfax School in Pittsburgh, where gifted children from grades 1-3 make up what is known as the junior workshop; those from grades 4-6 a senior workshop. Students in the Colfax School meet approximately one-half day per week to work on academic skills and related enrichment activities. Their work is conducted very informally in small group seminars, led by one of the members of the class. The remainder of the time, in their regular class, they work with "average" students in nonacademic subjects such as art, music, science, physical education, and library.[18]

The Masterman School, a public school in Philadelphia, Pennsylvania, is another school for gifted children. In 1967, this school was awarded a small grant to establish an electronic music laboratory. The laboratory operated five days a week, sometimes until late afternoon, with students selected from performing groups working in pairs on their experiments. The results, which were published by the Music Educators National Conference[19] were indeed spectacular, opening up a whole new range of creative endeavor to these gifted children.

A number of public schools have instituted special summer schools for music and the arts. These range from elementary schools with special emphasis on music, art, dance and dramatic activities to summer band and choral camps both on and off regular school sites.

In these schools, students with high interest, motivation and skill in music spend the regular school year with classmates in the normal range of academic and enrichment classes, but during the summer are provided with many opportunities for special training and acceleration in their special interest fields. A number of school districts set up programs both in breadth as well as depth. For example, students particularly gifted in music may spend one hour of special training in voice or their instrument, one hour of ensemble, then have two hours devoted to pursuits entirely outside of music, including arts, crafts, literature and dramatic activities.

Teachers may also provide many opportunities in regular class situations to challenge gifted students by providing opportunities for special research and creative endeavors, and in sharing the results of their work with classmates and others. Additional opportunities in music may be provided by means of "quest" time (i.e., free module) practice, released time to work with artist-teachers on or off-campus, attendance at special concerts and musical events, individual or small group field trips, participation in special summer music activities, all-city band, chorus, orchestra--and serving as teacher aides in other classes to make their special talents and expertise available to students and teachers alike.

Music In Therapy

While not directly related to the work of the public school, the field of music therapy is a growing area of special interest with many challenging opportunities for the young student in music education. It should also be pointed out that due to the stress on analytical processes involved in a study of abnormal behavior, a considerable insight is gained into the working of the "normal" mind.

Thayer Gaston, the "father" of music therapy in this country, stresses the relationship of music to human behavior, saying that it can benefit handicapped and ill persons by helping them change their behavior by acquiring or inducing (directly or indirectly), positive behavioral change.[20]

Music therapy, as an endeavor closely related to music education, received its impetus largely as a result of the forming of the National

Association for Music Therapy and the resulting programs initiated by this organization for up-grading and standardizing professional activities. One of the purposes of the NAMT was to train music therapists in appropriate areas of music, applied psychology, and clinical procedures related to these fields and medicine. The NAMT also publishes a quarterly, the Journal of Music Therapy, which is devoted to discussions of various aspects of the profession.[21]

The formal activities of music therapy are applied in mental institutions and hospitals which devote all or part of their efforts to treating mental illness. Therapeutic aspects include several applications which are specifically tailored to the needs of mentally incapacitated individuals. These stress applied music, performance, and listening activities. It is not uncommon to find listening clubs, square dancing, orchestras, bands, choruses, and solo music activities prominent in applied music therapy programs. In addition, prescriptive uses of music to influence passive-active behavior are found in some mental institutions. Such programs are handled by music therapists working in conjunction with their medical colleagues. Sears contends that as in other aspects of music education, the musical appropriateness of the behavior must always be judged with reference to the ability of the individual.[22]

Music is of great value in therapy due to many of the unique qualities which have been discussed in previous chapters. As an "experience in self-organization," Sears suggests that music may provide for (1) self-expression; (b) compensatory endeavors; (c) socially acceptable activities; and, (d) an enhancement of pride in self.

Music in Other Areas of the Curriculum

Music may be used to enhance a variety of learning endeavors in the school. The most common are correlations of appropriate areas of musical experience with other disciplines, such as social studies, language arts, art, physical education, and, physics (principles of acoustics). Lately, combined or interdisciplinary courses such as the humanities or allied arts class in the secondary school or college provide a means of making meaningful combinations. Most successful correlative experiences of this type have been experienced in introductory courses, or at lower levels of experience where perceptions begin and relationships do not involve experiential or conceptual problems which are unique to individual disciplinary fields. Thus, the elementary school usually is a very logical place for making meaningful relationships between music and other areas of the curriculum, provided that learnings enhance each other, are done with the principles, values, and concepts of each field being utilized, and by avoiding correlations which are artificial and meaningless.

Allied arts courses should be "true" to the respective disciplines which comprise the "fused" courses, since they can be successful only to the extent that the added materials become completely integrated into the characteristic materials of the host art. Occasionally, it may be possible to circumvent problems created by fusing disciplines by means of what Reimer calls "multi-media events," or simultaneous presentations, each in its own idiom.[23] In addition, carefully planned courses which are team taught by specialists in the contributing disciplinary fields may correctly present experiences and concepts unique to these specific fields, while at the same time interweaving threads of appropriate commonality. It is suggested that courses in the humanities consist of appropriate humanistic considerations, such as knowing about influences, studying ideas, historical derivations, principles, theories, and trends. However, actual experiencing and conceptualizing of the art form or its related academic discipline must be done in terms of the particular area of study, since, for reasons discussed in Chapter One, there is no precise way of relating one experience of a dissimilar nature to another, especially in terms of the unique way in which music is experienced.

Music In Recreation

A practical setting for many values and functions of music and one which can enhance school applications of music education is the field of music in recreation. With the advent of the 3 and 4-day week and the increasing use of leisure time by great segments of people of all ages and occupations, this field is becoming a potent means for experiencing music, arts, and related activities. In some communities, the recreation department of city government also works closely with public schools to extend programs of music education into leisure-time activity. Certainly if music educators feel that "music students have nowhere to go after they finish the school's program," this is one solution which should be explored by leaders in music education. The wise use of recreation agencies, both public and private, can extend a variety of music learning opportunities to the community at large. There is little need to consider this field the exclusive prerogative of physical education majors!

There are several types of music activity which may be conducted by agencies dealing with recreation. Some of these, according to Kaplan, include:[24]

* Training facilities (these refer to public or private schools, universities and colleges, and private teachers of music)
* Production units and performing groups (these may be sponsored by agencies such as churches, lodges, symphony and choral associations etc.
* Distributive agencies (stores, libraries, musicians unions, etc.)
* Consuming agencies (homes, clubs, concert associations, and other places where music is "consumed.")
* Extended recreational opportunities (summer music camps, etc.)
* Recreation departments having bureaus or sub-departments of music which conduct regular programs of participation in music on a funded basis.

Some programs by city recreation departments have achieved national prominence in the field and offer widely diversified programs in performance, music study, concerts and exhibitions, and "consumer" music. Flint, Michigan, Champaign-Urbana, Illinois, and Los Angeles, California are examples--the latter having a Bureau of Music with a full-time director, many aides and directors, and sponsoring upwards of 18 adult choruses, 20 youth choruses, a community orchestra, 4 bands, and many other activities.

Influences From Abroad

The field of comparative music education is barely established in this country, with few universities or colleges devoting courses to this subject as yet. Through the efforts of a few individuals, the broadening scope of international interest engendered by the Music Educators National Conference in the Western hemisphere and abroad, the situation is rapidly improving. In particular, the founding of the International Society for Music Education has now brought together professional persons and interests in Europe, Asia, Africa, Australia and the United States for the study and betterment of music education (both private and public). The biennial conferences of this organization which are held in such places as Sidney, Tokyo, and Moscow have attracted many persons, particularly leaders in music education from the United States.

Concerning the impact of foreign influences in school music education, a variety of influences have had profound affect in our classrooms. Perhaps the most prominent of these have been:

* the Orff-Schulwerk program
* Dalcroze eurhythmics
* notational and improvisatory techniques engendered by Zoltan Kodaly
* Suzuki techniques for teaching instruments to young children (with special emphasis on violin)

Although the literature in this field is by no means complete, there are several good sources which should be read by all music educators. Reference to these is made in the Suggested Readings at the end of this Chapter.

Music For Lifelong Learning

Reimer charges all music educators with the challenge that one of the chief missions of aesthetic education is to improve the quality of every person's life at every stage of his development.[25] If this is to be accomplished, it is important that leaders in music education understand the extended role of music learning, by which the influence of music may begin in pre-school and early childhood and extend through continuing education after the normal span of school years has been completed. Because of the opportunity of meeting the diverse needs and interests of adults who have completed secondary education, the promise of continuing (i.e., extension, adult) education is enormous. Some of the possibilities were suggested under music in recreation.

Some of the specific functions of music in lifelong learning or continuing education are:

* training (learning a new music skill)
* re-training (perfecting or taking up a skill dropped at some period during regular school years)
* production (providing outlets for solo/ensemble performance)
* study groups ("listening" and studying about music--extending the range of interests to other fields of music)
* consumption (audience-type situations)
* institutional music (various music activities provided for use in hospitals, industry, business, clubs--and non-educational institutions--for furthering music study and performance particularly related to the interests of the institution)

In communities where adult and continuing education in music is minimal or non-existent, it will be important for leaders in music education to work with the community leaders and administration to develop an on-going program along the lines outlined in the foregoing.

Summary

Since learning is an activity which should engage individuals in various ways throughout their lifetime, music education should be adapted to a wide range of interests and learning needs, some extending beyond the ordinary definitions of curriculum. Some of these applications are made in terms of the regular academic structure of the school, while many extend into the school-community.

The special adaptations which are included in the school include: (a) school resource centers for individual development of a wide range of learning needs; (b) music programs for the disadvantaged;

(c) music for exceptional children; (d) music for the gifted: (e) music in other areas of the curriculum; and, (f) adaptations of foreign music influences.

Programs which are chiefly community-sponsored and oriented include: (a) music in therapy; (b) music in recreation; and, (c) music in industry. Music programs for lifelong learning extend from pre-school and nursery school through organized adult education programs and spread into a variety of other music activities of the community.

Music educators should realize that whether organized as part of the school's regular program of learning activities or those of the community, the need for total music education is clear if we are concerned with music as a vital force in the complete development of human potential. Where community resources are insufficient or lacking, it is the responsibility of leaders in music education to assist in their nurture and development.

Topics For Discussion

1. Describe some of the most effective ways in which students may utilize school resource centers, (a) during regular class hours, and (b) during the school day.
2. What types of materials would be included in these centers to be most beneficial to (a) studies generated in performance classes, and (b) humanities or allied-arts classes?
3. Discuss how schools built on traditional lines might develop such centers.
4. Ideally, how would the school day be re-ordered for maximum use of learning and resource centers?
5. How would you stimulate students to use community resource centers effectively?
6. Discuss some of the special school adaptations which you feel are most urgently needed in communities with which you are familiar.
7. Does the concept of disadvantaged youth apply to any except minority or underprivileged socio-economic groups?
8. How does your community meet extended learning needs in music education through (a) recreation department programs; (b) organized community music activities; and, (c) adult education?
9. How can educational leaders be more effective in organizing and developing some of the resources of the community as adjuncts to formal education?

Suggested Readings

Committee for Economic Development. *Innovation in Education: New Directions for the American School.* See sections dealing with individualizing instruction, providing for disadvantaged learners, and building design to accomodate resource centers.

Kaplan, Max. *Foundations and Frontiers of Music Education.* New York: Holt, Rinehart and Winston, Inc., 1966. See Ch. 4, 5 and 7.

Leonhard, Charles. *Recreation Through Music.* New York: A.S. Barnes and Company, 1952.

Knirk, Frederick and John W. Childs (Ed) *Instructional Technology: A Book of Readings.* New York: Holt, Rinehart and Winston, Inc., 1968. Readings by several authors include systems design and materials programming, media characteristics, information storage and retrieval, and school plant design to accomodate a variety of individual and group learning needs.

Lehman, Paul R. *Tests and Measurements in Music.* Englewood Cliffs, N.J.: Prentice-Hall, Inc., 1968.

Nye, Robert E. and Vernice T. Nye. *Music in the Elementary School, Third Edition.* Englewood Cliffs, N.J.: Prentice-Hall, Inc., 1970. See Ch. 7, 15, 16 and 17.

Sur, William R. and Charles F. Schuller. *Music Education for Teen-Agers.* New York: Harper and Row, Publishers, 1966. See Ch. 8.

Thomas, George I. and Joseph Crescimbeni. *Guiding the Gifted Child.* New York: Random House, 1966.

Stoumbis, George C. and Alvin W. Howard (Ed) *Schools for the Middle Years: Readings.* Scranton, Pa.: International Textbook Company, 1969. See Part 4.

PART THREE

dimensions of music leadership — (organization)

CHAPTER TEN

THE MUSIC INSTRUCTIONAL STAFF

A teacher who is attempting to teach without inspiring the pupil with a desire to learn is hammering on cold iron.

Horace Mann

Because of the unique relationship which exists between teacher and learner, the art of teaching should occupy a very special place in any consideration of teaching and learning. Teaching, then, is the first consideration of leadership in music education which forms the basis of Part Three of this book.

In preceding sections, we have dealt with the foundations and structure of music education. If the *raison d' etre* of the substance, process and content of music is the musical growth of individuals, our concern ultimately must be with those who are most intimately connected with the classroom--the teacher and the supporting instructional staff.

Characteristics of Good Teachers and Teaching

Let us examine some of the dimensions, the yardsticks and special qualities by which good teaching is characterized. Whether it be "goodness" or "excellence" which is to serve as a criterion for teaching, the music educator of the Seventies must somehow be cut from the same cloth as his academic counterpart. He/she should be interested in human beings as well as in the processes by which they learn. This indicates a person who is:

* intelligent
* alert
* considerate
* open
* responsive
* democratic
* creative
* aware
* a leader

He/she is genuinely interested in finding new ways of arriving at goals; of discovering new applications for information--new ways of experiencing and making experience meaningful. He/she avoids sham, hyprocrisy, and triteness and inspires those with whom he/she works to become intellectually and artistically curious. The effective teacher is inventive and encourages others to become equally anxious to delve into the unknown to discover their own potentials and modes of operation. Rules, regulations, theorems, principles and guidelines are adopted to give inner meaning for educational process rather than becoming arbitary, imposed and restrictive.

From the research of Combs, other characteristics of good teachers are those two:[1]

* feel identified with, rather than apart from others
* feel basically adequate rather than inadequate
* feel trustworthy rather than untrustworthy
* See themselves as wanted rather than unwanted
* See themselves as worthy rather than unworthy
* Perceive their purpose in teaching as one of freeing, rather than controlling students
* Tend to be more concerned with larger, rather than smaller issues
* Are more likely to be self-revealing, rather than self-concealing
* Tend to be personally involved, rather than alienated
* Are concerned with furthering processes, rather than achieving goals

Although the effective music educator must possess qualities like those of his academic associates, there are also other considerations if this person is to aspire to be truly an artist-teacher. To be successful, the music educator also must have experienced success in making music and in understanding its principles. Several of these qualities, as recommended by the MENC Commission on Teacher Education, were presented in Chapter One. It should be stressed here that the good teacher of music need not be a performer of first calibre--but it is essential that this individual has been able to discover musical meanings in musical ways. He/she must also be convinced that the route which is pursued for musical experiencing is not necessarily the only route--and that if this person is to be considered a music educator, he/she will be anxious to help students find their own ways of experiencing and finding satisfaction from music. Most important of all, the effective music educator will consider the job unfinished if he/she does not continue to grow musically. Continued performance, in one or more idioms, will go a long way toward making music more meaningful and insightful for the music teacher as well as for those whom this individual teaches.

Contemporary Modes of Teaching

It is not difficult to understand why tradition and ritual have occupied such an important place in American education. Early America felt that its schools must be concerned with the transmission of knowledge, culture, and moral principles. The early concept of education was to provide the individual with the necessary skills for literacy as a God-fearing, capable member of the church. Teachers of the Nineteenth Century were expected to conform rather than to innovate--hence, great stress was placed on order, punctuality, and neatness, together with the nominal academic abilities in such fields as history, mathematics, English, geography, and so forth.[2] Music and the arts did not occupy an important place in normal school education until late in the Nineteenth Century.[3] Methodology and pedagogy followed the pattern of lecture, recitation, rote-memorization, and the like. It was not until well into the Twentieth Century that teaching began to change substantially and to become something which could be considered "professional." Old patterns still persist, however, and vestiges of them are still present today perhaps more so where communities feel their schools should reflect "stable" values of the past, rather than look to the present and future.

There is nothing wrong with tradition, nor does change necessarily imply goodness and quality. Indeed, it can be argued with some degree of success that American society is too prone to accept change rather than to inspect the effects which change brings about. Yet, if the concern of education is to find the most promising ways of releasing human potential, stagnation and status quo are undeserving of being equated with desirable elements of tradition. And, if traditional tools are found wanting, they should be discarded.

It has been said that schools in the United States lag fifty years behind the times. Yet, it is sometimes the American public which creates conditions and constraints which are not conducive to change. To a degree, each of us, whether educator or lay person, feels that the way in which we were taught is automatically the best---particularly if we have become relatively successful in our endeavors. Yet, for many students, school has been failure-oriented, and no amount of that tradition can justify continuing on the same track. Any child can learn in an atmosphere of inquiry and meaningful problem-solving.

Individualizing instruction helps to create such an atmosphere. What we are after is how the skills and potentials of teachers and students can be utilized most effectively. No one can say with any degree of certainty what releases human potential in any given situation, yet the factors which effect release are apparently numerous and complex. Certainly, what strikes a response in one student will leave another relatively untouched. In addition, a given stimulus may reach a student after the same stimulus, tried earlier, had failed. We have mentioned the tremendous capacity for growth on the part of individuals--part of this phenomenon may be explained simply by acknowledging that the individual is growing and changing in many ways--that he is adding new experiences and forgetting old ones continually.

Thus, the concept which must be applied either to teachers or to students is the emphasis on the individual as a human being, and the unique interaction which transpires in the act of teaching and learning which requires each person involved to be aware, genuinely interested, and accepting of others engaged in the process. This implies a recognition and response to emotional reactions of learners and to their academic achievements as well as to extensions of ordinary achievement. Individualization occurs when the teacher is willing to accept the student as an individual having unique perceptions, values, concepts and needs--and creatively fashioning learning opportunities which enhance these qualities.

Charles E. Silberman, one of this decade's most concerned yet constructive critics of American education, cites numerous examples of failure in the schools, pointing out that reform has left relatively untouched one of the most critical areas of the curriculum--the arts. His observations leave little doubt as to the reason. The examples are of schools with ugly design, and an almost total absence of esthetic environment--the disparagement of the arts by placing them in highly specialized or trivial segments of the school curriculum--and, if taught at all, relegating them to completely isolated experiences offered once or twice a week at best![4]

Part of the problem is that we have not met individual needs of learners in music, as well as in other areas of the school curriculum. American education has been concerned with priorities and "instant" striving to reach goals. We adopt or adapt systems such as the "open" classroom and program planning and budgeting systems--or spend sums of money to secure hardware--all without considering whether it will work, or whether intrinsically it is good for education. Values and valuing, discussed in Chapter III, have a great deal to do with this. Educators cannot continue to deal with dichotomous absolutes--to consider "what is wrong with- - -" rather, they must deal with the notion that schools can be both concerned with the development of individuals as well as being subject-centered.

The British infant and primary schools provide examples of a form of flexibility which may well be considered in this country.[5] Surely the concept of placing children's needs foremost and removing unnecessary administrative restraints in the pursuit of this goal is highly praiseworthy. Whether educators in the United States can develop the same individual autonomy within schools or can remove some of the artificiality of over-centralized administration remains to to be seen. With our penchant for organization, efficiency, and business acumen which has characterized school practice and unfortunately has dominated the leadership training of universities and colleges, teachers and schools tend to be dominated and regimented rather than led.

As in the Piaget model of learning discussed in Chapter IV, children in British Infant and Primary schools are encouraged to assimilate the external facts of experience and to integrate them into their individual mental structures. And, like Dewey's concept of progressivism, discovery through invention and activity becomes crucial. Intellectual development cannot be accomplished in isolation, but depends to a great degree on social interaction. The learner must progress at his own rate in an appropriate classroom environment arranged to accomodate individual pacing. The teacher in such a classroom serves as a creative stimulator, expediter, and orchestrator of experience.

To the traditionally-minded person who is accustomed to a formal classroom environment, a view of the informal British school is, to say the least, a disconcerting experience. The classroom may give a jumbled appearance, being filled with quantities of different materials, experimental centers, and activity areas. When children are in the room, there is apt to be a general "buzz" of conversation and hum of activity. Students all appear to be engaging in different, yet highly motivated and exciting work experiences. Occasionally a group or the entire room comes together (not always with the teacher or an aide in charge) to record, interpret, and discuss the range of activity going on in different centers. Although there is a lack of conformity and the silence which seems desirable to many teachers, it should be pointed out that there are few problems of misbehavior or disruption requiring disciplinary action in most British schools! The answer--this is meaningful activity which engages each child at his own level of motivation and skill![6]

Children in British infant and primary schools are continually exposed to artistic influences, of which music is one of the most important. Considerable emphasis is given to experimentation with a variety of sound-producing media from which the child successfully learns how to work with music in a musical context, even while ostensibly at play. Unlike carefully structured, rote-directed group exposure to singing and the use of instruments, the child begins to cope successfully with performing and composing music by being given virtually unlimited access to music instruments. Educators have been very successful in providing great flexibility, individualization, and innovation in all areas of music learning. Discovery and involvement are key elements in this process--and it is important for our music educators as well to recognize that music makes unique personal demands for direct experience in which these factors are essential.

Few infant and primary schools have music specialists in the American sense of the word, although there are traveling instrumental instructors in many areas. However, nearly every school has at least one teacher with expertise in music who serves as a special resource person. There are also "music organisers" (the term for supervisor, coordinator, or "status" leader) in approximately one hundred of the largest cities of Britain.

Promising School Models in the United States. American educators too are concerned with ways to help children identify with their curricula. Although many schools are experiencing success with open education and individual discovery-learning, there are as yet all too few in music and the arts, particularly at the secondary level. Part of this stems from the rigidity and traditional orientation of the music curriculum which was discussed in Chapters VI and VII, having to do with a heavy emphasis on performance and training for technical skill rather than viewing performance as one aspect of complete musicianship and understanding.

Examples of successful projects in music and the arts include some previously mentioned, such as the Julia R. Masterman Laboratory and Demonstration School in Philadelphia (see Chapter IX) and the fifteen experimental schools of the Manhattanville Music Curriculum Project. Until recently, the Contemporary Music Project composers-in-residence and participating schools program provided excellent opportunities for both elementary and secondary schools throughout the country. The more recent Arts-Impact Schools, in which federal funds were provided as "seed money" to assist schools in approaching the total curriculum through the arts, have also shown promise. Some of the findings of the Final Report from this Project are worthy of inspection:[7]

1. Most teachers in the projects believed that a greater parity had been reached between the arts and music--and that a desirable balance had been reached between affective and cognitive learning.
2. Although "quality" is important in performance in terms of so-called (and debatable!) absolute criteria, the Impact teams believe that their programs were at least comparable in level to traditional programs, but that they focused on other things--particularly products as well as performances.
3. In-service models were rated as either "great" or of "moderate" value to teaching--but all were felt to be stimulating and enriching for teachers.
4. Wherever classroom teachers, arts resource teachers, and principals worked unselfishly to change a school's learning atmosphere, change took place!

It may be noted that the author visited the Edgewood Elementary School in Eugene, Oregon, one of the five Arts-Impact Schools, during a recent trip to inspect "innovative" elementary and secondary schools in the Western part of the United States. This school was discovered to be a most exciting adaptation of the combined arts approach to the total school curriculum, utilizing a six-team horizontal structure devoted to contributions of the arts and humanities (particularly music, the visual arts, dance, and drama), with correlary emphasis on individualized instruction. Tentitive conclusions from the teaching staff of this team would tend to corroborate the findings of the Final Report.

At the secondary level, the model schools of the National Association of Secondary School Principals also provide good examples of "newer" approaches to curriculum and method. Of the thirty-four NASSP schools operating in 1970, thirty-two are in the United States, one in Canada and one in Germany. Most are public, although one is a private school. Although many operate with "new look" buildings, flexible scheduling, and differentiated staffing, several model schools have rather traditional buildings and curricula--although all are attempting to achieve excellence in a variety of ways. During the author's visits to several of the NASSP secondary schools, several were found with considerable emphasis on music and art in the experimental model suggested by Lloyd Trump and associates. One example, Highland High School of Bakersfield, California was discovered to have an unusual combination of "pontoon" scheduling, open-modular (or "pod") structure, team teaching and both an excellent performance and allied-arts-humanities program which utilized the concepts of the Contemporary Music Project and the Manhattanville Music Curriculum Program. Although most music and arts programs visited still appear to operate on a rather traditional design (emphasizing performance rather exclusively) in these otherwise innovative secondary schools, the Highland model proved without a shadow of a doubt that fine performance can be consistent with broader goals of music education.

The National Endowment for the Arts has also provided a most innovative program of "Artists in Schools" by means of which artists, poets, writers, musicians, actors, film-makers, dancers, and others were made available to schools during 1972 for the purpose of bringing students into close daily and personal contact with creative artists. These programs, limited to a four-week period in each community, were provided in several communities in Alabama, Minnesota, Wyoming, California, Nebraska, and Rhode Island. It may be noted that persons involved in this program have been convinced that the structural flaw in the general processes of education in the United States has been the failure to include ways of nurturing aesthetic awareness and participative experience in the creative arts as integral parts of education.[8]

Youth concerts made available at no or little cost to school students have been another means of affecting large numbers of students. A 1971 report of twenty cities throughout the United States revealed that there were some 717 concerts alone during the 1967-68 school year played before 1.2 million students, and over 2,000 ensemble programs were played in school buildings.[9] This report does not cover scores of communities where similar activities have been taking place.

A newer development which may have an even greater impact on bringing music to schools throughout the country is the medium of Television. A recent publication by the Music Educators National Conference reports a variety of activities by which TV is becoming a potent force for music education in the classroom--consumer programs, televised instruction, microteaching, etc. in such areas as Albuquerque, Duval County (Florida), Alabama, Georgia, Pennsylvania, Indiana, Michigan, New York, California and others.[10]

It must be stressed that no amount of re-designing of curricula, nor open-ness of school plant will in itself guarantee that instruction actually is good. Many innovative programs operate within fairly conventional school organizations, and conversely, many widely heralded innovations may be overly structured or are poor operating examples of what this book has been emphasizing. The important thing to consider is what happens with individual teachers and their efforts to release and develop individual student potential.

Team or pontoon teaching and differentiated staffing present several possibilities for moving in the direction which has been mentioned.

Team or Pontoon Teaching may operate either in traditional or "new look" schools. Team-teaching, the older of the two methods, provides the learners with the expertise and point-of-view of several persons who work together as a team on a continuing basis, or who come together periodically for designated presentations. In music education, team-teaching probably is most common at the elementary level where the music specialist and classroom teacher often combine skills to provide children with better music experiences than might be available either periodically or if only one person exclusively were available. This practice is also used in the so called "open" elementary schools where it is not uncommon to find from two to four teachers, assorted aides, paraprofessionals, and others working together as a team with as many as one hundred children at a time. At secondary and higher education levels, team teaching customarily is practiced in instances where it is desirable to have more than one subject-matter specialist involved. As we shall see presently, differentiated staffing also is derived from this concept.

Pontoon teaching is a modified form of team teaching and is occasionally referred to as the "pontoon-transitional design," since it contains elements of traditional team teaching as well as more innovative practices currently in vogue. Whereas team teaching may involve large group presentations, small discussion groups, and individual study, the pontoon concept incorporates all of these plus the interrelationship of various disciplines in a flexible block of time. Thus, pontooning interrelates two or more subjects under the leadership of teachers from different academic disciplines, functioning in a block of time which would ordinarily be used for independent teaching. The three prevalent forms of pontoons are:

1. Compatible correlation (Example: English, history, and art)
2. Periodic correlation (Example: Algebra II and chemistry)
3. Non-correlated

Experts in pontoon planning claim that while correlation between some subjects is not ordinarily desirable, the pontoon arrangement still can be advantageous inasmuch as it enhances certain flexibilities in terms of time and size of learning groups which are allowed in the "block." Some of its advantages are:

1. Helping teachers solve common problems in working together.
2. Correlating subject matter in meaningful ways.
3. Adjusting amounts of time internally (within the "pontoon" team) to suit the activity or nature of instruction.
4. Encouraging teachers to vary instructional procedure.
5. Requiring less large group activity for total presentations (example: every-other day, once a week, etc.).
6. Using "conventional" teaching methods wherever these are best suited without disrupting other disciplines and schedules.

Differentiated Staffing combines many of the advantages of team teaching and pontooning, but assigns specific instructional tasks to a hierarchy of persons involved in teaching and learning. These roles place greater emphasis on the professional role of the master teacher and assistant teachers who are primarily responsible for designing and directing curricular matters--with supporting and subordinate roles played by a variety of aides, instructional assistants, clerks, media technicians, staff specialists (including central office personnel), and community and university consultants.

Trump and Baynham stress the three related phases of instruction which they feel to be important to differentiated staffing. These include (a) using varied teaching roles, assistants, specialists, and other designated aides involved in specified jobs (for which, it is suggested, carefully worded job descriptions should be written); (b) changing school building design to support the resulting flexible educational plan; and, (c) providing flexible schedules which allow varying amounts of time on different days for large-group, small-group, and individual instruction (this is the so-called "modular" rather than "period" organization of the school day). These authors and others emphasize the use of resource personnel, specialists, and consultants from the professions and specialized fields who may be working either in the school system or in the community.[11] Such resource personnel may have a full-time staff assignment in the school (typically as department chairmen, librarians, psychologists, counselors, etc.), a part-time responsibility, or may make only occasional visits on an informal basis.

The total professional components of the differentiated staff team include the following persons:

* master (senior) teachers responsible for curriculum design, major instructional duties, staff assignments, and other administrative duties.
* staff (or assisting) certificated teachers who take a more limited responsibility for the conceptual outline of courses but who assist with curriculum development and have substantial instructional responsibilities.
* interns (beginning teachers and/or student teachers) who assume responsibility for curriculum assistance, more limited instruction and administrative detail.
* paraprofessionals (non-certificated) who are used for limited areas of instruction and areas of their expertise.
* aides and externs who serve as instructional helpers, take care of routine duties (including supervising individual

instruction and otherwise working with instruction in a limited way), and take charge of minor clerical and administrative details.

* support staff (those having professional status in school, such as departmental specialists, librarians, media technicians, psychometrists, psychologists, counselors, assistant principals, deans, medical personnel, etc.) to provide specialized assistance.
* "others" — including, where pertinent, lay persons, teaching assistants, clerks, technical assistants, proctors, etc.

Staff requirements and loads for differentiated staffing team members are dependent upon such factors as curriculum design, course organization, availability of qualified personnel, student grouping, scheduling arrangements, limitations in facilities, and financial support. With respect to the latter, it is interesting to note that interviews conducted by the author with administrators in many of the NASSP model schools indicated that they operate within identical budgetary limitations as do non-model schools in the same school district. Many have traditional buildings and schedules, modified slightly to meet the demands of differentiated staffing and flexibility of curricula.

An illustrative guideline for computing staff loads proposed by Bush and Allen is based upon a total of eighty half-hour modules per week.[12] These are divided between classroom presentation-preparation-evaluation, guidance instruction, staff meetings, correction of student material, evaluation-instruction, conferences with students and parents, supervision of students out of class, and clerical. Of the total number of modules available, certificated staff personnel (teachers, interns, teaching assistants) are assigned to a range of from 50 to 60 weekly, or roughly from five-eighths to three-quarters of their total assignment. There are seven categories of staff responsibility indicated in Figure 22. For the master teacher, all of these are oriented to classroom responsibility. Classroom time, however, is rather arbitrarily suggested, and depends upon the nature of the work being presented and techniques of instruction employed. Staff coordination and planning is essential due to the increased need for overall planning and availability of several persons assigned to different responsibilities. Minimal emphasis is placed upon "paper work," such as the physical preparation of materials and correcting of student assignments, since this is a responsibility of teaching assistants. Of great importance is the time suggested for evaluation and conferences, since the teacher must be available as a resource person and counselor both to students and their parents in programs which place stress on self-motivation and direction.

A method of computing the weekly staff load of members of the instructional team, in 1/2-hour modules, is shown in Figure 22.

Figure 22

Weekly Load of Instructional Staff - In 1/2 Hour Modules

Activity	Master Teacher	Assistant Teachers	Interns	Aides & Others
1. Teaching (preparation, presentations, eval.)	55	52	50	↑
2. Preparing and organization of curriculum, supervising and organizing work of staff	13	8	4	
3. Supervising and correcting student work (group)	3	8	8	Hours as
4. Instructional guidance (individual)	3	4	12	required for activity
5. Staff meetings	2	2	2	
6. Conferences-student and parent	4	4	0	
7. Routine and clerical	0	2	4	↓
TOTAL LOAD	80	80	80	80

In computing loads, some authorities suggest the following load factors for various types of instruction:

* large-group instruction 2 to 1
* small-group instruction 1.5 to 1
* laboratory 1 to 1
* individual 1 to 1

From this, it will be noted that it will require twice as many persons to supervise individual activities as for large group presentations, etc. This requires more persons in "support" categories--but, fortunately, for budgetary reasons it is possible to have more persons in lower salary categories, yet maintain curricular excellence due to emphasis and the way personnel are utilized in differentiated staffing.

Differentiated staffing, like team-teaching or pontooning, depends for its success largely on the personal as well as professional qualifications of the individuals involved plus the type of leadership exercised in the school organization. Recent research in psychology in the area of group processes indicates that the following are highly important ingredients:

1. Members of the team should be skilled in the various leadership and membership roles required for effective group interaction.
2. Members of the group should know each other sufficiently to be attracted to and respect the personal as well as professional qualifications of the other members of the team.
3. The group should be in existence long enough to have established an informal, open-ended working relationship between its members.
4. There must be mutual give-and-take between working members of the group and a willingness to accept helpful criticism as well as praise for individual accomplishment.
5. The group must develop by concensus both long and short-range goals which it feels to be both desirable and realistic. Moreover, there must be a willingness to modify goal structure when the need arises.
6. It is important that the group function as a goal-seeking, problem-solving, interdependent and interacting entity and that information, ideas, suggestions and criticisms be both sought and welcomed. Respect for other points-of-view is essential.
7. Group leadership should be informal, non-rigid, and may change

according to the needs of the particular problem being worked upon (However, it is important that there be group concensus on who is responsible for a given assignment). The support of leadership by members of the group will depend largely on their understanding of the leadership role, as well as the degree of cooperation and democracy practiced.

8. Although practical limitations on group projects must be recognized, "dream goals" should not be dismissed as utopian until sufficiently discussed and tested. Failure to accomplish tasks sometimes is an important ingredient to creativity and innovation. Imagination should never be summarily curtailed.
9. Skills of communication should be developed for effectibe group processes. Although communication should serve the best interests and goals of the group, it is important that individual members be encouraged to "speak out" in order that all ideas and dimensions of problem-solving be explored. Irrelevance and domination of discussion are to be avoided.
10. The group should agree on procedural and administrative matters governing its activities, but should avoid over-conformity where this becomes restrictive rather than conducive to enhancing its work.

The Music Curriculum Team is much like differentiated staff. In essence, its composition represents all teaching as well as non-certificated, who are involved in the school's program of music education. Team membership will vary according to the complexity of learning experiences, customarily requiring more personnel at the secondary school level due to the greater number and depth of music offerings available to junior and senior high school students. When applied to larger segments of organized instruction, such as city, county and state units, the music curriculum team functions only where the enterprise is mutually desirable and necessary to implement a specific activity or endeavor, never from the top down if individualized instruction is the goal. Decentralization of leadership and curriculum development is axiomatic (and currently practised) in this concept. The only exception to this principle is where legal requirements or desirable administrative coordination are necessary.

In recent years, the practice of decreasing the pyramid of organizational hierarchy and of decentralizing supervisory staff has had a beneficial effect in most school systems. Rather than concentrating on music administrative and advisory staff operating exclusively at the central office level, the trend to have more persons "in the field" has made services more readily available to instructional staffs. Building principals and their staffs thus have had a greater say in the improvement of instruction directly related to their own schools. These persons are made accountable to the central office in terms of priorities for their school, rather than arbitrarily mandated goals handed down from on high. The shift in relationship between the building staffs and top administrators has been accompanied by changes in the relationship of administrative-supervisory personnel to the building staffs. For example, most "status." leaders in music--directors, coordinators, consultants, etc. are now assigned to "staff" rather than administrative positions, and their role in working with building instructional units now becomes one of coordination, consulting, and assisting rather than directing.

As we shall see shortly in the following chapters on Leadership Behaviors, a new type of leadership and followership is necessary if the term music curriculum team is to be truly appropriate. Yet, it will be necessary to remove at least two critical organizational blocks if this is accomplished; namely, (a) the aversion of principals and supervisors to becoming part of a team of which the classroom teacher is the coordinator; and, (b) the preparation of classroom teachers to become effective team leaders capable of using a supportive staff.

The team approach is a major answer to the dilemma of the creative, competent teacher who is hopelessly enmeshed in a tangle of organizational and routine duties which might otherwise be entrusted to assistants. The all-encompassing notion of the efficacy of the self-contained teacher, classroom, and school has become largely obsolete. In its place, the roles of teacher, aide, and specialist have become truly interrelated and interdependent in order to make the learning environment more stimulating and productive.

Figure 23 indicates the responsibilities of the professional staff of the music curriculum team. Figure 24 reveals how the interrelated structure is applied to the total music curriculum team. This organization consists of the categories of (a) in-group (meaning local school personnel) professional staff, (b) in-group auxiliary personnel, and, (c) out-group specialists (refering to area, district or community personnel).

Figure 23

Responsibilities of the Professional Staff of the Music Curriculum Team

MASTER TEACHER(S) AND ASSISTANT TEACHERS (Certificated):

1. Curriculum planning and development
2. Unit Planning
3. Assessing student potential and learning problems
4. Designing appropriate learning and teaching strategies, according to individual pupil needs and interests
5. Designating time, space, personnel, and materials requirements
6. Instruction
7. Instructional conferences and student resource activity
8. Evaluation of pupil progress

} INSTRUCTIONAL FUNCTIONS

INTERNS, PARAPROFESSIONALS, AND AIDES (Non-certificated):

1. Supervised study and/or practice
2. Securing and preparing materials
3. Routine correction of student material
4. Duplicating and secretarial
5. Music library and filing duties
6. Student files and records
7. "Special" arrangements (busing, festival routine, programs, marching band, uniforms, etc.
8. Housekeeping

} SUPPORTIVE FUNCTIONS

Figure 24
The Music Curriculum Team

In-group Professional Staff:

(Have a major responsibility for curriculum planning and instruction on a continuing basis.)

Master teacher(s)
Assistant teachers
Interns & paraprofessionals
Instructional aides assigned to the classroom (clerks, secretaries, etc.)

In-group Auxiliary Personnel:

(Have a tangential, contributing, or consultative function on an intermittent basis.)

Department chairmen or school music specialists
Allied arts or other instructional personnel, as appropriate
Principal and school administrative staff
Development specialists (such as curriculum, differentiated staff, and scheduling coordinators)
Counselors, psychometrists, guidance, and health personnel
Librarians (where school is large enough, to include a trained music librarian)
Media technicians (including computer specialists), audio-visual specialists, TV technicians
General clerks and aides (including laboratory clerks, where required)

Out-group Specialists:

(Have a consultative responsibility, or function for specified amounts of time to aid in completion of designated tasks.)

Area or district music consultants and coordinators
Other consultants and coordinators, as appropriate
Paraprofessionals (see also, "In-group Professional Staff")
Community musicians and musical groups
Community consultants, librarians, and other specialists in music
College or university consultants and specialists

INSTRUCTIONAL UNIT:
STUDENTS
LEARNING EXPERIENCES
MATERIALS

The music curriculum team may function at any given level, either elementary or secondary, and within the normal ranges of school size, from small to large. It may operate either in a traditional or "open" school design, with or without the benefit of modular or modified-conventional scheduling--yet the benefits of the latter, due to increased flexibility, are more conducive to certain team requirements. The team may consist of a single elementary teacher, the school music specialist, a parent volunteer aide on a part-time basis, a college intern, the school principal and secretary, and an interested and qualified community professional musician functioning as needed in a consultative or paraprofessional capacity. Or, depending on the nature of the resources and size of the organization involved, the team may approximate the resources previously outlined.

Reorganizing Teaching Structures

Interpersonal Relationships and Group Goals. The trend to change certain educational designations, such as "curriculum or educational resource center" from "administration building," and "consultant or resource teacher" from "supervisor or administrative assistant" is indicative of certain changes which are taking place in the schools. Similarly, the term "department chairman" is being replaced by "project coordinator, curriculum specialist, lead teacher," or other descriptive terminology indicating a coordinating function of educational leadership.

Changes in the concept of curriculum and instruction have resulted in changes in leadership and the way in which leaders and team members work. It is highly important that interpersonal relationships of group members be flexible, personally and professionally operable and that group goals be actually those of the group. In addition, if a multiunit-differentiated staffing design is to be accepted and maintained, certain structural changes must occur within the school organization. To be effective, members who are expected to work within the new structure must receive appropriate training to prepare them for new behavioral expectations. According to Arends and Essig, this involves:[13]

Specifically:

1. If new teacher-leaders are to provide the leadership expected under their role description, then:
   a. They must receive appropriate training to insure competency in the needed skills; i.e., group communication and leadership, supervision, and curriculum development.
   b. The teaching units must be organized to afford direct interaction by the teacher-leader and other members of the team.
   c. They must be given appropriate time to perform the prescribed leadership functions.
   d. They must be compensated for added responsibility.
2. If the paraprofessionals are to provide the service expected of them, then:
   a. They must receive appropriate training to perform the tasks expected of them.
   b. The teaching units must be organized to afford the paraprofessionals opportunities to interact directly with other members of the team.
3. If all members of the organization are to change their behavior to be consistent with the new structural organization, then:
   a. They must receive appropriate training in interpersonal relations group problem-solving, and communication skills.
   b. They must receive training as a unit so that they can understand each other's role and behavioral expectations.

Many authorities believe that it is particularly important in a time of discontinuity, unresolved conflicts, new forces, and dissimilar modes of teaching and learning that education leadership be devoted to helping the teacher have a primary and authentic commitment to the basic concept of how children grow and learn. This means that all available strategies be used; all methods for professional and personal self-renewal be examined; all methods for experimenting and solving problems be employed; all resources both in terms of material and personnel be utilized. It also requires that not only will the teacher and supporting professional staff take a careful look at individual children, their needs, and potentials--but will assess their own capacities for understanding and growth as well.

The Development of Repertoire Potential is a more recent adaptation of the notion of "in-service training," and is meant to cover the full range of the development of personal and professional capacities of the professional staff. In this day when no one person can be expected to keep abreast of the full range of educational change, or even the knowledge and developments in a single field, it becomes increasingly important that each member of the music curriculum team continue to develop a full range of repertoire resources and new techniques for instructional performance. It must be evident even to the dyed-in-the-wool traditionalist, that he probably is ill-equipped to cope with compositional or electronic music strategies in the classroom if he has not been recently exposed to contemporary modes of music theory. Or, to the performer who is impressed with the violinistic abilities of the pupils of Shinizi Suzuki--how can he experiment successfully in such techniques of group instrumental instruction without having first been personally involved with these concepts and tools? Perhaps his knowledge of current musical literature (or even historical!) has dimmed due to lack of exposure or use--how then will he extend and refresh himself if he remains aloof to such matters? Can he be effective in teaching a humanities or allied arts course if his knowledge is wanting in these areas or if he is actually unaware of the ongoing nature of art forms which surround him? If he ignores or denigrates contemporary music and art forms, can he be expected to communicate as a "real" person to youth in the seventies?

Sheer skills in handling old devices require an extension of the music educator's repertoire potential. When we magnify the task of working as a contributing, knowledgable member of an instructional team, the problem of repertoire development is further magnified. In addition, it must be remembered that modern team members need to have more than a passing acquaintance with new hardware and instructional technology. Consequently, there are additional demands for the development of staff resources and competencies.

Modes for developing repertoire potential are many and varied, depending on the nature of the school organization, its resources, and the individual needs of the instructional staff. Educational leadership in music in the current scene seems to offer such opportunities for persons to participate at many levels of involvement in both program and repertoire development. Bessom, Hermann, House, and Klotman are among writers who address themselves to a variety of techniques applicable to the field of music education. In general, developmental experiences are either individualized (on a one-to-one basis) or depend upon group structure. Some typical methods of organizing these activities are (a) building music committees, (b) departmental committees, (c) horizontal committees (grade level, topical, procedural, etc.), (d) vertical committees (such as festival committees, grading standards, policies and educational opportunities, K-12), (e) system-wide music curriculum committees, (f) area or geographical professional activities (MENC and its affiliated units, area conferences, meetings, etc.), (g) workshops, (h) clinics, (i) microteaching (for perception of individual, specific teaching techniques, and for self-evaluation of individuals concerned), (j) conferences (individual and group), (k) university and college extension and in-service courses, (l) visitation days, (m) applied research and experimental activities, (n) participation in music-making activities in the community, (o) demonstration-observation of master teachers and specialist-experts in the field, (p) research and advanced study, (q) work at curriculum centers, and many more.

The development of repertoire potential hinges upon the individual perceptions, motivations, and capacities for growth within the individuals who comprise the educational staff. The success of professional development depends upon the continuous involvement of each member of the profession. Consequently, repertoire development is not the exclusive responsibility of teachers, but should be a major concern of each person, whether he be teacher, status leader, or staff member.

Summary

Due to the unique and intimate relationship which exists between teacher and learner, education in the seventies will demand a high level of personal and professional skill on the part of the instructional staff. If they are to meet new demands in this decade of changing conditions, music educators must possess the qualities of objectivity, identification, openness, personal involvement, creativity, and inventiveness. They must be intellectually aware and artistically involved and able to make music and discover musical meanings for themselves in musical ways. They must be capable of capitalizing on the unique skills and potentials of individuals (including themselves) and be skilled in group processes. They must be involved, aware, and genuinely interested in and accepting of others engaged in the process of education.

While there are many effective American schools, a larger proportion of British Primary Schools are felt to be capitalizing on promising aspects of innovative and individualized instruction. These centers, while tending to be more informal than their American counterparts, provide an atmosphere in which children are highly motivated to experiment and create. The resulting educational mileu has been observed to have fewer disciplinary problems among children who appear better adjusted and vitally interested in their educational endeavors.

American schools recently have begun to realize the importance of providing opportunities for the release of individual human potential in a more "open," innovative atmosphere. While many such programs take place in traditionally oriented schools, such ideas as team or pontoon teaching and differentiated staffing utilize the combined expertise of several persons and present encouraging departures in education. With the additional flexibility of new arrangements in use of space, time, and personnel, individualization can be further enhanced.

The music curriculum team presents an adaptation of the concept of differentiated staffing, providing additional strength by using the skills of specialists, aides, paraprofessionals and others from the district and community to augment the local school instructional staff. Teaching structures are modified and strengthened by the development and application of skills of leadership and followership to the educational team. To a great degree, the development of repertoire potential, as an expanded concept of in-service training, can strengthen the skills of each member of the instructional staff and make learning more effective.

Topics For Discussion

1. What are some of the characteristics of formal organizations in our society which demand a high degree of skill in interpersonal relationships?
2. Discuss some of the most desirable personal qualities which you have observed in persons in public life or of your own acquaintance. Why do some persons appear to succeed in working with others while others fail to relate well with people?
3. Discuss ways in which you could develop team-teaching, pontooning, or differentiated staffing in a traditional school.
4. Discuss ways in which you as a "status" leader (music consultant or coordinator) could implement a music curriculum team in a specific school.
5. Present a detailed plan for staffing a secondary school of average size (1200-1500) under the differentiated staff concept.

Suggested Readings

Bessom, Malcom E. *Supervising the Successful School Music Program.* West Nyack, New York: Parker Publishing Co., 1969.

Bush, Robert N. and Dwight W. Allen. *A New Design for High School Education.* New York: McGraw-Hill Book Co., 1964. See flexible scheduling examples.

Elsbree, Willard S., Harold J. McNally, and Richard Wynn. *Elementary School Administration and Supervision, Third Edition.* New York: American Book Company, 1967. See Ch. 3.

Fisher, James L., "The New Teacher Education: Prospects for Change," in *The Teacher and His Staff: Differentiating Teaching Roles,* A Report of the 1968 Regional TEPS Conferences. Washington, D.C.

Jones, James J., C. Jackson Salisbury, and Ralph L. Spencer. *Secondary School Administration.* New York: McGraw-Hill Book Company, 1969.

Klotman, Robert H. *The School Music Administrator and Supervisor: Catalysts for Change in Music Education.* Englewood Cliffs, N.J.: Prentice-Hall, Inc., 1973.

Lucio, William H. (Ed) *The Supervisor: New Demands; New Dimensions.* Washington, D.C.: Association for Supervision and Curriculum Development, 1969.

Petrie, Thomas A. "To Improve Instruction, Supervision, and Evaluation," in Robert R. Leeper (Ed) *Supervision: Emerging Profession.* Washington, D.C.: Association for Supervision and Curriculum Development, 1969.

Roush, Donald C. "Educating Teachers Through Differentiated Roles," in *The Teacher and His Staff: Differentiating Teaching Roles.* Washington, D.C.

Smith, Frederick R. and R. Bruce McQuigg. *Secondary Schools Today: Readings for Educators.* Boston: Houghton Nifflin Company, 1965.

CHAPTER ELEVEN

ORGANIZATIONAL STRUCTURE AND LEADERSHIP BEHAVIORS IN MUSIC EDUCATION

Leadership is the activity of influencing people to cooperate toward some goal which they come to find desirable.

Ordway Tead

At the beginning of the book, we dealt with the identification and competencies of the music educator as an instructional leader. In this Chapter, our purpose will be to examine the nature of organizations, contemporary theories of leadership, and behavioral characteristics of leaders in music education. In the succeeding chapters (Functional Designs I and II) the skills and managerial aspects of leaders in music education will be delineated. Resources will be discussed in Chapter XIV.

The terms administration and supervision have almost disappeared from the educational scene, due in great measure to their negative connotation and the more recent concepts of educational leadership which stress cooperative and coordinative endeavors of the staff as a whole.

Although an official "status" leadership role in music appeared in the schools of Cleveland, Ohio in 1869, it was not until well into the Twentieth Century that this position exceeded that of a somewhat glorified music teacher. The Music Supervisors National Conference (MSNC) organized in Keokuk, Iowa in 1907 actually was a misnomer, since its membership consisted chiefly of music teachers. This designation was changed appropriately in the 1930's to the Music Educators National Conference (MENC) and today the official leadership activities of its members are recognized by such organizations as the MENC affiliate, the Council of State Supervisors of Music (CSSM) as well as the national, state, and regional music committees of the Association for Supervision and Curriculum Development (ASCD), a department of the National Education Association.

Tapper was among the first to recognize the principle of the interrelated role of music supervisors with their fellow teachers of music.[2]

. . .no one lives and works unto himself alone. Though we pursue our ambitions along individual pathways, these constantly cross and intercross, bringing us unto frequent and intimate relationships with our fellow beings. The fact that we are, in countless ways, related to contemporary individuals and institutions is the basis of all work for service. That we are all, and in a greater degree than we commonly realize, workers of intercommunicating interests must be the basic consideration.

Of current importance, however, is the influence provided by researchers, writers, and practioners in the field who have related theories of human behavior to leadership practice. The need for behavioral theory in instructional leadership for the Seventies is acute, due to a resurgence of interest in applying a more humane dimension to an area which formerly was conceived almost exclusively in managerial terms.

In essence, educational leaders should provide opportunities for the abilities and talents of members of the staff to thrive and make their own contribution. If educational leadership exists principally for the improvement of instruction, the primary goal and definition of this activity is achieved. The real purpose, however, has to do with facilitating, coordinating, and releasing human talents in the process of teaching and learning. Thus, leadership depends to a great degree on the individuals who lead as well as on an environment which is conducive to free, creative, cooperative, and happily-productive endeavors. In any organization, most members desire and require leadership. Such leadership must recognize the objectives and aspirations of the component members, yet must also encourage individuals to work toward group goals through mutually acceptable means.

It must be remembered that every organization will have informal as well as "status" leaders, the latter being those persons officially designated to perform leadership functions. It will be the status leader's task to encourage individuals to act, to synthesize, and to coordinate activities--and to help individuals within the group to assume a variety of leadership and followership roles.

Organizations and Organizational Structure

The Nature of Organizations. The term organization implies some activity which is coordinated as a unified whole. Our society is comprised of organizations and organizational hierarchy, whether the latter be social, economic, religious, political, or merely the family structure, And, even in death, organization is inescapable since the largest organization of all--the state--must grant official permission for burial. Carried to the illogical extreme of the Peter Principle, society consists of a hierarchal order of organizations in which each worker tends to rise to his "level of incompetence," and in which group functions are actually carried out by workers who have not yet reached this level.[3] In *The Organization Man,* William Whyte Jr. contends that the organization, as a form of bureaucratic endeavor, is fashioned from a so-called "social ethic" and that its demands for fealty are rationalized from a sort of sense of individual dedication to the group. Just as a student trainee may believe management to be an end in itself, organization members may come to accept expertise as relatively independent of the content of what is managed. This view tends to restrict society's organizations to narrow and fairly immediate activities, rather than to allow them to discharge the greater service of which they are capable.

Organizations may be either formal or informal. Formal organizations, such as those in schools, depend upon a rather complex structure, wherein individuals occupy roles in which behaviors are either implied or prescriptively described. If an individual is replaced, his successor customarily is expected to fill the position with some knowledge of the parameters of his job. Owens feels that complex organizations have two specific characteristics; namely, (a) the constancy of role structure which exists in schools, industry, government, and the military; and, (b) the delineation of authority of one role over another.[4] Less is known about informal organizations, however, there is some evidence that these are essential to formal organizations and that they also have considerable power derived from the manner in which people work with one another. Behavioral norms are often governed by primary informal structures. A music consultant, for example, may experience little or no impact on teacher performance if the primary informal group feels it does not have the consultant's support and confidence and consequently opposes his actions.

Power to act is essential to all organizational activities. One view of power as expressed by Lucio and McNeil is described as ". . .the ability to propose and achieve objectives." These authors further contend that, in order to exercise power, one must be able to control the means to the ends sought.[5] Control may come about in terms of who acquires it and how material resources and personal skills are used. In addition, power will depend upon how goals are achieved as well as the manner in which people give and use the tools of control.

Human Values and Organizational Change. Throughout this book it has been our purpose to stress the importance of individuals, whether students, teachers, or leaders. In the preceding chapter, such qualities as openness, identification, creativity, inventiveness, and so on were described as ideally suited to the needs of music educators and members of the music curriculum team in an era of change. Ideally, since organizations are comprised of humans who possess these desired qualities, they too should reflect many of the same characteristics.

Organizations, on the other hand, are more amorphous and lack readily identifiable humanistic features. While they are amenable to modification, organizational change is slow and sometimes more radical and destructive of individual goals. For example, school organizations are occasionally terminated at the option of the electorate or their elected officials, due to a lack of fiscal resources or some untoward act which is not generally understood or accepted. Consequently, organizational structure may be modified or stopped entirely as a result of forces outside the organization's membership, no matter how individually and collectively effective their efforts may be.

Four conditions aiding change, according to Griffiths are:[6]

1. The major impetus for change in organizations is from the outside.
2. The degree and duration of change is directly proportional to the intensity of the stimulus from the supra-system.
3. Change in an organization is more probable if the successor to the chief administrator is from outside the organization.
4. Living systems respond to continuously increasing stress first by a lag in response, then by an over-compensatory response, and finally by catastrophic collapse of the system.

Griffiths also feels that innovations occur in inverse proportion to the tenure of the leadership, and its complexity of hierarchal structure, and that they likewise result from conditions which tend to occur from the top down, rather than from the bottom up. This concept places an acute responsibility on the official status leadership structure in education.

Leadership begins, according to Wiles, where it can contribute to the establishment and attainment of group purposes. Official leadership, he contends, is appointed by some authority outside the group or elected from within the group by the group.[7] In this view, emerging leadership may come from any member of the organization and is recognized as the group adopts the leadership contribution within its own objectives and methods. Organizational modification is effected on the basis of a careful evaluation of goals and means, based on objective evidence at hand. Change must be both desired and accepted by group members before it can be effective.

The importance of organizational structure and leadership which is essentially humanistically oriented is of paramount importance in music education. If for no other reason than the unique feelingful qualities of musical experience within humans, any structure for the implementation of music education must be assumed to be dedicated to such experience. As has been previously pointed out, there are also unique goals in education which are not present in industry, economics, government and other organizations. Growth in these fields implies something other than behavioral growth. Consequently, we cannot conceive of an educational enterprise nor an on-going developmental program of music education in strictly managerial terms.

Impediments. British Primary Schools have been mentioned in a foregoing section as good examples of organizations which do change and innovate. It can be argued, however, that disparities in flexibility result from structural differences which exist between schools of Great Britain and the United States. British schools are in fact a concern of Her Majesty's Government which exercises nominal control over the local district (salary schedules, funding, and terms of employment are national rather than local). This removes many social pressures from local classrooms, as in many public universities of the United States, and gives English teachers and heads much greater freedom to experiment and innovate. The head in each school enjoys an autonomy unheard of in most American schools--consequently, a school wishing to experiment in an arts curriculum is free to do so. English schools and classrooms are also much smaller than in the United States, thus, further aiding individualized instruction.

It should be pointed out that most heads of British schools function quite differently than do their counterparts, the American principals, who do little if any direct classroom teaching. English heads subscribe to the theory that they should spend up to seventy-five percent of their time in the classroom where they remain in contact with learning.[8] The difference is perhaps subtle but important--one who chiefly administers may not actually be involved and concerned with the act of teaching and learning--and administrative chores have a tendency to proliferate with the amount of administration one does. Part-time teaching on the part of the status leader not only puts him into an immediate and continuous relationship with the cause and effect of educational process, but can help to make him a more effective group leader as well. This same principle recently has been enunciated for persons who have a responsibility for guiding teacher education at the higher education level by the Commission on Teacher Education of the Music Educators National Conference.[9]

There is no royal road to change in educational structure, and, indeed, many imperfections and impediments exist in society which make innovation difficult. There is also the distinct possibility of undesirable mutations of change which will make the new pattern less effective and acceptable than the old one, for, all organizational change goes through three separate and distinct phases: (a) enthusiasm, (b) vulgarization and spread, and, (c) institutionalization. An example of this was observed by this writer in a so-called team teaching effort, which was quickly adopted by a school principal after having been highly touted by his music coordinator. The result was spectacularly unsuccessful since the experiment did not present new alternatives for action for the consideration of the team itself, having followed a well-worn, albeit successful example in another school.

The chief impediment in educational organizations, according to Abbott is that we have become unwittingly if not specifically receptive to the concept of bureaucratic control. Thus, we have incorporated some of the worst bureaucratic practices in educational leadership. These are:[10]

1. The school organization has clearly been influenced by the need for specialization and the factoring of tasks.
2. The school organization has developed a clearly defined and rigid hierarchy of authority.
3. The school organization has leaned heavily upon the use of general rules to control the behavior of members of the organization and to develop standards which would assure reasonable uniformity in the performance of tasks.
4. Despite frequent proclamations regarding togetherness and democracy, the school organization has made extensive application of Weber's principle of impersonality in organizational relationships.
5. Employment in the educational organization has been based upon technical competence and has constituted for most members a professional career. Promotions have been determined by seniority and by achievement; tenure has been provided; and fixed compensation and retirement benefits have been assured.

Members of organizations should be ensured the right to share in decisions which affect their work, to freely communicate and make known their ideas to status or informal group leaders, and to be accorded the privilege of affirming, or of vetoing or disengaging from activities which they cannot support without fear of recrimination.

Recent Developments. During and immediately following World War II, a resurgence of interest in human behavior was evidenced in the research and writings of social scientists, psychologists, sociologists, and political scientists. Behavioral science began to draw more heavily from theory, applied research, and specialized knowledge of human behavior to provide a more adequate background for administrative leadership. In the quest for better models of administrative behavior, theory, according to Owens, passed through three successive stages.[11]

1. Scientific management era — rigid technological principles for organizational management--primary goal: increased efficiency and output.
2. Human relations era — specific attention to psychological and social aspects of organizations--primary goal: furthering human and social elements as a coordinated, functioning whole.
3. Current era; synthesis — combines previous era goals with new behavioral insights--primary goal: development of a conceptual framework through which we may systematize and integrate our knowledge of the various types of administration.

McNeil likens present day school organization to an "ailing monster," claiming that while there are serious cultural lags between school and society, some of these may be bridged by a re-definition of educational goals translated into workable curricular structure.[12] It is contended that whereas specific problems can be solved (as in industry) by employing the specific talents of specialists, education should be wary of adding together each of the available narrow, specialized, or departmental viewpoints to obtain better meaning-purpose-direction for its activities.

Thus, a new research and development role is called for occupying a leadership position free of the usual demands of department and discipline and fulfilled by an individual who is able to focus on the broad view of the past, present, and future of education. The initial academic training of this person is probably less relevant than the breadth of vision that he or she possesses. Although the current goal is to adapt models from other disciplines to educational administration, the uniqueness of learning demands that leadership behaviors in schools raise new questions, test new hypotheses, and develop new theories of behavior particularly appropriate to educational goals. With this concept in mind, leaders in music education must also develop a set of behavioral goals and skills which will assist them to:

1. Become familiar with a wider range of music experience.
2. Become more perceptive of human and aesthetic needs and values in a changing society.
3. Develop more adequate theoretical foundations for experiencing music.
4. Discover and apply new knowledge of education and educational leadership.
5. Examine, test, and use new and innovative concepts of music education.
6. Develop theories and expertise in fields of pre-service training and development of repertoire potential.
7. Become informed concerning and disseminate findings of research applicable to music and music education.

Contemporary Theories of Leadership

Flexibility Versus Conformity. It is interesting to note that current research suggests that flexible, loosely structured enterprises are probably more efficient for given situations than are highly structured, formal organizations. The foregoing suggests that such a principle is equally true of educational as well as other organizational models. This is probably due to the explicitness with which role expectations and leadership behaviors were established and regulated by formal organizational structures. Activities which were carefully prescribed in terms of efficiency and output goals were too impersonal and found lacking for group processes. This notion also depended upon the theory that situations were nearly identical and that the tasks of human components of the organization were largely predictable and repetitive. It also assumed that there is an insignificant degree of discretion and decision-making on the part of subordinates in the enterprise.

There is some recent evidence to indicate that (a) for each task a worker performs, he is confronted with the opportunity and/or necessity of exerting a certain degree of discretion; and, (b) discretion on the part of the worker is brought into play when the character of the work itself and the routine governing how the work is done do not automatically determine the "best" way for an individual to perform.

A desirable type of organizational structure suggests the importance of more flexibility, less rigidity of authority, better horizontal and vertical communication, coordination only to the degree of assisting the work effort of those involved, high normative control by leaders, better work commitment (improved understanding of leadership-followership roles), and improved interpersonal relationships. In addition, as Campbell and Gregg point out, educational leadership requires a distinctive value framework since it has a greater responsibility for cherished human values than do many other kinds of administration. Schools also are closer to values of the community, hence they have a high degree of interaction with their school-community, requiring a different set of skills on the part of school leaders. This close interaction is a relatively new phenomenon occasioned by American's deep-rooted belief in education, by the increase in the school's functions, and most importantly perhaps, by the fact that people feel a need to remain close to the institution whose *raison d' etre* is direct help to them on their fundamental problems.[13]

Components of Leadership. The components of leadership are both personal and professional. Studies of the trait approach indicate that specific personal characteristics are incomplete, since the degree to which an individual exhibits leadership ability depends not only on his own attributes, but the characteristics of the situation in which he finds himself.[14]

If considered as desirable leadership behaviors, however, the following are important guidelines for music educators:

1. Leaders need to develop a concept of situational variables

applied to certain areas of responsibility.

2. Leaders need to experience different ways of working with various reference groups.
3. Leaders need to assess values and characteristics of people with whom they are expected to work.
4. Leaders need to understand informal as well as formal organizational structure in any given area of work.
5. Leaders must develop a "tolerance factor" which will assist them in acting objectively in a variety of situations.
6. Leaders must develop appropriate skills of interpersonal relationships which will help them to be more effective contributing (as opposed to dominating) members of various groups with whom they are expected to work.
7. Leaders must assist individual members of the group to clarify and understand their role in given situations.
8. Leaders must provide greater latitude in group expectations which will allow them to accept unpredictable results.

Theories of Leadership. A situational approach to leadership in education derived from the research of Halpin and associates leans heavily on behavioral science for its model. Halpin's model becomes a "hypothetico-deductive" rather than speculative theory, in which a systematic terminology is used for the purpose of clarity and consistency. The components of leadership are reduced to:[15] (1) The task, (2) The formal organization, (3) The work group(s), (4) The leader(s).

Halpin's model is based on human behaviors as applied to various levels of leadership (situational, democratically elected, officially designated status persons in formal organizations, etc.). This concept could be applied equally to any member of the music curriculum team (see Chapter X), according to the situational variables involved. Accordingly, if leadership is to function effectively, goals must be clarified and agreed upon. Furthermore, the organization must allow itself to remain in a dynamic rather than static mold, since the nature of the task changes from time to time, each change requiring a different approach or emphasis. An example of this would be where rapid shifts in student characteristics brought about by population shifts may render certain curriculum emphases inappropriate or obsolete. Consequently, an acceptance of new dimensions of the task resulting from change is one of the primary obligations of the music education.

In this paradigm, it is pointed out that it is necessary to make a distinction between a task and the problem, the former representing the mission of the organization as defined by the observers of the organization proper, and the latter referring to the perception of the tasks at a given time by significant members of the organization. These are not necessarily identical. The most important person in this dual process is the status leader--that is to say, the person formally charged with the responsibility of leadership. Thus, a person in the task, as viewed by an observer, reacts according to conditions set externally for following specified rules of behavior in given situations, and for satisfying (hence, also being rewarded by) specified criteria by which his acts are judged as being successful. In contrast, although the observer and participant may share the same view of a given set of circumstances, the approach to the problem is internalized. In the problem, the "in-group" member (group member other than the official status leader) himself sees the stimulus situation, then acts by way of modifying the situation to realize the desired outcome which he perceives. These perceptions underscore the importance of the status leader's help in assessing real group goals, and assisting the group in translating verbalizations into operational objectives by which the activities of the group may be accomplished and measured. Just as in behaviors for learning, organizational goals should be expressed in behavioral terms stated in descriptive (what is) rather than normative (what ought to be) language.

Another model of leadership theory outlined by Campbell, Corbally, and Ramseyer defines the activities of leaders in terms of specific situational variables each of which is dependent on group interaction.[16] Figure 25 indicates how the leader (A) would react under given conditions. In diagram 1, the status leader attempts to exert leadership by efforts to attract the group to himself and his way of thinking and pulls on the group in an attempt to overcome group pressures that are exerted in the opposite direction. Diagram 2 shows the leader as an accepted member of the group--influence in this situation is from within, and, while the leader affects group decisions,

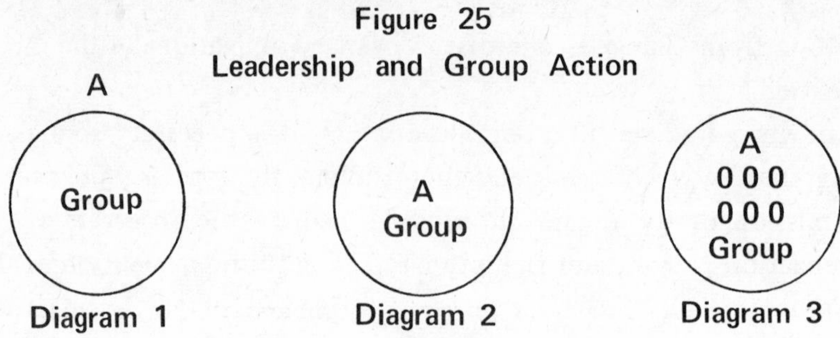

Figure 25
Leadership and Group Action

A=leader; 0 0 0=informal organizational structures.

they are nonetheless group rather than leader decisions having group approval. Similar to this concept, diagram 3 is intended to point out a situation in which the leader may recognize that within a given group there is a nucleus of power (informal organizational structure) that must be dealt with in order to get group action. When the power group has given its approval, the group is ready to act also. In this instance, the leader has the alternative of obtaining approval of the power group or of by-passing them in his relationship with other members of the group. Decision-making is delicate and requires a thorough understanding of group processes. It is also important to recognize that the leader's own behavior is likely to follow one of these three patterns, depending upon how he understands group action and his responsibility and relationship to the group.

Status leaders in music education ("out-group" area or district coordinators and consultants) have additional responsibilities which provide another dimension to the role of working with groups. In this instance, the music status leader does not function independently as a member of the music curriculum team at all times. Since he has district responsibilities delegated by the superintendent's office, works with other schools and groups and functions in a variety of community musical endeavors, he is additionally responsible for coordinating and integrating the work of these groups. To be an effective member of a working group (i.e., music curriculum team), the music leader must avoid imposing other ideas and goals, instead helping the group to understand and accept only those which are appropriate to its own work. In figure 26, the shaded area represents

Figure 26
The Dynamics of Intergroup Relationships of Music Education Leaders

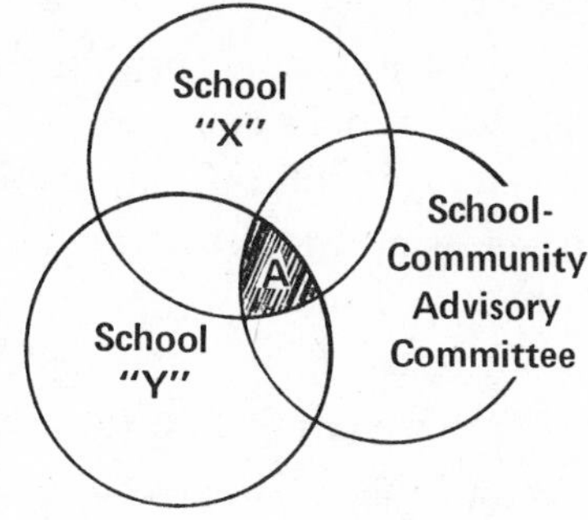

"A" = status leader in music education

these areas of common agreement. If the status leader in music is an effective influence in coordinating interrelated work activity of his various constituent groups, the centers of these circles move closer together indicating a considerable area of common agreement. Conversely, if the circles move farther apart, common agreement decreases and the effectiveness of the leader in accomplishing common goals is impaired.

Behavioral Dimensions of Leadership

Individual Actualization. Any set of behavioral terms used to describe the goals of a given activity should be self-actualizing; that is, they should contain built-in statements for attaining desired goals. Since leadership is essentially another dimension of individualization, the terms should be capable of being individually actualized.

In terms of broad behavioral goals, educational leaders should:

1. Work toward an understanding and appreciation of the dignity

and worth of human beings.

2. Seek personal insight and work toward a better understanding of themselves in relationship to groups.
3. Develop the ability to express as well as receive ideas.
4. Become socially responsive and insightful concerning society in a broad as well as specific sense.
5. Develop expertise as coordinators and facilitators of human action and interaction.
6. Develop an understanding of concensus in assessing and acting on goals. Conversely, they should come to understand and accept a varying spectrum of opinion on the part of their associates.
7. Develop ways of releasing the creative and inventive energies of themselves and others.

The literature and research in the field of status leaders in education also stresses the importance of (a) insightful understanding which will govern how the individual operates within a given situation; (b) the taking as well as giving of ideas in which leaders may strengthen areas of their own weaknesses; (c) differences between those who hold only a "two-value" (i.e., "yes" "no") logic and those who perceive several facets to the problem; (d) awareness of the role of leadership in which empathy and rapport between leader and group are of greatest priority; and, (e) the importance of general rather than specific traits in leadership behaviors. The latter would include such things as have been mentioned for successful teachers, with special emphasis on adaptability, emotional stability, judgment, originality, "popularity," and communicative skills.

Most traits seem to be more significantly related to the personality of leaders as opposed to the position itself. These traits are more closely allied to the interaction of persons in social situations rather than with status. The reader should be cautioned, however, that most studies of traits per se point out that these factors alone are insufficient to a determination of leadership behavior since they must be studied in terms of relationship to roles in educational settings.

Behavioral Characteristics of Leaders in Music Education. In considering the desired behaviors for leadership, we should first identify the roles which are being described and the general nature of the enterprise. Prior reference has been made to "in-group" and "out-group" leadership, the former as applied to local members of the music curriculum team (the staff of a given school) and the latter referring to persons outside the local group (area, district, or community) who contribute to the efforts of the "in-group" team. In the terms of this book, we refer to bòth, hence, the behavior characteristics depend on the variables of the role as it is practiced in a given situation. To understand the requirements, we should make the following assumptions concerning operational and decision making expectancies:

1. Educational leadership is concerned with the improvement of instruction.
2. Instruction and curriculum are inseparable; hence, leaders in music education have a responsibility both for developing the music education program desired as well as learning opportunities provided in the classroom.
3. Leadership (whether "in-group" or "out-group.") exists as a service (staff) rather than administrative (line) function and the responsibility for carrying out leadership rests on both "status" as well as other (including informal) group leaders.
4. "Out-group" leadership should coordinate and facilitate appropriate work activities of individual teachers and groups. It should never impose its will, activate programs, or dominate learning situations where it will hamper the creativity of the local staff and individual teachers.

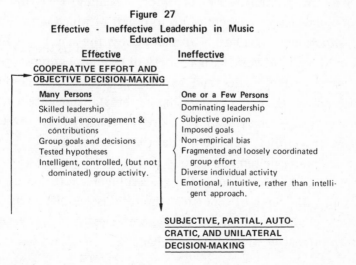

Figure 27
Effective - Ineffective Leadership in Music Education

Effective	Ineffective
COOPERATIVE EFFORT AND OBJECTIVE DECISION-MAKING	
Many Persons	**One or a Few Persons**
Skilled leadership	Dominating leadership
Individual encouragement & contributions	Subjective opinion
Group goals and decisions	Imposed goals
Tested hypotheses	Non-empirical bias
Intelligent, controlled, (but not dominated) group activity.	Fragmented and loosely coordinated group effort
	Diverse individual activity
	Emotional, intuitive, rather than intelligent approach.
	SUBJECTIVE, PARTIAL, AUTOCRATIC, AND UNILATERAL DECISION-MAKING

In describing general behaviors of leadership, Wiles suggests that status leaders in education should develop skills of leadership, human relations, group processes, personnel administration, and evaluation. He also indicates that the successful supervisor is one who can develop situations in which people work cooperatively and in which leaders assist personnel in making more effective use of their own skills and abilities.[17] Snyder outlines the behaviors of status leaders in music education under such activities as defining purpose, planning, organizing, directing, evaluating, and improving.[18] Snyder is in general agreement with Wiles on the importance of personal qualities and leadership acceptance and stresses the importance of such additional factors as good group working climate and democratic processes. This author suggests that the effective music status leader also has great need for artistic as well as educational leadership. According to Ostrander and Dethy, a favorable climate for creative action by staff members occurs when leaders endeavor to adopt a transitional style of behavior which blends nomethetic (governed by law) and idiographic (characteristic of the individual) considerations in relationship to a specific social situation.[19] In decision-making, he will draw upon those elements of theoretical systems and models to predict results of leadership behavior which have tentatively been verified by behavioral science.

Campbell draws from research to adduce the effects of situational variables on administrative behavior, claiming that the leader (a) should develop a concept of his job (part of which must deal with these situational variables); (b) should, by the nature of his job, prepare himself to work with a variety of reference groups; (c) assess situational characteristics and expectations (including community characteristics, values, and leadership patterns); (d) maintain contacts with the "power structure;" (e) clarify roles; (f) learn to face and work with conflict; (g) learn that it is impossible to meet the expectations of one reference group since other reference groups may be ignored in the process and their goals submerged; (h) be knowledgable about the "area of tolerance" limitations; and, (i) do his best to remain a student of how situational variables affect his leadership behavior no matter what his involvement.[20]

Halpin's research indicates that there are essentially two dimensions of leadership behavior for the status leader, namely, "initiating structure" and "consideration."[21] To be effective, a leader should be strong in initiating structure (how to initiate action and get things done) while at the same time high in consideration for members of his work group. While these two types of behavior are somewhat independent, they indeed are compatible. Leaders among school administrators who were considered to be neither "highly effective" nor "ineffective" were characterized as being high in consideration but low on initiation of structure. Halpin speculates on the possible dichotomy which may appear between the behaviors under initiation of structure as being undemocratic and postulates that what is referred to as democratic leadership actually is a combination of high initiation of structure and high consideration. Moreover, he contends that while this type of leadership is highly to be desired, it is not sufficient for the leader to be democratic--he must also demonstrate definite acts of leadership. Furthermore, it is the group's perception of the behavior patterns of the status leader rather than the individual's self-image of these behaviors that the real role of leadership is determined.

Schools differ markedly in organizational climate--that is, their working environment. In turn, these climates have a great deal to do with leadership behaviors, in many instances resulting directly from these behaviors. In the 1950's, Argyris was among the first to study factors which comprise the organizational climate in banking institutions, suggesting that it is important to find ways of managing internal environments in which a certain amount of conflict exists, and to keep these differences within bounds. A few years later, Etzioni contended that the manner of "fit" within the organization depended to a large extent on the theory of "compliance," that of attracting and involving people.[22] An interesting study carried on in the formal atmosphere of a faculty lounge reports what every seasoned leader knows, that new teachers are quickly apprised by older teachers of "how things are done." Younger teachers had to abandon ideas which they thought to be worthwhile if they wanted to conform with the established way of doing things and fit in comfortably. They could submit to the "old" norm, suffer a certain amount of conflict, or leave the group. Whether group behaviors can be influenced positively for effective group action is dependent on the organizational climate effected by group leaders.

The six organizational climates of schools and their educational leaders, as measured by the Halpin research, are:[23]

1. Open climate
2. Autonomous climate
3. Controlled climate
4. Familiar climate
5. Paternal climate
6. Closed climate

There are impelling reasons why, when confronted with changes in leadership, "in-group" members are faced first with relatively closed climates, then more open ones. Such changes frequently not only challenge (or threaten) teacher behavior, but also induce periods of relative inactivity and ineffectiveness while all members of the organization are attempting to assess their new roles. The range of alternatives must be assessed by the leader who will then act in a manner most consistent with his philosophy, and in so doing use the proper climates and administrative behaviors to allow the particular group to function most effectively. Since change is sometimes regarded as a threat, however, success can never be fully predicted in change patterns. An understanding of these implications is crucial to the leader in music education who must solve this before attempting to move toward massive changes in the music curriculum. Degrees of "open" or "closed" climate may also be influenced by a variety of factors entirely external to the school organization, such as legal and administrative regulations, community attitudes, parent and student opinion. In the Halpin investigation, he reports validating a concept of authenticity--that is, some schools organizations appeared to be "for real" while others had learned the pattern by rote and were merely going through the motions.

Paradigm for Music Leadership: A Behavioral System. A redefinition of systems as applied to leadership behaviors is in order at this point. It will be remembered from Chapter VII in which this approach was used to define the curricular framework for music education, systems focus on types or integrated relationships rather than units of the system, such as individual behavior in the performance of leadership roles. Systems theory evolves from interdisciplinary research (such as economics, education cultural anthropology, political science, psychology, management, and sociology), particularly from the behavioral sciences. The concern is for the organizational enterprise and its human derivatives rather than specific individual and institutional problems. The goal is integration, coordination, synthesis, and release of power by and among individuals who cooperatively act in leadership or followership roles.

A departure is indicated here from the "classical" notion of systems which are frequently theorized to be rationalistic as opposed to behavioralistic. Therefore, it shall be the intent to assume that our organization shall be considered as an open system, comprised of human interactions and behaviors. At the same time, it is well to remember that educational systems have special properties that set them apart from other organizations, particularly in their emphasis on the uniqueness and desirability of helping individuals within groups to attain their maximum human potential. Consequently, we shall attempt to describe a behavioral system which places emphasis on individuals who operate within the group in a leadership capacity to facilitate the organizational enterprise.

As in the consideration of the nature of music and music education, our systems approach is heuristic and holistic—it is concerned with the processes of inquiry, study, and problem-solving as applied to a whole approach to music content, learning, and leadership. What follows is that learning and leadership behaviors are different not in kind but in application, whether one be an instrumental, vocal, or general music consultant. Our systems model also is dedicated to the fullest development of repertoire potential on the part of the entire staff, of which the status leader in music education is a component.

In Figure 28, the total working structure of the music education system is indicated. The foci are in the primary subsystems--the classrooms; the principal system is the Music Curriculum Team. Leadership is a two-way process between these two units. The status leader's behavior will be predicated on facilitating the work of these systems and subsystems--individual growth (student and instructor) augmented and complimented by group interaction.

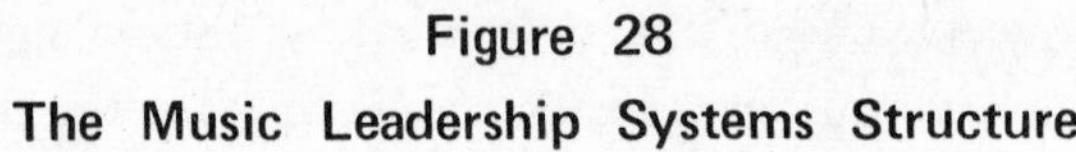

Figure 28
The Music Leadership Systems Structure

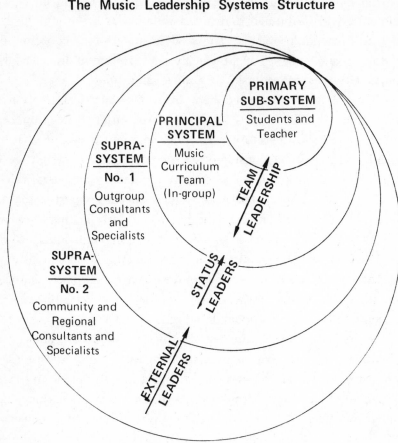

Leadership behaviors in music education may be subsumed under (a) skills of instructional leadership, and (b) managerial functions. While the principal thrust should always be on the former, a certain amount of managerial skill is necessary and desirable to provide opportunities for the exercise of leadership and group activity in the improvement of instruction. Both will be examined in chapters immediately to follow.

Generally speaking, the behavioral skills of good leaders in music education are:

Insights – Cognitive Area:

1. To acquire knowledge concerning the nature of music as one of the important arts of mankind.
2. To understand the relationship of music to other cultural influences in our society.
3. To comprehend the difference between musical and ordinary experience, and to experience music in musical ways. (feelingful experience)
4. To acquire and develop personal skills of musical expression.
5. To comprehend the unique behaviors (cognitive, psychomotor, affective, critical judgment) which apply to the experiencing of music in learning situations.
6. To develop an eclectic background of educational philosophy through which one's own philosophical structuring of music education may be developed.
7. To acquire an understanding of individual human needs, interests, and motivations in learning (in general).
8. To understand and relate knowledge of teaching-learning theory as a successful practioner of teaching.
9. To develop a background and understanding of school organizations in society and their contemporary position in American education.
10. To understand the dynamics of human interaction and communication.
11. To acquire a theoretical and practical background of all common areas of the music curriculum.
12. To become knowledgeable concerning the specific resources in music education.

Skills – Leadership Area:

1. To demonstrate personal skill in representative areas of music teaching at levels which one is expected (or designated) to lead; to acquire additional specialization competency in one or more areas of expertise.
2. To be able to communicate one's ideas and expertise to others in helpful ways.
3. To develop skills of interpersonal relationships in working with individuals and groups.
4. To acquire the fullest possible knowledge of the possibilities for repertoire development and to be able to apply this effectively.

5. To assist in the fullest implementation of the Music Curriculum Team concept at all levels, and to extend the range of expertise of individual teachers and staff members of the Team.
6. To assist in assessing goals, planning, organizing, implementing, and evaluating outcomes of instruction (curriculum development).
7. To participate in recruiting, selecting, training, and evaluating personnel who are members of the Music Curriculum Team (Note: cooperative rather than administrative evaluation).
8. To coordinate the work activities of in and out-groups in music education.
9. To serve as an interpreter, facilitator, and coordinator of work efforts of individuals, groups, central office staff, and community in music.
10. To assist in acquiring and developing resources for music education (equipment, materials, physical plant).
11. To implement effective ways of using time, personnel, and physical resources.
12. To institute and/or apply programs of theoretical and applied research designed to study and improve music teaching and learning.

Summary

Organizations exist to unify and coordinate the work of individuals in common endeavors. Although the educational structure described in this chapter has to do with formal organizations, informal organizations within schools also exert considerable influence on the former. Complex organizations such as schools have two principal characteristics; namely, (a) constancy of roles of members, and, (b) delineation of authority of one role over another.

Educational organizations lack personal qualities but assume many of the characteristics of their individual human components, especially, as pointed up in the research of Halpin and others, those of their leaders. Leadership may be exerted by any member of a group (status, elected, or informal) but change must be both desired and accepted by the group to be an effective instrumentality of group endeavor.

There are several impediments to leadership, the principal ones being those of (a) elements outside the control of the organization; (b) rigid bureaucratic hierarchies and autocratic control, and, (c) poor communication and the inability to make one's ideas heard.

Organizations have passed through the eras of scientific management and human relations to the present one of synthesis, based on behaviors of individuals who lead and those who follow. Currently, flexible organizational models appear to be more efficient and productive in education than are overly rigid, formal, and closed ones.

Status leadership is comprised of both personal and professional components. From research in several disciplines, it appears important to apply the knowledge of behavioral science to leadership functions. Situational variables and group goals must be appropriately recognized and acted upon for effective educational operations. Status leaders in music education also must assist groups in working with other influences and organizations in the school-community.

The acquisition of general and specific behaviors of leadership are essential for status leaders in music. These include Halpin's theory of "initiating structure" and "consideration," as well as other skills of democratic individual and group activation. They must also acquire specific skills of musicianship, educational philosophy and practice, communication, group leadership, and be able to lead effectively in helping members of the Music Curriculum Team reach their human potentials in planning, organizing, implementing, and evaluating products of the music curriculum in action.

Topics For Discussion

1. In what ways are organizations essential to the achievement of societal goals? Theoretically and practically, could our society operate without them?
2. From your collateral reading and prior knowledge of educational administrative structure, explain the statement, "Education is a federal interest, state concern, and local responsibility."
3. Present and discuss some of the conflicting views of organizations and leadership from the research and writing of specialists and others in the field.
4. Classical models of open organizational systems have certain characteristics such as self-regulation, outside influences as a major impetus for change, inputs and outputs (principle of feed-back), and rather finite boundaries of human responsibility and interaction. How desirable is this concept in relationship to the more flexible model described in this chapter?
5. What situational variables do you feel to be most important for the consideration of the status leader in music?

6. Describe how you feel the Music Leadership Systems Structure (see Figure 30) can be the most effective instrumentality for music learning in the classroom.
7. From your own experience, describe how leadership behaviors influence the "open-closed" climate of schools and the ability of individuals and groups to operate effectively.
8. Why is the cooperative expertise and objectivity of several persons more productive than dominating, subjective leadership? Do you feel this principle should be violated under certain "closed" circumstances, or is it possible eventually to effectively circumvent these restrictions using the "ideal" model as an operating concept?
9. Describe and give the rationale for the various leadership behaviors which have been mentioned as being essential for the status leader in music education. How may these also be applied to other members of the Music Curriculum Team?

Suggested Readings

Campbell, Roald F., John Corbally, and John Ramseyer. *Introduction to Educational Administration,* Third Edition. Boston: Allyn and Bacon, Inc., 1966.

Campbell, Roald F. and Russell T. Gregg (Ed.) *Administrative Behavior in Education.* New York: Harper, 1957.

Carver, Fred D. and Thomas J. Sergiovanni (Ed.) *Organizations and Human Behavior: Focus on Schools.* New York: McGraw-Hill Book Company, 1969.

Halpin, Andrew W. *Theory and Research in Administration.* New York: MacMillan, 1966.

Klotman, Robert H. *The School Music Administrator and Supervisor: Catalysts for Change in Music Education.* Englewood Cliffs, N.J.: Prentice-Hall, Inc. 1973.

Landon, Joseph W. "The Arts Deserve Quality Leadership," *Music Educators Journal,* Vol. 52, No. 1, Sept.-Oct., 1965, pp. 73-75.

Leonhard, Charles and Robert W. House. *Foundations and Principles of Music Education.* New York: McGraw-Hill Book Co., 1972.

Lucio, William H. and John D. McNeil. *Supervision: A Synthesis of Thought and Action,* Second Edition. New York: McGraw-Hill Book Company, 1969.

Ostrander, Raymond H. and Ray C. Dethy. *A Values Approach to Educational Administration.* New York: American Book Company, 1968.

CHAPTER TWELVE

FUNCTIONAL DESIGN I: SKILLS OF EDUCATIONAL LEADERSHIP

A leader is best when people barely know that he exists, not so good when people obey and acclaim him . . . When his work is done, his aim fulfilled, they will all say, "we did this ourselves."

Laotzu

Skills of educational leadership have to do with those factors which are utilized primarily for the improvement of instruction. These are the principal skills and functions of persons who are responsible for the development and implementation of curriculum. This Chapter is concerned with the nature and function of such skills, as applied to music educators.

BACKGROUND

At the turn of the century, a new era of child study followed a rapid expansion of the public school curriculum. At that time, there were many conflicting theories concerning the general aims and methods of public school music teaching. As a more scientific approach toward teaching gained support, the present role of music education, teaching, and leadership began to take shape.

As music became more common in the curriculum of American public schools, there was a greater need to develop a more precise role for music leadership. As was noted in Chapter Eleven, music supervisors in the mid-Nineteenth Century were little more than itinerant vocal music instructors. With the rapid expansion and diversification of the music curriculum in the Twentieth Century, however, a need arose for better prepared teachers and leaders--music educators whose skills of leadership would compare with the most sophisticated of professional fields.

The skills of educational leadership have undergone many changes since the enactment of the first public school law of 1827 in Massachussetts. At first inspectorial in nature, supervisory activities originally centered on such matters as providing textbooks and taking a "firm hand" in matters of classroom discipline. To a limited extent, early supervisors also were concerned with insuring that students evidenced habits and proficiencies which were scholastically satisfactory.

Supervisory leadership is characterized by educational practices emphasized during four eras in United States Education; namely:

1. *Inspection by Laymen* – Colonial period until the Civil War.
2. *Inspection by School Administrators* – Civil War until the beginning of the 20th Century.
3. *Close Supervision by Principals and Special Supervisors* – from 1900 until approximately 1935.
4. *Democratic Practices of Cooperative Supervisory Leadership and Differentiated Staff Roles* – emerging development beginning prior to World War II; leadership vested in many persons is the trend of the Seventies.

The earliest supervisors were not considered leaders as much as inspectors whose primary responsibility was to direct the work of others. Even at the outset of the Twentieth Century and continuing through the Thirties, supervisors and principals were considered to be analagous to military and business leaders. The resulting "line-and-staff" organizational charts showed status leaders at the top of the educational hierarchy, followed by those whose work they "directed." In this scheme, teachers and students--and all classroom activity--was the last and bottom rung of the educational ladder. As will be noted in Figure 29, descriptors of supervisory leadership centered on such terms as supervise, direct, tell, inspect, and rate.

The present concept of educational leadership, while maintaining certain elements of the "line-and-staff" organization for purposes of administrative management, may be characterized by such descriptors

Figure 29

CHANGES IN EDUCATIONAL LEADERSHIP

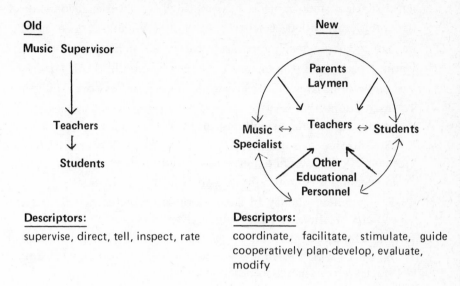

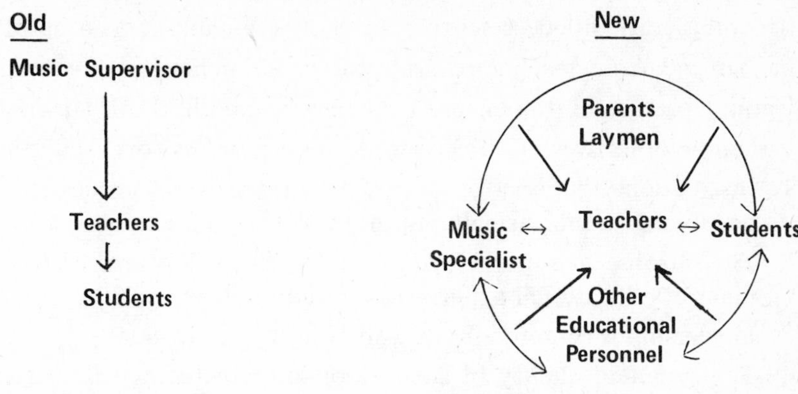

Descriptors:
supervise, direct, tell, inspect, rate

Descriptors:
coordinate, facilitate, stimulate, guide cooperatively plan-develop, evaluate, modify

as coordinate, facilitate, stimulate, guide, cooperatively plan-develop, evaluate, and modify. A diagram of this type of leadership reveals interacting, coordinate roles in which status leaders and members of the instructional team have somewhat equal status and are concerned primarily with the improvement of instruction rather than stratified position. Even salary differentials, which once tended to make implied separations between status leaders and teachers, have begun to disappear. In the differentiated staff concept, a master teacher member of the Music Curriculum Team may be compensated similarly to certain status leaders, thereby helping to insure the equality of in-group leadership.

Modern society cannot accept strict authoritarianism and stratification in public institutions which are designed to incorporate democratic principles. The change in leadership skills is a clear illustration of the impact of scientific and human research, new and more efficient utilization of human resources, and a growing spirit of cooperation in the conduct of human affairs. Leadership in public education now may be compared to other highly technical services in which the primary aim is on the product rather than the process.

In music education, the goal is the study and cooperative development of effective programs for teaching and learning. Rather than authoritarian and subjective, functions of music leadership are becoming diversified, scientific, and individualized. The spotlight has shifted from teacher to students as the central element in the learning process. Burnham and King have emphasized this concept by listing the objectives of objectives of modern supervisory leadership:

1. Instructional supervision is a dynamic, growing process that is occupying an increasingly important role in the schools.
2. The purpose of supervision is to offer leadership in the improvement of educational experiences for children and youth.
3. Leadership is centered in a group, not in an individual.
4. The type and quality of supervision are affected by the situation, the organization, in which supervision exists.
5. The climate of human relationships within the group and the degree to which members are committed to group goals influence the degree of change in practice.
6. The way in which individuals perceive the problems and the tasks inherent in the situation affect their behavior.
7. The actual role of supervision--and of instructional leaders--is a composite of all the expectations held for the role by the people associated with it.
8. A primary goal of supervisory leaders is to foster leadership in others.

It is important that the goals of leadership in music education be consistent with the goals of education in general. Status leaders must also recognize that instruction will flourish best where leadership services are aimed at a greater measure of self-determination and self-direction on the part of teachers and students. At the same time, leaders must anticipate the need for assistance where highly trained expertise will lead to qualitative music experiences. Group morale which is engendered by perceptive leadership also will help members of the Music Curriculum Team work together more effectively toward a common purpose. Status leaders in music must also acknowledge the need of all individuals, including themselves, for developing repertoire potential. They should also be aware of the musical values which are important areas of human aesthetic experience, and are in fact the *raison d' etre* for their educational endeavors.

Specific Skills of Educational Leadership

The functional design for skills of leadership in music education requires several guidelines which may assist in an interpretation of leadership behaviors which must be applied to situational variables. The notion that good teachers or leaders are "born and not made" is a mystique which cannot be justified under any objective knowledge of human behavior. In this Chapter, we shall examine nine specific skills of leadership which may be applied to music education. These skills are:

1. Teaching
2. Communication
3. Interpersonal relationships
4. Repertoire development
5. Team effort
6. Planning, organizing, implementing and evaluating instruction
7. Personnel selection, training and evaluation
8. Coordinating Work
9. Instituting and applying programs of research

Skills of Teaching

The increasing complexity and knowledge of the learning process places special demands on master teachers and status leaders for improved skills of teaching. Furthermore, if music educators are removed from the day-to-day process of teaching and learning, the greater is the need for maintaining and improving one's instructional skill. In order to be an effective instructional leader, one must be intimately acquainted with the art of teaching!

Special requirements in the field of music education place unique demands on its educational leaders. Persons who are entrusted in an official capacity (status leaders) with the responsibility for setting up, promoting, and carrying out programs of music education in the schools should possess highly developed and recognized skills of musicianship, performance and teaching. By reason of his/her special expertise and understanding of instruction, the status leader in music should be a recognized authority to whom school administrators, teachers, students and laymen may turn. In short, this individual should be equally at home as an instructor in the classroom or as a "teacher of teachers."

The need for status leaders who are effective teachers has obvious implications for teacher training. It should be evident that leaders in music education can ill afford to play the role of the "marginal man," but must be fully possessed of a wide range of skill in each of the areas in which leadership is to be exercised--plus a high degree of potential for professional repertoire development. In addition to competence in producing, organizing, and describing sounds, leaders in music education must possess a knowledge of music history, repertoire and performance practices. They should also have a recognized area of music specialization and give evidence of teaching experience in the widest possible range of school levels and teaching situations which have relevance to their leadership roles--hopefully, all members of the Music Curriculum Team will have some elementary and secondary experience during the pre-service and/or actual professional assignment. Status leadership roles also have practical as well as legal requirements for a minimum of from three to five years of successful teaching in most states.

Hopefully, leaders will first consider themselves to be qualified as music educators in the broadest sense; secondarily as specialists in the humanities, or in one of the applications of music--vocal, instrumental, or theory.

Skills of Communication

An effective leader must be able to communicate ideas effectively to others. Due to his skill in music and in educational processes, it is assumed that he/she possesses the ability to conceptualize ideas essential to the teaching and learning of music; can analyze those elements which will be helpful to transmit to his associates; and, will be competent to assist them in developing their own powers of conceptualization of the task. As a corrolary, leaders must understand the practical process of analyzing, interpreting, and applying concepts to learning situations. His/her familiarity with musical resources and processes will assist in responding imaginatively and significantly to the diverse situations and demands that arise in the classroom.

Since one of the major responsibilities of group leadership is helping groups develop skills by which others may examine and communicate ideas, effective leadership should use the principle of feedback. There are many special devices useful in interactive analysis, but feedback provides members of the Music Curriculum Team with special tools of communication by which a profile of leadership and followership performance can be evaluated in a variety of situations.

In addition to skills of interpersonal communication, the status leader is responsible for a variety of informal as well as structured oral and written communications. As a recognized leader in the community, you are frequently called upon to interpret the music education program to the lay public. Also service in an official capacity on an arts council or governing board of a symphony orchestra or concert association where it is necessary that you be able to communicate the philosophy and practice of music in the schools. At the organizational level of the school district, status leaders serve as official specialists in music education whose obligation it is to assist the central office staff to understand the influence of music in learning, which will bring about coordinated efforts with these persons and the various Music Curriculum Teams in implementing qualitative music programs throughout the district.

It is also important that the music education leader be capable of carrying out effective written communication. This is particularly important in large, complex educational structures. In this respect, ideas may be communicated by letter, memorandum, bulletin, announcement of meetings, information concerning materials, festival lists, schedules of music activities, summaries of legislative and professional association activities, publicity releases to the information media, announcements of music courses and workshops, curriculum guides and leaflets, information regarding pertinent research and recent literature, resumes concerning on-going activities of special committees and curriculum teams, questionnaires seeking information and feedback from the staff, announcements of student scholarships and awards, and information concerning special activities.

Skills of Interpersonal Relationships

The Report of the Tanglewood Symposium suggested that the broad concept of music education requires teachers who are sensitive to the many self-fulfilling needs of people and how music can be related to these ends.[3] As has been noted from the research of behavioral scientists such as Halpin and others, many desired group goals may be effected through skills of leadership on the part of group members and the status person. If professionals in school organizations (as well as society at large) can accept behavioral change as an important function of the schools, then group leaders must help develop sound interpersonal relationships by which (a) behavioral change is understood, and, (b) desired behavioral goals are developed and transmitted into action programs.

In applied school situations, it will be the responsibility of leaders in music education not only to work with individuals (teachers, students, administrators, parents, community, and other "out-group" persons) but to develop skills by which their special talents can be used to full effect in group situations. Whereas informal or appointed in-group leaders may work more or less continuously on an immediate one-to-one basis with their students and associates, status leaders may have many individuals and groups with whom they are expected to function. Consequently, limitations of time may make it necessary to work more frequently in groups. The music leader, therefore, should expect to help in the formation of appropriate operational groups such as Music Curriculum Teams, informal groups which meet to work on specified activities, central office and community groups. In addition, leaders must develop ways of meeting a variety of individual needs through group techniques such as conferences, meetings, clinics, demonstrations, and workshops. Several of these will be discussed under the next category.

Skills of Repertoire Development

A very important aspect of music leadership is helping individuals reach their maximum efficiency through the full development of repertoire potential. On the part of teachers, this implies that they will develop a range of skills in planning, establishing realistic goals, developing pupil interest and motivations, developing curricular materials for class use, applying sound principles of learning, using appropriate and varied instructional techniques, making appropriate assignments for reinforcing class learning activities, providing for individual differences and encouraging individual initiative and creativity, using effective instructional resources and materials, planning optimum use of available space, time, and facilities, using appropriate techniques for review and evaluation, and making suitable adjustments and changes in the curriculum. Since a large part of repertoire development is theoretical or simulated during pre-service education, teachers must be aided in acquiring and improving skills requisite to these needs as professionals in service.

Research conducted by the author revealed a wide range of repertoire development activities in which status leaders were engaged, the most popular being those in which personal participation was involved. Those activities of a cooperative and diversified nature were found to be significantly correlated with professional opinion and practice. From this it was found that the effectiveness of such programs was highly dependent upon the role of the status person as a leader as well as upon how individuals and groups were helped in working on problems which for them had significance.[4] It was also found that teachers must be assisted in identifying their problems before experiences may be of any practical help.

It is important to recognize that: (a) teachers are undergoing successive stages in their professional lives; (b) individual differences exist among teachers; (c) experiences must be planned which meet the problems and needs in terms of the realities of beginning as well as experienced teachers; (d) repertoire development programs must be diversified and developmental and should include a variety of appropriate techniques by which this may be realized; and, (e) the role of the teacher at any given time in the group may be that of participating member, originator and leader, or group resource person. Each of the foregoing teacher roles calls for a variety of situational solutions.

Recent literature in the field of music education lists a variety of repertoire development activities, to include:

1. Pre-service orientation meetings
2. Staff and teacher planning meetings
3. Studying and defining differentiated teaching roles
4. Studying the characteristics of specific classes from which

operational plans will be cooperatively made

5. Participating in clinics, workshops, and demonstrations
6. Conferences
7. Interim evaluation and assessment sessions
8. Applying evaluative techniques to processes and material resources of education
9. Study groups
10. Informal discussion meetings
11. Inspection, trial, and evaluation of material resources (music, instruments, learning aids, textbooks, etc.)
12. Conducting action (applied) research in the classroom
13. Becoming aware of results of research in fields related to one's endeavors
14. Participating in activities of professional music education associations (local, area, state, national; general and specialized)
15. Writing for publication
16. Communicating ideas concerning the music program to appropriate individuals and groups outside the instructional staff (parents, community organizations, professional musicians,
17. Participating in special summer workshops
18. Taking advanced (and hopefully, related) study at an institution of higher education
19. Participating as a performing musician (player, conductor, composer) in a community music organization
20. "Keeping alive" by doing continual professional reading
21. Becoming aware of new and innovative practices--trying those which are applicable to specific situations.
22. Participation in inter-visitations for the purpose of gaining and sharing new ideas between other members of the local teaching staff as well as in other schools.

Status leaders should provide many opportunities for teachers to share in the development of these programs and should encourage members of the Music Curriculum Team to initiate, lead, or serve as consultants where possible.

Skills for Team Effort (The Music Curriculum Team)

The heart of dynamic organizational effort is the group. If individuals achieve their full human potentials as students or instructors, it requires the active phenomenon of group interaction. Not only is there a limit to individual potential, but horizons are often obscured by personal factors. These same factors, if used cooperatively, may help individuals establish higher goals, provide new insights and meanings to instructional endeavors, and compliment each other in a variety of ways. The democratic leader-follower process may also establish better interpersonal relations, provide group solidarity, give a sense of belonging, achievement, and accomplishment not individually possible. Individuals operating as members of a group may be stimulated to think more profoundly, to recall something that may have "slipped below the threshold of memory," or to put forth a new burst of effort because of what a member of the group says or does. Reasoning may be improved, attitudes modified, and expressions made more effective because of the influence of fellow-group members.[5]

Music Curriculum Team

An operational example of team effort is the Music Curriculum Team. The size of this Team will depend on formal as well as informal attitudes and organizational structures within the school--as well as such assessed factors as the likelihood for proper interaction, group functioning, and communication in a common effort. Leaders in music education must be aware of these personal and situational factors and will help in the creation and development of Music Curriculum Teams wherever feasible.

Skills in Planning, Organizing, Implementing and Evaluating Instruction

Good programs of music education depend on the ability to assess needs, formulate, and carry out adequate plans. To be effective, planning must incorporate both long and short-range objectives expressed at the program level of instruction (curriculum) and in terms of desired student learning behaviors.

Successful leaders in music education should be able to define the major goals of the music program, develop a plan by which these may be achieved, organize the necessary material and personnel resources required to implement these plans, assist those involved in getting started and following through, and evaluating the final result. Once this cycle is completed, the status leader will use the principle of cybernetics described earlier to make such changes in the program as are necessary to improve the teaching-learning process.

In working with individual members of the group, it is advisable for the leader to remember that planning and implementing music programs are a phase of repertoire development which will reflect the competence and expertise commensurate with each person's professional development. It may be helpful if the status leader develops an organizational outline by which relatively inexperienced groups may learn to operate. The following questions are examples:

What do you wish to accomplish?

For whom is this intended?

Over what period of time is the project envisioned?

What material and personnel resources will be needed?

What will be the most productive way(s) of accomplishing this?

Are there possible subdivisions of the project--and, if so, which should receive the highest priority in getting started?

Do you envision any possible obstacles or difficulties?

How should data concerning this project be recorded?

What are the proposed outcomes and how will they be evaluated?

Has this idea been used elsewhere, and, if so, what were the results?

A school or district steering committee is frequently one of the most effective ways of organizing and carrying out group goals and in coordinating various individual and committee activities. For short-range projects, ad hoc committees may be developed for attacking a wide-range of limited problems and activities. Group planning in either case provides a positive climate which may result in (a) stimulating a consideration of a wide range of alternatives; (b) initiating cooperative processes; (c) providing an incentive toward fuller realization of individual and group goals; (d) providing for a friendly exchange of ideas pro and con; (e) developing in-group leadership; (f) indicating the concern and understanding of the status leader in music in the problems and ideas of teachers; and, (g) providing for cooperative planning and coordination which will help all sub-committees and individuals operate more effectively.

One aspect of planning which is important to the status leader is the development of comprehensive plans for systemwide programs of music education. As the designated music specialist for the district, this individual must provide a broad range of planning and organizational expertise for the benefit of the administration and central office staff. In this capacity, it will be his job to:

1. Articulate the broad goals of music education in contemporary American life.
2. Interpret the knowledge from research, related literature, and recent developments in the field which he feels to be applicable to the district.
3. Develop a comprehensive music program expressed in behavioral terms which will be presented for adoption by the district as objectives of the total music program.
4. Formulate general working plans for the position consistent with policies of the district.
5. Recommend the adoption of working policies and procedural plans (these to include how the leader may function at the district and school level).
6. Develop and present plans for needed personnel and material resources.
7. Suggest situational plans for the use of time, space, and personnel (flexible scheduling, "new" uses of school plants, planning of new buildings, differentiated staff concept leading to development of Music Curriculum Teams, etc.)
8. Develop plans for joint community and staff participation.
9. Develop and coordinate schedules of music activities within the district.
10. Develop adequate programs for assessment and improvement.

Evaluation of programs implies a more comprehensive assessment than does measurement, which is applied almost exclusively to objectively obtained data. In the process of evaluation, emphasis is placed on the formulation of objectives and appraising the result in terms of stated behavioral changes. Statements of objectives in behavioral terms, as we have previously noted, should contain built-in evaluative criteria. Adequate evaluation thus requires the identification of relevant behavioral objectives, the collection or observation of conditions and/or data pertaining to the realization of these objectives, comparing these data with the original statements of objectives, and interpreting the findings. At the classroom level, short-range objectives also make possible a means of self-satisfaction and self-evaluation which may be valuable in helping the student view his own progress.

The Music Curriculum may be evaluated in terms of:

* objectives — what it is designed to do
* context — how it is initiated and planned
* input — how the original components are incorporated into the planning
* content and process — "on site" evaluation as curriculum is being developed
* final product — final quality of the work in terms of its original objectives

Examples of evaluative instruments for use with the total school music program have been developed by various accrediting agencies, such as the California Association of Secondary School Principals, the Music Educators National Conference, and the National Association of Schools of Music.

The principal purposes of evaluation, as applied to status leaders, are to:

1. Clarify objectives and provide for continuous assessment of the total program of music education.
2. Provide for the evaluation of individual curricular programs.
3. Assist in diagnosing, re-thinking, and revising program goals and means.
4. Serve as a means of feedback for ideas of individuals and groups.
5. Assist individuals directly involved in teaching in using tools of self-study and evaluation.
6. Provide means for testing new techniques and materials.
7. Establish and test hypotheses related to experimental programs of instruction.
8. Establish appropriate testing procedures for classroom performance.
9. Discover student interests, motivations, and involvement in the learning process.
10. Serve as an instrument for student counseling and guidance.
11. Furnish records concerning the quality of individual and group

performance, such as:

   a. Pre-tests and auditions to assist in an assessment of learning needs and class placement.
   b. Musical performance and progress levels.
   c. Cumulative pupil records.

12. Serve as a source of comparative studies with other schools and districts of similar composition.
13. Encourage individual staff members in conducting applied research and studies of classroom musical behaviors.

Skills in Personnel Selection, Training, and Evaluation

The foremost concern of personnel administration in the schools is to provide qualitative programs of instruction. As the music specialist responsible for the music program in the schools, the status leader in music education should become involved in the various processes of recruitment, selection, placement, orientation, development of repertoire potential in professional service, and evaluation. The manner and extent to which this should operate is, of course, a matter of local district policy. Since in personnel matters, the status leader usually serves in an advisory capacity to the superintendent and administrative staff, his involvement at each step in the process will be that of helping secure for the district the best qualified teachers, and thereafter to assist them in achieving their maximum potential for teaching. Districts which bypass this important phase of coordinated effort cannot be expected to achieve effective programs of music education.

Personnel policies. Most school districts follow fairly consistent rules based on accepted human and educational needs. It is important that the status leader recognize the principles and procedures which form the basis for such policies.

1. The basic functions of personnel management fall within the purview of the office of the superintendent of schools. As chief executive for the school district, the superintendent recommends, the board acts on all personnel matters. Only those personnel functions which have been delegated to other members of the administrative-curriculum staff may be performed in the name of the superintendent or the district, and in each case, the channel of management and control is vested in his office.
2. Written personnel policies should be developed by the superinten-

dent and staff and adopted by the governing board. These policies should first be concerned with the quality of education as a guideline for the activities of members of the staff.

3. Personnel administration should provide channels of communication for each member of the staff. Every person should have the right to be heard and consulted on matters affecting the individual's professional welfare.
4. Policies and procedures should be fair and impartial, allowing each individual equal access to receive recognition, appointment, promotion, salary, and other benefits of merited performance.
5. Up-to-date personnel records should be maintained for each employee of the district. These data, including both objective data and performance evaluations should be available for the inspection of the employee. Only legally or otherwise specified items of privileged communication (such as professional confidential recommendations) should not be open to his inspection.
6. The superintendent may delegate specific functions of personnel management, such as placement recommendations, appropriate programs for repertoire development, and scheduling of traveling personnel to appropriately designated persons, such as the status leader in music. The latter individual thus becomes responsible and is answerable for fulfilling these prescribed duties.
7. Selection, retention and promotion of personnel should be based on demonstrated competence. It should be remembered that if the quality of education is the fundamental concern, schools deserve the finest available teachers who are competent in the field of academic assignment. Although the status leader in music should serve in an advisory capacity in these matters, the superintendent and administrative staff should seek his counsel in appropriate ways and act in ways consonant with his recommendations.
8. The appraisal of teaching performance should be fair and objective and should safeguard not only the educational welfare of the district but the teachers and others concerned. A cumulative evaluation program, based upon several appraisals of more than one evaluator (including self-evaluation by the individual) are desirable. These should be made periodically, discussed fully with the person concerned, and kept in the individual's personnel folder. The right of dissent and appeal in all matters relating to teaching performance is fundamental.
9. Ordinarily, except for music personnel assigned to the central

office or who serve in more than one school as traveling teachers of music, the music status leader participates in formal evaluation only in an informal and/or advisory capacity.

Recruitment and Selection. Specific attributes and qualifications for teachers of music have been previously described in Chapter I. It is important for status leaders in music to be well acquainted with available sources of teacher supply, bearing in mind those which have produced persons who have proven themselves in teaching assignments. They must be aware of the colleges and universities whose philosophy and programs of teacher education meet the expectations of their own school districts. Music leaders must also recognize and respect accepted policies and avenues of communication between their school districts and sources of teacher supply. If leaders are empowered to act somewhat autonomously or in cooperation with designated administrators, they must keep these persons informed of all actions taken in terms of proper communications and should avoid actions which may be confusing to outside agencies. Printed recruitment brochures (including those which describe the music education program) and application forms may be made available to individuals and sources of teacher supply.

After formal applications have been received by the school district, the status leader in music may assist the personnel administrator, principals, and teacher-committees in evaluating these documents and making recommendations based on the training, experience, and personal recommendations of the candidate's work. Tape recordings, programs, and other documents showing more detailed work of the applicant may in certain instances provide a better profile of the individual's qualifications. Personal interviews should be required before a final selection is made. It is often desirable for a committee, including the status leader, to observe the candidate in an actual teaching situation where such arrangements may be conveniently made.

Placement and Orientation are also advisory functions of personnel management which should be performed in consultation with or assigned to the status leader in music. District handbooks and curriculum guides are helpful; however, teachers new to the district should obtain adequate personal and group guidance from the various members of the Music Curriculum Team in understanding the nature of their teaching duties. Workshops, group and individual conferences, and planning sessions are also helpful in this process.

While music philosophy and policies often may be discussed fruitfully at this time, the perceptive leader understands that he must take up a variety of immediate, pertinent problems, leaving less pressing matters to subsequent meetings. New teachers are justifiably concerned with immediate matters of instruction and personal problems relating to such items as special services, salary, insurance health care and retirement. In addition, they may wish to know what to expect in the way of physical plant and resources for instruction. Questions regarding students, student records, musical programs and policies, parent and public relations also may be important to them. Teachers usually are anxious to know about methods of classroom organization, discipline, teacher evaluation, and policies relating to reemployment. A brief word about the role of in-group leadership services also may be pertinent.

Training and evaluation. Growth in repertoire potential is probably the most important single functions of music leadership since it is directly related to the improvement of instruction. The status leader in music should make effective use of the resources of the various music curriculum teams, teaching and administrative staff, outside resource-consultants, college and university personnel and courses, and in every way devise and utilize every avenue for effective training and repertoire development in-service for both new and experienced teachers.

Self-evaluation check-lists may be used with effectiveness by teachers who have access to the services of status leaders in music. These evaluation devices also are extremely helpful to the leader and may furnish clues concerning the effectiveness of those services which are provided for personnel whose work he/she coordinates. Techniques employed in self-evaluation check-lists are based on the assumption that in an open, democratic society where self-supervision is the desired goal, teachers are anxious for self-improvement and that supervision by others is unnecessary in achieving maximum growth and professional competence. The services of status leaders are utilized where this individual's special expertise in music will make for greater effectiveness in instruction. In this concept, two factors are involved; namely, (a) evaluation should be based primarily on pupil change, and, (b) evaluation should relate to the degree of achieving goals of personal and professional behavior.

Figure 30 provides an example of a check-list which may be used for requesting as well as evaluating special services in music. The questions listed are just a sampling of the many items you might wish to include in a comprehensive request and evaluation form.

Skills in Coordinating Work. Coordinating efforts of individuals who comprise the instructional staff is an essential skill of leadership. Since many groups may be operating within a large school system, coordination requires an understanding not only of the dynamics of interpersonal relationships, but ways of steering work efforts toward mutual, compatible, and frequently interrelated goals. This requires an assessment of group operational parameters and responsibilities and occasionally, where resources and activities overlap or conflict, an assignment of working priorities. In such cases, the advice of a steering committee from the instructional staff may be helpful to the status leader.

Figure 30

Check-List For Requesting And Evaluating Special Services In Music

To the Instructor: Please evaluate the special services in music by circling the number which most applys: 1. Very helpful, 2. Helpful, 3. Occasionally helpful, 4. Of no help. Check and date the far left column if this service is desired. Cut on the dotted line, (in order that your request may be identified but your evaluation remain anonymous) and return both sides to your music office.

	SERVICE	EVALUATION	
_____	1. Planning of classroom music activity.	1 2 3 4 5	(1)
_____	2. Consultation of specific problems.	1 2 3 4 5	(2)
_____	3. Class music demonstration.	1 2 3 4 5	(3)
_____	4. Curriculum planning.	1 2 3 4 5	(4)
_____	5. Securing resource material in music.	1 2 3 4 5	(5)

Name ________________ School ________________

Phone ________________ Date ________________

My special needs (describe on back side).

Activities of groups working on instructional problems in music should never be dominated by their designated or official leaders. Groups are often best left alone to work after the purposes for their existence are well established. This is particularly true of ad hoc or special problems committees. The work of the various Music Curriculum Teams is on-going and reasonably constant; therefore, their activities ordinarily include status leaders as working members. Questions directed to the group may assist its members in an assessment of needs and working priorities--for example:

What is the nature of the work you are doing?

Have you established interim or long-range goals?

Do you have working procedures (informal or otherwise) which you can apply to the situation?

When do you expect to finish this task?

Are there special needs at this time for information or materials?

Would you like any kind of specialized help at this point?

Do you foresee any particular problems in trying to find solutions to your activities?

Will you notify me when I can be of further assistance to you?

Skills in Instituting and Applying Programs of Research in Music Education. Ongoing research is necessary to provide more objective data and answers to a variety of problems affecting the music program. Techniques employed may range from informal to highly sophisticated procedures by which data may be gathered and evaluated. All persons affected by instruction--status leaders in music, music specialists, classroom teachers, administrators, research directors, and students should be involved in various types of research. One of the most important levels of research is the classroom itself, where teachers and students should be encouraged to pose hypotheses, observe and test data, solve problems, and seek answers to a variety of questions. In this way, individual perception, musical growth and cognition takes place. It is of utmost importance that teachers apply this principle in checking and validating their own procedures. The closer the research to actual instructional problems, the more effective it is as an agent for evaluation, improvement, and change.

The term research is often misleading and repulsive to many music educators since it implies little more than seeking solutions to theoretical problems, or perhaps simply a device for personal academic achievement. Its relevance to music instruction has been demonstrated, however, by the growing impact of field research conducted by members of the school staff working on problems significantly and directly related to the classroom.

Certain traits or characteristics of a good research climate are essential if projects are to be successfully initiated and completed. According to Phelps, these include:[6]

1. The inquisitive mind
2. The perceptive mind
3. An objective viewpoint
4. Discrimination in selecting and using material
5. Impartiality and objectivity in reporting
6. A candid accounting in presenting results
7. Diligent attention to details
8. Persistence, despite obstacles
9. Creativity in organizing and executing the project
10. Erudition--as a result of knowledge gained from the project

The status leader in music should be thoroughly conversant with the various methods for conducting applied research, including experimental designs such as the equivalent-group-comparative, and factorial models, as well as a variety of descriptive research designs which use less sophisticated tools of measurement and comparison. The latter includes surveys, correlational studies, relationship studies, and anecdotal observation. The leader should also be familiar with the resources available in the district which will be useful in conducting field research, including the availability of computer hardware and personnel. It is also his responsibility to help individuals and groups find the most appropriate research tools to apply to specific problems.

There is great need for finding research solutions to such classroom problems as:

1. How are attitudes affected by certain types of musical experience?
2. How do out-of-school experiences affect musical growth in the classroom?
3. What is the relationship of motivation to musical achievement?
4. Are humanities and allied-arts courses more or less effective in

developing (a) concepts, (b) skills, or (c) attitudes about music than are independent discipline courses (such as a survey of music)?
5. What is the result of ________________ technique as applied to a given learning situation?

Summary

The status leader in music education must acquire a variety of skills in his role for the improvement of instruction. It is first assumed that he/she must be a master teacher, capable of using and applying superior skills of music instruction to the work of others. Such a person should be capable in a specialized area of music as well as being broadly trained both as a musician and educator who is fully knowledgable and supportive of the music education program in the context of the total school curriculum.

The status leader must also be skilled in communicating with individuals, groups, administrative leaders, and the community, whether this be done informally, through speaking engagements, or by a variety of written communications. He/she must be skilled in interpersonal relations and capable of helping groups come together to find solutions to problems or to plan, organize, and implement ideas and instructional programs. One of the most important skills is that of helping individuals (including himself/herself) grow professionally be applying a variety of repertoire development techniques such as meetings, conferences, workshops, clinics, study groups, action research, intervisitation, and applying new and innovative techniques. The leader will help to coordinate and regulate activities of groups where these oppose, overlap, or compliment each other. The leader will also develop skills of planning-organizing-directing-evaluating programs of instruction. One of the chief duties will be to serve in an advisory capacity as music specialist for the district in matters of personnel management--particularly in the selection, training, and self-evaluation of teachers.

Finally, the music status leader will conduct and/or assist the instructional staff in developing and applying appropriate tools of research related to practical matters of instruction in the classroom. Some of this research should be conducted by the status leader in seeking information which will be useful to the leader and to the central office staff in the further development of the music education program.

Topics For Discussion

1. The MENC Commission on Teacher Education has recommended that the training of music educators (a) not require continuous performance in a specific major performance group for four years, and, (b) have terminal solo performance requirements other than the senior recital. Take positions "pro" and "con" for discussion.

2. Why is general culture (general education) helpful to the complete music educator?

3. In terms of your own training, do you feel the recommendation for a four-year exposure to field work in the schools (observation, aide, student teaching, and other differentiated staff assignments) as recommended by MENC would be helpful to teachers and prospective status leaders in music?

4. Visit a music consultant or coordinator and study the manner in which the skills of leadership, as outlined in this chapter, are performed. Comment on those which you feel to be most related, those least related to effectiveness as an educational leader.

5. Interview a school principal or personnel administrator to obtain his views concerning the selection, training, and evaluation of teaching personnel. Why do you feel it may be important for the music specialist or status leader to participate in this process? Have you discovered good examples of participation by a Music Curriculum Team in these activities?

6. Which techniques of repertoire development do you feel have been most helpful to you in your professional career? How would you go about setting up such a program as a status leader and which activities would you include first?

7. List some of the activities and problems which you feel warrant further study and research.

Suggested Readings

Andrews, Frances M. and Clara E. Cockerille. *Your School Music Program: A Guide to Effective Curriculum Development.* Englewood Cliffs, N.J.: Prentice-Hall, Inc., 1958.

Glenn, Neal E., William B. McBride, and George H. Wilson. *Secondary School Music: Philosophy, Theory, and Practice.* Englewood Cliffs, N.J.: Prentice-Hall, Inc., 1970.

Hermann, Edward J. *Supervising Music in the Elementary School.* Englewood Cliffs, N.J.: Prentice-Hall, Inc., 1965.

Hesch, Clarence J. (Ed) *State Supervision of Music, Second Edition.* Washington, D.C.: The National Council of State Supervisors of Music of the Music Educators National Conference, 1965.

Harrison, Raymond H. *Supervisory Leadership in Education.* New York: American Book Co., 1968.

Klotman, Robert H. *The School Music Administrator and Supervisor: Catalysts for Change in Music Education.* Englewood Cliffs, N.J.: Prentice-Hall, Inc., 1973.

Landon, Joseph W. "Changing Status of Music Supervisors," in *Music Education in Action: Basic Principles and Practical Methods.* (Archie N. Jones, Ed.) Boston: Allyn and Bacon, Inc., 1960.

Phelps, Roger P. *A Guide to Research in Music Education.* Dubuque, Iowa: Wm. C. Brown Co., Publishers, 1970.

CHAPTER THIRTEEN

FUNCTIONAL DESIGN II: MANAGERIAL ASPECTS OF LEADERSHIP

He leads who least manages and manages best when he most leads.
Anon

Management is the functional aspect of leadership which involves "getting the work done." Successful performance of managerial aspects of leadership requires recognizing the nature and demands of the task, understanding how these activities are related to instructional goals, assessing time and energy priorities, and organizing and implementing the necessary work involved. Consequently, management of music education programs requires persons who have the ability to (a) conceptualize the nature of the task; (b) organize the components of the task; (c) discard extraneous items; (d) obtain and exchange information which may assist in performing the task; (e) make an accurate analysis and assessment of the necessary working parameters and needs of the task; (f) assign priorities; (g) program the task: act on matters of routine; delegate items of lesser importance to clerical assistants; share those best suited to group action and decision-making; (h) coordinate, as necessary, work activities of groups and individuals; (i) follow-through to insure completion of the project; and, (j) summarize, evaluate, and apply to future action where pertinent. The foregoing abilities also pertain responsibility and accountability.

Scheduling of Time, Space, and Personnel

The Need for Flexibility. The performance of instructional tasks by teachers and members of the staff depends to a great extent on how time, space, and personnel requirements are met. Scheduling of these elements is one of the most important functions of educational leadership. Flexibility in scheduling the music curriculum will help to achieve greater adaptability to the changing needs of the student and the music program.

The music curriculum must reflect adequate provisions for a variety of learning needs at all schools levels. This requires the consideration of the following types of curricular experience:

1. Common curricular experiences - for all students. (classroom music, general music, allied arts, humanities, general chorus, guitar class, etc.)
2. Optional or alternative curricular experiences - specified types of activity for some students. (choice of more specialized work in vocal, instrumental, theoretical, keyboard, music literature, etc.)
3. Periodic curricular experiences - special "quest" activities for specific or limited interests. (usually from one day to a week in length).
4. Individualized curricular experiences - those elements of the foregoing experiences (items 1 - 3) which require individualized applications.

Elementary Scheduling. Flexibility should be exercised when scheduling the elementary music curriculum. Two useful curriculum models involve the relatively conventional team of classroom teacher and music specialist, while the team-teaching example consist of persons acting in differentiated staff roles. In the latter, five 30 minute music periods are planned per week by a team of three teachers. These teachers are responsible for presenting one combined session (usually once weekly) to cover large group activities such as part-singing, using instruments, or notational concepts. Supplementing this are several small-group and individualized experiences, some as follow-ups to the combined presentation; others include a variety of activities including dancing, resonator bell choirs, choral ensembles, and orchestral instruments. Supplementary assistance is obtained from P.E. and special music teachers.

Individual interest or "quest" activities (including music listening clubs, guitar, electronic composition groups, and field trips) also should be considered in making schedules for elementary schools. These activities, many of which are of limited (short-term) duration, may be scheduled during club, homeroom, or special periods provided expressly for them.

Secondary Scheduling. Problems of secondary school scheduling are more complex--hence, junior and senior high school schedules are less likely to be as responsive to individualization and change as are those of the elementary level. With increasing differences in maturation, interests, and learning rates--to say nothing of widely diversified curricular offerings and built-in requirements--ways must be found to organize the curriculum in order that teachers and students may exercise well-defined options regarding content, space and time. It should be assumed at the outset that for maximum learning, it is not necessary for every student to receive equal amounts of instructional time nor to use the same materials as every other student. This implies a careful consideration of the various forms of scheduling and the proper application to fit the situation.

The following description of traditional and innovative models of curriculum scheduling is designed to introduce to the reader the many scheduling options available for consideration. This discussion is not meant to be all inclusive but hopefully will glean some creative approaches to a most challenging area of music leadership. There are basically three schedule patterns used in secondary schools; namely, (1) conventional, (2) transitional, and, (3) flexible.

Conventional block schedules consist of fixed, daily periods of time which are provided for each activity of the school curriculum. In a typical day, there are from five to seven periods, each ranging from 40 to 60 minutes in length. Instructors and students know, that the first period of the day will always be concert band or a cappella choir--each day of the week, Monday through Friday. Unfortunately, however, first period may also be the only period in which advanced English composition is taught! Thus, the conventional block schedule has the greatest number of conflicts which threaten music programs.

Transitional Schedules provide a number of variations of the conventional block which are advantageous for the music program. Each of these provides flexibility which the fixed block does not. Examples of transitional schedule patterns found in secondary schools include:

* Varied Block Schedules
  1. Short-term seasonal schedules
  2. Extended day schedules
  3. Student "contracts"
* Combined Block and Flexible Schedules
  1. Extended-day area schools schedules
  2. Conventional team schedule
  3. Rotating
  4. Modified block
* Pontoon Schedules

Short-term seasonal schedules provide opportunities within the conventional blocks of time to combine "back-to-back" classes, such as concert and marching band. During the football season, when all personnel are needed, these classes may be combined, following which they revert to their individual separate class status. Seasonal schedules also permit combining the marching band with the girls drill team during football season--each for physical education credit!

Extended day schedules are basically conventional-block in nature, but provide additional flexibility by providing period extensions for special classes and activities. These are frequently referred to as "X" and "O" periods (before or after the "regular" school day)--or they may utilize double noon hour scheduling possibilities. In this way, six-period days may be lengthened to seven or eight. Care must be exercised, however, to make sure that music is not the only subject scheduled in the extended day and that there is no interference with bus and atheletic schedules.

Student contract schedules provide opportunities for students to audit courses during "open" periods and receive credit when the contract obligations are fulfilled. Contracts are frequently exercised upon the completion of required courses during the senior year --or may include options to pursue "honors" programs in music at a nearby college or university.

Extended day area schools music schedules provide a means of combining instructional facilities and personnel from more than one school. Ordinarily, combinations are made between elementary and junior high, or junior and senior high schools in which the host school serves specified instructional needs for its area "feeder" schools. This is most common at the junior high-elementary levels in order to provide advanced performing group opportunities and specialized instruction during the "X" period (before school). Basic music instruction is still handled at each elementary school.

Conventional team schedules: These provide augmented instructional resources for learning, plus some flexibility and individualization within the class. Otherwise, the examples shown are common to conventional block scheduling.

Figure 31

Allied Arts-Humanities Team: Single Period Model

Period*	Mon.	Tues.	Wed.	Thurs.	Fri.
55 minute allied arts class	(A) B	Special Presentations or small group discussions		A or B	A (B)

Instructor A: music major, art minor
Instructor B: drama major, English minor
○ = discussion leader

*Note: allied arts period may be scheduled during any hour of the day when the two instructors are jointly available. This is an elective, interdisciplinary class. The arrangement of time within the class is not prescriptive and varies with the demands of the unit.

Rotating schedules: Figure 32 indicates a typical example of a rotating schedule in a school in which the major performance groups (A - Choir and B - Band) are scheduled on a rotating basis with other academic and music classes of the school. By eliminating one period daily and rotating classes in sequence, all students may elect a performance group, since the net effect of this schedule is to achieve seven courses within a six-period day.

Figure 32

Rotating Schedule - High School Level

	Mon.	Tues.	Wed.	Thurs	Fri.
7:25-8:20 Special Interests	Orchestra, Stage Band, Madrigals, Solos, Etc.				
	A, B	6	5	4	3
	1	A, B	6	5	4
	2	1	A, B	6	5
	3	2	1	A, B	6
	4	3	2	1	A, B
* 2:50-3:30	5	4	3	2	1
"X" Period	Mu. Lit.	Mu. Theo.	Mu. Lit.	Mu. Theo.	March B. Sp. Cho.

*School day ends officially at 2:50. "X" period provides for special "extra" activities, including athletics, drama, clubs, and seminars such as shown (music theory and literature) for college-bound music majors.

Modified block schedules: Certain modifications may be made by means of simple administrative changes to block schedules such as omitting or re-arranging periods (for example: on Mondays--first period meets during the time normally allocated for periods one and two, but period two is omitted.) The pattern may be varied throughout the week to provide for extended class meetings and some rearrangements of activities within these classes, but each class forfeits its fifth meeting, although in so doing it gains one double period. This may be particularly advantageous for longer music rehearsals. Figure 33 presents a system used to combine periods with certain possibilities for art-music team teaching.

Figure 33
Modified Block - Extended, Varied Period Model

<table>
<tr><th>PERIOD</th><th>Mon.</th><th>Tues.</th><th>Wed.</th><th>Thurs.</th><th>Fri.</th></tr>
<tr><td>1</td><td rowspan="2">ART</td><td>MUSIC</td><td rowspan="2">ART</td><td>MUSIC</td><td rowspan="2">ART</td></tr>
<tr><td>X</td><td rowspan="2">ART</td><td rowspan="2">ART</td></tr>
<tr><td>2</td><td>MUSIC</td><td>MUSIC</td><td>MUSIC</td></tr>
</table>

Note: Period 1 provides 3 long periods of art and 2 of music weekly. Period 2 is two extended art periods and 3 shorter music sessions. The time distribution can be reversed weekly or by semesters. May be used for other academic subject combinations.

Pontoon Schedules: One of the most promising of the newer approaches is called a "pontoon transitional design." This design utilizes some of the best aspects of team teaching, large-group, small-group, individual-study, differentiated staffing, and flexibility. It is not as radical an approach as computer-assisted modular or daily demand scheduling; hence, it is more readily adaptable to traditional physical facilities and other conventional aspects of secondary school schedules. Figure 34 indicates how scheduling would be handled by team teachers within a specified time allotment. This allows for large-groups, small-groups, and independent study as required for meeting instructional needs. There is also planning time for the team to meet regularly to design units, behavioral objectives, and allot appropriate time. The example indicates a team consisting of sixty students, two teachers, and a paraprofessional. Students are broken into groups A, B, and C, and the small groups each into two sub-groups, A_1, A_2, B_1, B_2, C_1, and C_2. The small groups have twenty students and the sub-groups ten students each. The team effort is within a one hundred ten minute block of time.

Figure 34
Pontoon Schedule Design for Allied Arts Class
(An Interdisciplinary Team Approach)

Lecture Schedules

Teaching Team	**55 min.**	**55 min.**	
*Music (English)	A B C		Total lecture time available = 110 min. Leadership according to needs of the unit.
*Art (Drama)		A B C	

( ) = academic minor

A,B,C, = student groups, 20 each

Resource centers for subject matter needs are within or near study and lecture facilities and are an integral part of the pontoon design. These centers contain a wide variety of music and art materials and media which may be used during independent study time, as needed by small groups, and before or after regular school hours.

Flexible Pattern

Modular and Computer-Modular Schedules: The concept-design for flexible scheduling is sometimes referred to as "continuous progress." By "continuous progress design" we mean that provision is made for students to progress from one learning activity (or module) to another on the basis of demonstrated competence rather than at a predetermined pace. This curricular program is arranged into modules of varying lengths for speicfied and alternate days of the week. A typical example of a working plan for modular-flexible scheduling is handled as follows: there are twenty-one 20-minute modules per school day available (on a weekly cycle of 105 modules); courses are organized within the number of modules felt to be desirable for each academic discipline (examples: orchestra--3 modules; chorus--2 modules; allied arts--2 modules); each subject matter discipline may provide large group presentations (up to approximately 250 students), laboratory groups of from twenty to fifty, small groups or seminars of ten to fifteen, and independent and/or directed study. The number of meetings per week varies usually from one or two to as many as five or six, but each day's schedule is different and subjects may require different amounts of time for each meeting, depending on the nature of the discipline and the work being done.

Flexible Pattern; Daily Demand Modular Schedules: A new-type schedule which is tailor-made for the school and for each student each student each day of the week. Each student determines their own time for required, elective, and quest classes--and may have a wider range of remedial, "normal" or enrichment activities in a more individualized manner. Students may also program special study or practice time within the regular school day. This program may be the ultimate in providing for individual learning needs but it also requires a great deal of computer hardware and trained technicians to insure its success.

Schedules of the Central Office

Coordinating Music Specialist Services. The coordination of music activities of the central office staff is one of the direct managerial functions performed by the status leader in music. There are three principal forms of schedules at this level of operation including those of (a) the status leader, (b) consultants and special music teachers assigned to the central office, and (c) district music activities schedules or calendars.

Study of leadership activities in music reveals that school administrators and nationally recognized leaders in music education favor providing some regularly scheduled as well as informal and on-call services for teachers. In preparing such a schedule, both long and short-range goals should be anticipated by means of yearly, monthly, and weekly activity outlines.

Flexibility in scheduling is desired so "on-the-spot" needs can be dealt with. Problems of working with new teachers or with special activities of any member of the instructional staff may be anticipated by providing larger blocks of unscheduled time. Time should be allotted for certain recurring and special activities such as workshops, meetings, clinics, conferences, and all-district music programs. In addition, adequate time must be allowed for conferences with members of the Music Curriculum Team, principals, administrators, and students--for individual and group planning, committee meetings, and for representing the district at various civic and professional meetings. Not to be overlooked is the need to budget adequate travel time from school-to-school and time for creative planning as well as the necessary details of office routine.

Schedules of other central office personnel, such as music consultants or traveling music teachers likewise must be carefully organized in cooperation with these personnel and the schools involved. Since teaching schedules of traveling music specialists are superimposed on existing school schedules, coordination with building principals is imperative. Frequently the specialists' classes may be arranged on a rotating basis to insure, for example, that the string class does not always occur during the classroom reading period, the chorus during the study of a mathematics problem, and so on. If the Music Curriculum Team concept has been established, classroom teachers, the music specialists, principals, and others concerned will make plans to integrate important music experiences with other academic work.

District music activity schedules or calendars are helpful in coordinating dates of all-city festivals, programs, children's concerts, meetings, workshops, clinics and other events involving the school district as a whole. If the district also includes educational TV or radio as an integral part of its instructional program, separate schedules and information leaflets for the use of the staff should be developed in a weekly or monthly format.

Financing The Music Education Program

Fiscal Planning. An important aspect of management is that of fiscal planning and control--the financial aspect of leadership which allows the district to plan, budget, and allot its available monetary resources to instruction. School budgets may best be defined as the philosophy of the district expressed in dollars and cents. Like all other functions of leadership, budgeting serves the primary goal of improving instruction, within the realistic confines of the school's ability to finance its desired educational program.

Since fiscal policy affects personnel at all levels of the instructional program, all persons affected by these policies should have a voice in fiscal planning. Although the budget is primarily a responsibility of administrative leaders such as the assistant superintendent for business services, purchasing agents, and building principals, policy development and certain assigned responsibilities of budget preparation and implementation are also the advisory responsibility of members of the Music Curriculum Team and the status leader in music.

Careful planning of fiscal aspects of education not only will enable the district to take care of current instructional programs, but also will enable the staff to make long range plans for improved music education. Thus, long and short-range fiscal goals are a necessary corollary to sound educational objectives.

Budgetary Design and Control. Since public education is administered by local school districts in accordance with strict legal codes prescribed by the state, the over-all design of school budgets is comparable throughout the United States. The purpose and general procedures followed are also similar, although there are obvious variances in precise applications from state-to-state and community-to-community.

The principal purposes of school budgets are to:

1. Establish district educational needs--analyze and estimate their cost together with fixed costs of operation.
2. Estimate amounts of revenue which will accrue to the district from available sources.
3. Allot monies from available funds--establish priorities if needs exceed funds available (working budget).
4. Establish uniform procedures for the collection and disbursement of funds.
5. Provide for continuous procurement of material and personnel according to needs and standards of operation adopted by the district.
6. Establish methods of auditing and reporting.
7. Establish procedures for continuous evaluation and planning of present and future fiscal operations.

The music status leader, working in cooperation with members of the Music Curriculum Team, principals, and other responsible administrators, will have a responsibility for four types of budget, each of which demands a different type of service (Figure 35).

Figure 35

District Budgets - Responsibilities of Administrative and Curricular Leaders

	Type of Budget	Person Responsible	Person(s) Assisting
1.	Over-all district budget	Assistant Superintendent for Business Services	Central Office Staff (including music status leader)
2.	Central office music budget	Status leader in music	Music staff of the central office
3.	Individual school and departmental budgets	Building Principal	Department chairman, instructional staff, status leader in music (district)
4.	"Special" music budgets	Person responsible for developing and administering (status leader, department chairman, advisory group leader, etc.)	Others concerned with the budget function

The over-all district budget is the specific responsibility of the superintendent of schools. Its preparation and operation typically is assigned by the superintendent and governing board to the assistant superintendent for business services, or a similarly accountable school officer of the administrative staff. This budget contains the total fiscal plan for the school district, including all items of anticipated revenue and expenditure. Policies for its administration are the responsibility of the board and superintendent, except for those expressly indicated by law. The district budget also includes the various budgets for which the status leader in music is responsible.

Central office music budget. The music status leader exercises a primary responsibility for the preparation of the central office music budget, aided by members of the operating staff. This budget includes estimates of material and personnel resources necessary for functions of the district as a whole. Typical items for which this budget provides include (a) salaries of traveling music specialists, (b) central music and record libraries, (c) instruments and equipment centrally housed and distributed, (d) audio-visual aids, (e) educational TV and radio program services, (f) children's concert funds, (g) "special use" funds, such as those prescribed by governmental and foundation sources (USOE title funds, Contemporary Music Project, Rockefeller, Ford, and Carnegie Foundation funds for specified music projects), (h) consultant fees, (i) professional library, (j) piano tuning and maintenance, (k) instrumental repair, (l) festivals and all-city music programs, (m) experimental and research projects, (n) professional association conference fees and expenses, and, (o) other supplies and equipment used by the music status leader and his staff in performing their duties.

Individual school and departmental budgets. Each school within the district customarily is charged with the responsibility of estimating its budget needs. These planning budgets also include those of the various departments and academic disciplines represented. The music status leader serves in an advisory capacity to the principal and the members of the Music Curriculum Team in the preparation of the individual school budgets. If department heads have been appointed, these persons are customarily expected to exercise primary leadership for the development of the departmental budget, which is then incorporated into the principal's school budget. It is incubment upon the department chairman, with appropriate assistance from the music status leader, to develop his budget with careful balance between the desired aspects of the total music program, including vocal, instrumental, theoretical, allied arts, and other instructional areas involved.

"Special" music budgets. This category refers primarily to operations which are not dependent upon public funds for their source of revenue. Because these sources also constitute a very small

portion of the total school support and vary from district to district, they are less typical of school budgetary operations. "Special" budgets may, however, constitute important supplementary means of supporting district music education activities. They may operate either at the district or the individual school level, sometimes (with the exception of student association funds) involving both. The principal types of "special" budgets include:

1. Title or foundation budgets. These include funds for specified purposes, according to the nature of the proposals submitted to federal or independent foundation sources.
2. Student association budgets. Where permitted by law, schools may finance certain music activities, equipment, band and choral uniforms, at the discretion of student governments who assume sponsorship.
3. Parent advisory organization budgets. At the discretion of the district (by policy) and if permitted by law, parent associations may underwrite specified music activities.
4. Student music auxiliary budgets. Where student auxiliary activities are an important function of the music program, such budgets are fairly common. The source of revenue may be from student organization membership dues, special sales and/or assessments. Typical expenditures include field trips, school concerts, financing music department publications, awards, scholarships, and, in certain instances, the purchase of equipment not available from other budget sources.
5. Gift and donation budgets. Some school districts encourage programs by which individuals and organizations may contribute capital outlay items such as musical instruments, or may provide grants-in-aid and music scholarships to enable students to study privately or to attend special events such as summer music camps. Typically such programs are developed and administered at the district level.

Principles of Program Budget Design. In the late 1960's the Research Corporation of the Association of School Business Officials began a three-year project to develop a budgeting-evaluation system, now known by the initials PPBS, or, "program-planning-budget-system."[1] It was felt by this means that educators would be capable of improving the management of educational and financial resources by determining desired quality and costs of the product. PPBS stresses the concept of evaluation of educational programs. In this day of mounting for public financial support, schools, like other agencies of government often must vie for the same funds. Hence, schools must be able to define not only broad educational goals, but must translate these goals into appropriate support costs, and finally justify (by means of careful evaluation) how effectively the program actually has been carried out. School systems must employ on a continuing basis the results of cost-benefit and cost-analyses in order to allocate in an effective way the resources which are available. It must be remembered that such analyses and evaluation must always be related to behavioral and instructional goals as the primary determinants.

Several guidelines pertaining to PPBS are in order at this point, including the following:

1. Teachers and other members of the instructional staff should be involved in curriculum building and the corresponding budgetary planning.
2. This planning must be on the basis of sound and realistic goals which are developed from behavioral objectives.
3. The process must allow for adequate evaluation and feedback at all points.
4. It must contain flexibility for innovation and experimentation related to the stated behavioral goals.
5. PPBS must also allow for differences between schools and between various disciplines within schools.
6. It must seek more efficient educational models by which behavioral goals and change processes may be effected.

Leadership Activities With Students

Evaluation, Counseling, and Guidance. Evaluation, counseling, and guidance are closely related to scheduling and comprise, in operation, an advisory function of the music status leader. The objective is to assist students in reaching their maximum potential for personal and musical growth. The purposes served are principally those of assisting each student in having experiences which for him are personal and have aesthetic validity. Another aspect of service also enters the picture, since if teachers and status leaders can locate potential interests and aptitudes--then provide individually appropriate courses and learning activities, the most important idea is discovered.

Attitude surveys, interest inventories, informational indices, performance auditions and "challenges," teacher-made tests, standardized achievement and aptitude tests may be used as important sources of information about student progress and interests. Many of these may be developed and administered by the music status leader in cooperation with school and district research and counseling offices. The status leader should always possess up-to-date information concerning tests and other measures of standardized evaluation from sources such as *Burros Mental Measurements Yearbooks,* one of the most complete listings of available standardized measurement instruments.[2] Locally devised surveys and tests made by members of the Music Curriculum Team also may be effective in providing data readily applicable to the student population of the school.

To help insure each student having maximum opportunities for participation in the district's music curriculum, status leaders and teachers require a variety of data. Several helpful guidelines which may be useful in the evaluation, counseling, and guidance of students listed by Andrews and Leeder:

1. All marks used in grading should serve diagnostic purposes (avoid too much emphasis on the acquisition of factual information).
2. Classroom testing should be based upon actual musical experiences provided for all children in the classroom.
3. Progress reports which give parents a whole picture of his child's progress in school appear to be a more functional medium than traditional report cards.
4. Tests of musical capacity are useful in estimating what may be expected of a child in musical achievement and in guiding him, but should never be used as conclusive evidence.
5. Standardized tests of musical achievement have a limited value because too often they are chiefly concerned with measuring factual information rather than musical experiences, and because musical opportunities vary in different schools.

6. A cumulative record of pupils' musical experiences is a valuable source of information and guidance for the music teacher.
7. The whole process of pupil evaluation should be regarded as a functional tool, contributing to the musical growth of the child.

Student Activities in Music. The status leader works in a variety of ways with student music activities of the district. In an advisory capacity, the leader works directly with and as a member of various Music Curriculum Teams in planning and developing musical programs. Wherever possible, students are encouraged to participate in school music organizations and to take part in festivals and programs which are a natural outgrowth of their instructional programs. They are also invited to participate in a variety of co-curricular and community music activities, according to their talents and interests, thereby endeavoring to make music education a continuing experience.

All district and honors ensembles. Since it is assumed that the status leader is a master teacher and musician who actively maintains his skills, he/she also may organize and direct appropriate all-city ensembles such as bands, orchestras and choruses in which students of the district participate. These activities in no way supersede those of individual schools; rather, they augment and embellish them in appropriate ways. Membership therefore should be open only to students who are participants in the musical life of their respective schools and who are recommended by other members of the staff more directly concerned with the day-to-day instructional program. Typically, such all-city groups are "honors" organizations and exist for the purpose of motivating highly gifted student musicians and providing performing groups representative of the best the district has to offer.

Summary

Leadership in managerial aspects of music education is an activity which facilitates communication, clarifies responsibility, coordinates services, and facilitates instruction. In the derivation of authority, the federal government delegates the responsibility for education to the several states, who in turn give local communities the authority to operate schools. Local administrative control is legally vested in governing boards, which appoint a chief administrator (superintendent) who is empowered to transact business in the name of the board. Some of functions of school management are in turn delegated to other members of the staff by the chief officer of the district. Music status leaders, as members of the curriculum leadership staff, customarily are empowered to administer only those segments of the music program specifically assigned as part of their position, most frequently serving the central administration and building principals in an advisory rather than direct role in these matters.

As the officially designated leader in music education for the district, the status leader must be familiar with the pattern of total administrative responsibility and authority for the district. Moreover, the designated music leader understands and supports the concept that leadership in managerial functions and skills of instructional leadership are operationally interrelated, particularly with regard to his principal role in the improvement of instruction.

Topics For Discussion

1. Define and illustrate what is meant by the expression, "Management is not an end in itself".

2. Conduct an interview with a school administrator for the purpose of developing a diagram of the district's chart of administrative control and delegated authority.

3. List and discuss the advantages of the various systems of scheduling presented in this chapter. Find other examples, including mutations and hybrid models which appear to be working to the benefit of music programs. Considering the importance of flexibility and innovation, which of the models do you prefer and why?

4. Visit a school utilizing computer-assisted modular scheduling and interview personnel involved. Trace the steps used in building master schedules, student schedules, and program counseling. What advantages are given by the staff; what disadvantages for using this particular system?

5. What is the primary purpose of scheduling? Describe the coordinate functions which are contributed by various persons including students, counselors, principals, music teachers, and music status persons (at the department as well as district level).

6. What is the purpose of the school budget? What are the most common types, and the responsibility of the music status person for their preparation and administration?

7. Discuss additional innovative budget practices which you feel to be worthy of note.

8. What are the principal advantages-disadvantages in PPBS budget accountability?
9. What specific activities do you consider most important for continuing music education (student and adult) in the community?

Suggested Readings

Anderson, Wesley R. *Planning a New High School With Pontooning as the Educational Design.* Los Angeles, California: Center for Excellence in Education, University of Southern California, 1970.

Bessom, Malcolm E. *Supervising the Successful School Music Program.* West Nyack, N.Y.: Parker Publishing Co., 1969.

Bessom, Malcolm, Alphonse M. Tatarunis, and Samuel L. Forcucci. *Teaching Music in Today's Secondary Schools.* New York: Holt, Rinehart and Winston, Inc., 1974.

Bush, Robert N. and Dwight W. Allen. *A New Design for High School Education. New York: McGraw-Hill Book Co., 1964.*

Hermann, Edward J. *Supervising Music in the Elementary School.* Englewood Cliffs, N. J.: Prentice-Hall, Inc., 1965.

House, Robert W. *Administration in Music Education.* Englewood Cliffs, N.J.: Prentice-Hall, Inc., 1973.

Klotman, Robert H. *Scheduling Music Classes.* Washington, D.C.: Music Educators National Conference, 1968.

Klotman, Robert H. *The School Music Administrator and Supervisor: Catalysts for Change in Music Education.* Englewood Cliffs, N.J.: Prentice-Hall, Inc., 1973.

Kuhn, Wolfgang E. *Instrumental Music: Principles and Methods of Instruction,* Second Edition. Boston: Allyn and Bacon, Inc., 1970.

Snyder, Keith D. *School Music Administration and Supervision,* Second Edition. Boston: Allyn and Bacon, Inc., 1965.

Sur, William R. and Charles Francis Schuller. *Music Education for Teen-Agers,* Second Edition. New York: Harper and Row Publishers, 1966.

Trump, J. Lloyd and Dorsey Baynham. *Focus on Change: Guide to Better Schools.* Chicago: Rand McNally and Co., 1961.

Weyland, Rudolph H. *A Guide to Effective Music Supervision,* Second Edition. Dubuque, Iowa: Wm. C. Brown Co. Publishers, 1968.

PART FOUR

the music educator as a professional leader — (realization)

CHAPTER FOURTEEN

LEADERSHIP IN THE PROFESSION AND COMMUNITY

Leadership usually begins with a vision of success, a glimmering intuition that solutions are possible.

Lance Morrow

Professionalism

From the outset, this book has stressed the necessity for good programs of music education. Good programs usually reflect successful leadership. The recognition of a music educator as a professional is important to the success and effectiveness of that leadership role when dealing with the school or community. Professionalism--the state of being professional--arises when individuals are competent, concerned and involved. Professional leaders in music education should also be imbued with the qualities of objectivity and foresight. They should be competent in handling the dynamics of interpersonal relationships. They must be intimately acquainted with the content and practice of their art in order to be able to analyze, diagnose, and apply appropriate learning strategies with the same degree of efficiency as the architect would design a building, an engineer plan a bridge or a scientist conduct an experiment. One of the most important qualities of professional leaders is the empathy and understanding of the needs of students for whom the music curriculum is designed.

The Role of the Professional Leader in Music Education.

Responsibilities. Individuals who serve as educational leaders in music education may be identified as either:

* In-group leaders - persons who exercise informal leadership (especially with students) depending on their instructional assignments, such as classroom or traveling music teachers and ad hoc music committee chairmen.
* Status leaders - persons who are officially designated to serve in a leadership capacity (especially with teachers and administrators), to include:
  department chairmen (schools or colleges)
  music resource teachers
  teacher-coordinators (serving as official spokesmen for their peers)
  music consultants
  district music coordinators
  directors of music education (those who head music programs for large school units, such as those of city, county, or state)

The primary task of the professional leader in music (informal or status) is to improve instruction. This individual must, therefore, relate to others (learners, colleagues) in such a way that all persons may work together to implement common goals and instructional procedures. Throughout this book it has been emphasized that leaders should coordinate rather than direct--implement rather than tell--and release the potentials of all persons involved in teaching and learning.

In Figure 36, we note the various levels of leadership responsibility, as related to designated status leaders.

The relationship of leaders to the instructional staff may be informal or well-defined. Teachers who exercise leadership with students, motivate, guide and provide special expertise for learning and experiencing music. Status leaders have broader and more well-defined leadership responsibilities. The subject of how they work

Figure 36
Responsibilities of Music Status Leaders

Teachers and ad-hoc music committee chairmen

teaching
leadership in instructional activities with students
informal leadership as members of designated committees

Teacher-coordinators (usually at the elementary level)

serve primarily as instructors in single schools
coordinate, help, and advise other teachers
coordinate and direct all-school music groups (choruses, band, orchestra)
meet with district music leaders, serve as spokesmen in two-way communications between district and school

Department chairmen (principally in secondary schools)

primary responsibility is teaching, but may also receive released time for administration and coordination of program
coordinates program (chiefly scheduling, budget, and curricular planning)
represents department in principal's administrative cabinet and at the district level
advises in matters of personnel and resource implementation
works with district music leadership to coordinate individual school program with that of the district

Music consultants and resource teachers

area of instructional leadership is generally confined to a limited responsibility, such as classroom music (grades 1-3 or 4-6), vocal, general, or instrumental music
resource teachers instruct and assist teachers on a 1-1 basis
consultants may demonstrate, teach, provide group leadership, cordinate budgets-schedules-facilities-resources, offer workshops or meetings
resource teachers and consultants rarely perform administrative duties, but may advise music leaders and administrators on matters of curriculum and instruction
work with district music leadership to coordinate and develop program in designated area or schools of responsibility

District music coordinator

serves as member of the central office curriculum staff in music education -- advises district and school administrators on matters of curriculum and instruction in music
coordinates budgets, schedules, facilities and resources at the district level
advises principals and local staffs in matters of personnel, curriculum, budget, and instruction
coordinates activities of special resource teachers and consultants
organizes and develops activities of a city-wide nature
serves as a representative for music education in school-community activities
provides leadership in curriculum development at the district level
establishes programs for in-service repertoire development of classroom teachers and Music Curriculum Team

Director of music education

duties in most ways parallel those outlined for the district music coordinator, except that this position generally denotes persons who serve as music leaders in large city school districts, county and state departments of education
activities are more those of coordination and management--hence they are related more to administration, however, as indicated earlier, the focus should always be on instructional activities

with teachers and instruction has been well-covered in previous chapters. In working with administrators, it must be remembered that status leaders in music are generally considered to be staff (advisory) rather than line (administrative) officials--therefore, most of their responsibilities are designated as coordinating, advising, or instructional functions. Only those administrative functions which are specifically delegated by virtue of title or job description should be considered administrative in nature. At the district level, status leaders plan and coordinate instructional resources (services and materials affecting the total music program), serve as advisors in such matters as budgets, building-facility planning, and personnel, and serve as a spokesman for music in the schools, community and profession. At the individual school level, status leaders advise and serve as music consultants to principals and assist the local instructional staff in realizing its goals in music education.

Preparation. In Chapter I we outlined the personal and professional skills of leaders in music education. The MENC model presented in this section assumes the acquisition of a minimum of a baccalaureate degree from a duly accredited college or university. This also requires completion of a designated teacher education curriculum by which individuals are certified for teaching credentials and licenses in the various states.

The explosion of curricula and instructional technology has placed increased emphasis on a high degree of skill by status leaders in music education. Increasingly there is a demand for the master's or doctoral degree on the part of persons selected as master teachers or district leaders. When in doubt about these requirements, individuals should consult a nearby university or the state or county department of public instruction.

Professional Organizations. The profession of music education has numerous professional organizations which serve the needs of its members. Since the aims and activities of these organizations are by and for music educators, they serve the individual as well as collective efforts of their constituencies. It is important for all music educators to belong and further the efforts of their professional organizations--to serve on study groups and committees, festival and convention planning, and to serve in any leadership capacity for which their interests and talents equip them. Any list of organizations will be incomplete--but, it is especially important that music educators belong and contribute to the activities of the *Music Educators National Conference,* its regional, state, and local affiliates--since MENC is the "parent" organization which serves and speaks for music educators in every specialization and at all levels of education. In addition, persons in music education should consider affiliation with one or more organizations having a direct relationship to their instructional assignment, such as the *Association for Supervision and Curriculum Development, American Bandmasters Association* and the *American Choral Directors Association,* and many other national, state and local groups which are readily identifiable.

Community Relations

The Professional Music Educator as a School-Community Leader. The values of parents and laymen are reflected in community educational institutions. Millions of dollars are spent annually for public and private schools in this country. Parental and civic aspirations thus are heavily invested in youth. These communities also consist of people who are or may readily become interested in providing a richer cultural environment for themselves and their offspring.

The music program is one of the most visable aspects of education and school personnel should capitalize on the many opportunities provided to serve their communities and to develop effective school-civic communications. The school and community should be viewed as partners in education, in which the school, as its most important enterprise, may be likened to a sort of corporate endeavor with its stockholders being members of the instructional staff and community. The school must be a sounding board and provide leadership for community betterment in music. Every legitimate channel of school-community relations should be explored in the process--one of the most obvious of which is public performance. This product is always attractive and interesting, and many musical programs are heard by parents and lay persons each year. Every effort should be made to see that these programs represent a wide spectrum of musical activity and reflect the best the school has to offer, as well as providing real educational experiences for the students involved.

Music leadership should be responsive to, provide an avenue of communications for, and exercise leadership in a total program for the musical development of the community which it serves. The community may be viewed as a total resource for improving curricula and instruction in terms of available commercial and organizational influences including clubs, newspaper, radio and television. The vision of educational and cultural excellence held by a community depend on educational leaders who capture the best the community has to offer and lead in developing the best resources available. Pride in program--plus vigor, candor, modesty and vision are desirable attributes for those who would capitalize on these community forces.

Undoubtedly, public relations is one aspect of leadership which must be stressed. Emphasis must be placed upon the importance of utilizing the various media (newspaper, radio, TV), as well as various "ready-made" sources such as journals, bulletins, pamphlets, etc., from professional music education associations. Pamphlets developed at the local district level are also valuable tools of communication.

Music educators should understand the policies and requirements of their local media outlets and be prepared to write (or direct the writing of) news releases which inform the public about on-going aspects of the music curriculum or special activities of a periodic nature. Wherever possible, spot announcements or programs should be prepared and presented via radio and television. Brochures and leaflets describing the program may also be made available for public distribution at concerts, via mail to community leaders and organizations, or through local chambers of commerce.

When preparing a news release include the following items: (a) your name, title, school and address, (b) date of release, (c) title of news release, (d) when (date, time), (e) what or who the article is about, (f) where and (g) why. These few suggestions may serve as the basis of your article and whenever possible be sure to include a black and white photo.

The Community Music-Arts Council. The music-arts council is one of the most effective of the structured agencies for school-community music development. Membership in the council includes directors of the music and art in city and county schools, college and university music department chairmen, city and county library directors, city recreation department heads, county museum director, music editors of area news media, presidents of music and art associations, concert and civic light opera association heads, lay leaders in the arts, and other actively connected with music and arts in education and in the community.

Relations with Music Teachers in the Community. The general objectives of music instruction provided by private music teachers in the community are analogous to behavioral expectations of students who perform in the various school performing ensembles. Not infrequently, however, communications between school music educators, status leaders and private instructors break down or are lacking or misdirected, to the detriment of the activities of all concerned.

Status leaders in music should take the initiative in developing procedures by which school and private instructional personnel may confer, plan, and coordinate mutually related efforts. The presence of representative professional associations of private teachers, such as the Music Teachers National Association, with its state and local affiliates, has helped to a great degree in professionalizing these relationships. School music educators generally recognize the importance of private study by talented students who perform in school musical organizations. The professional private teacher is viewed as an associate who provides invaluable assistance and may greatly extend the total individual development of music students.

Through the efforts of music status leaders, many boards of education throughout the country have developed policies whereby students may receive official school academic credit for outside study. It is customary for governing boards and music educators to develop a joint statement of requirements, including the recognition of suitable performance levels and requirements. These may include lists of required studies similar to university-college music jury levels.

Students applying for credit are provided with suitable application forms supplied by the school district and/or private music teacher associations. These forms, on which the performance level and proposed course of study are indicated, must be filed with the local school at the beginning of the semester. Typically, it is required that the proposed studies be verified by a jury (public school music personnel) at the beginning and end of the term for which the application is being made. Students must give evidence of successful completion of the prescribed work at a given level of competence, following which a grade and credit is entered on their permanent record. This practice has been found to be of importance to sutdents who later apply to enter college-university or conservatory music programs.

Another important aspect of leadership in this area has been the development of joint statements of ethical practice in relations between schools and private instructors of music.

Music Trades Industry. The members of the music trades industry are professional partners with the schools who may assist music education in a variety of ways. For nearly a half century, the Music Industry Council (formerly the Music Education Exhibitors Association) has served as a liaison between the music educators of the United States and the manufacturing, publishing, and retail firms supplying materials and equipment to the schools. At the local level, there are many state and regional affiliates of MIC which serve to coordinate activities of the trades with the professional instructional staffs of the schools. *The Music Educators Business Handbook* is an example of one of its publications which is available to music educators throughout the country.[1] Most leading firms of national stature maintain educational departments whose representatives are available for many services to the profession. Depending on the nature of the business, some have educational research departments, furnish clinicians and lecturers on stated occasions, conduct in-service workshops, provide a variety of useful publications for music educators, and encourage their local outlets to work cooperatively with members of the local school staffs. Even where MIC affiliates are not present, the status leader in music should develop strong working relations with the music trades representatives in his community. State and local music education associations may encourage exhibits by these organizations at their respective conventions, clinics and meetings. By inspecting the available literature, music educators may also enhance their efforts by using a variety of commercially prepared "hand-outs" and other aids, including music lists, sample materials, films, filmstrips, tapes, booklets, pictures, wall charts and other instructional aids.

Summary

The music educator is a leader in the profession and the community which he/she serves. Like other professions, music education provides an organized body of knowledge, a system of communicating this knowledge, and a means of up-grading itself. As a professional in the field, the music educator works with groups representing his discipline, such as the Music Educators National Conference, its affiliates, and those representing his/her own special competencies.

The roles and functions of leaders in music education vary with title and responsibility, the most common of which are in-group leaders (teachers and ad hoc committee chairmen) and status leaders (music resource teachers, department chairmen, consultants, and district coordinators and directors of music education). All are considered to be primarily staff leaders whose primary responsibilities focus on ways of implementing instructional goals--such as instructing, advising and coordinating. The preparation of music status leaders requires specified collegiate training, usually including a fifth year, special studies in professional education and leadership, field work or internship as an instructional leader, and, where indicated by the state or nature of the position, additional certification and appropriate graduate degrees.

The music educator should assume leadership in a variety of activities serving the community. Since music education is a most visable aspect of the school program which has high potential for community cultural development in general, music status leaders should serve in many ways to communicate, lead, and utilize community resources. The status leader uses various media and groups (including the important community arts-council) for the betterment of school programs and all cultural activity. He/she also works in a variety of ways with professional (private) music teachers and representatives of the music trades industry on implementing policies and procedures governing mutual relationships and activities.

As stressed throughout this book, the music educator is a professional leader among professionals who exercises total leadership in the schools and community. Since the profession and community are important adjuncts of the curriculum of the schools, these activities are important to leadership for learning in music education.

Topics For Discussion

1. Interview a music status leader who has an effective program of community leadership. List and describe his/her activities.
2. Prepare a press release and/or radio spot announcement for a typical school music activity.
3. Find and discuss examples of effective relations with private music teachers groups and the music trades industry.
4. If you were appointed as coordinator of music for the Centerpatch Public Schools, how would you go about setting up a community music-arts council? Describe some of its most important functions and show how these may be applied for effective school-community leadership.
5. In communities where community relations have been poor or non-existent (news media, public support, relations between private teachers and commercial outlets, etc.) describe how you might go about remedying problem areas and developing transitional procedures for improvement.

Suggested Readings

Bessom, Malcolm E., Alphonse M. Tatarunis, and Samuel L. Forcucci. *Teaching Music in Today's Secondary Schools.* New York: Holt, Rinehart and Winston, Inc. 1974. See sections on communications media and community performances.

Gaines, Joan. *Approaches to Public Relations for the Music Educator.* Washington, D. C.: Music Educators National Conference, 1968. Excellent "how-to" approach to media management.

Klotman, Robert H. *The School Music Administrator and Supervisor.* Englewood Cliffs, N. J.: Prentice-Hall, Inc., 1973. See sections on communities and administration and public relations.

Morgan, Hazel N. (Ed.) *Music in American Education: Music Source Book Number Two.* Washington, D. C.: Music Educators National Conference, 1955. See section on community music activities.

Sur, William R. and Charles F. Schuller. *Music Education for Teen-Agers,* Second Edition. New York: Harper and Row, Publishers, 1966. Excellent chapter on "School Music and the Community."

FOOTNOTES

CHAPTER I

1. Music Educators National Conference, Commission on Teacher Education, *Teacher Education in Music: Final Report* (Washington, D.C.: the Commission, 1972), pp. 26-35.

2. The term "status leader" refers to an official position of leadership, usually designated by such titles as chairman, consultant, coordinator, etc.

3. Adapted from *Student Teacher Evaluation Form,* California State University, Fullerton, 1974.

4. John I. Goodlad, *School, Curriculum, and the Individual* (Waltham, Mass: Blaisdell Publishing Company, 1966), pp. 148-152.

5. Robert J. Havighurst, "The Values of Youth;" in Arthur Kroll (Ed), *Issues in American Education* (New York: Oxford University Press, 1970), pp. 13-16.

CHAPTER II

1. Some of the statements of prominent figures concerning the importance of music in the school curriculum are found in the following publications:

California Association for Supervision and Curriculum Development, *Operation Quotation* (San Bernardino, California: CASCD, 1962), and Joan Gaines, *Approaches to Public Relations for the Music Educator* (Washington, D.C.: Music Educators National Conference, 1968).

2. Max Kaplan, *Foundations and Frontiers of Music Education* (New York: Holt, Rinehart and Winston, Inc., 1966), pp. 42-55.

3. John M. Culkin, "A Schoolman's Guide to Marshall McLuhan," in Harry H. Crosby and George R. Bond, *The McLuhan Explosion: A Casebook on Marshall McLuhan and Understanding Media* (New York: American Book Co., 1968), p. 188.

4. Leonard B. Meyer, *Music, The Arts and Ideas; Patterns and Predictions in Twentieth-Century Culture* (Chicago, Illinois: University of Chicago Press, 1967), p. 15.

5. Philip H. Phenix, *Realms of Meaning* (New York: McGraw-Hill Book Co., 1964, p. 7.

6. Bennett Reimer, *A Philosophy of Music Education* (Englewood Cliffs, N. J.: Prentice-Hall, Inc., 1970), Chapter IV.

7. Just as electronic media, our extended faculties and senses constitute a single instantaneous and coexistent field of knowledge, music requires us to be active creators-transmitters-or receptors; hence, the medium of the music is the "message." See Marshall McLuhan and Quentin Fiore, *The Medium is the Massage* (New York: Bantam Books, Inc., 1967).

8. William Schumann, "On Freedom in Music," a paper delivered in 1950 at the University of Pennsylvania. Reported in Lewis Mumford, *The Arts in Renewal* (New York: A. S. Barnes and Co., 1950), p. 67.

9. John Dewey, *Art as Experience* (New York: Minton, Balch, and Co., 1934), pp. 41-42.

10. Reimer, *op. cit.,* pp. 60-65.

11. Dewey, *op. cit.,* pp. 134-161.

12. Abraham A. Schwadron, *Aesthetics: Dimensions for Music Education* (Washington, D. C.: Music Educators National Conference, 1967), p. 80.

13. Dewey, *op. cit.,* Chapters IX and X; also, p. 192.

14. Suzanne K. Langer, *Philosophy in a New Key* (Cambridge, Mass: Harvard University Press, 1957), p. 222.

15. Leonard B. Meyer, *Emotion and Meaning in Music* (Chicago: The University of Chicago Press, 1956), pp. 35-38.

16. Allen P. Britton, "Listening to Unfamiliar Music," *NEA Journal* (51:8, November, 1962), pp. 38-40.

17. Meyer, Leonard B. *Music, the Arts and Ideas: Patterns and Predictions in Twentieth-Century Culture* (Chicago: The University of Chicago Press, 1967), p. 271.

18. Finis E. Engleman, "Not By Bread Alone," *Music Educators Journal* (November-December, 1958).

19. Judith Murphy and George Sullivan, "Music in American Society," *An Interpretive Report to the Tanglewood Symposium* (Washington, D.C.: Music Educators National Conference, 1968), p. 45. This idea is also supported by Claude V. Palisca, *Music in our Schools: A Search for Improvement* (report of the Yale Seminar) (Washington: USOE, OE-33033, 1964) and in the 1970 Yearbook of the Association for Supervision and Curriculum Development, *To Nurture Humaneness: Commitment for the 70's* (Washington, D.C.: ASCD, 1970), pp. 80-81.

CHAPTER III

1. Roald F. Campbell and Russell T. Gregg (Eds.), *Administrative Behavior in Education* (New York: Harper, 1957), pp. 121-124.

2. Hilda Taba, "Teaching Strategies for Cognitive Growth," in Eli M. Bower and William G. Hollister (Ed), *Behavioral Science Frontiers in Education* (New York: John Wiley and Sons, Inc., 1967), pp. 161-176. Taba also indicates that in sympathetic form, this belief is best expressed in the 1963 Conant report on teacher education.

3. Brameld, Theodore. *Patterns of Educational Philosophy* (Yonkers-on-Hudson, N. Y.: World Book Co., 1950), p. 57. See also, "crisis culture" p. 85 re immediate environment.

4. *Ibid,* p. 85.

5. A term used to denote a general tenet or moral principle which is interpreted identically and remains unchanged throughout repetitions under various circumstances.

6. D. W. Brogan, *The American Character,* Revised Edition (New York: Time, Inc., 1962), See p. 166. One of the idealistic difficulties which this author cites is that of "slogan affinity." Americans, Brogan claims, ". . .like absolutes in ethics. They believe that good is good, even if they quarrel over what, in the circumstances is good."

7. William G. Carr, *Values and the Curriculum* (Washington, D.C.: The National Education Association, 1970), p. 7.

8. William O'Neill, "Behaving and Believing," *Ibid, p. 8.*

9. Roald F. Campbell, John Corbally, and John Ramseyer, *Introduction to Educational Administration,* Third Edition (Boston: Allyn and Bacon, Inc. 1966), p. 100.

10. Andrew W. Halpin, *Theory and Research in Administration.* (New York: MacMillan, 1966), pp. 28-9.

11. Harold C. Cassidy, *The Sciences and the Arts.* (New York: Harper, 1962), p. 6.

12. Bennett Reimer, *A Philosophy of Music Education* (Englewood Cliffs, New Jersey: Prentice-Hall, Inc., 1970), p. 3.

13. According to McKay, when we turn to music itself to examine it for permancies, these basic types of "natural excitation" occur. See George F. McKay, "The Range of Musical Expêrience," in *Basic Concepts in Music Education,* Fifty-seventh Yearbook of the National Society for the Study of Education, Part I (Chicago: University of Chicago Press, 1958), pp. 129-131.

14. Bennett Reimer, *A Philosophy of Music Education.* (Englewood Cliffs, N.J.: Prentice-Hall, Inc., 1970), p. 143.

15. R. A. Smith and C. M. Smith, "Justifying Aesthetic Education," *The Journal of Aesthetic Education,* Volume 4, No. 2 (April 1970), p. 49.

16. See William C. Hartshorn, *Music for the Academically Talented Student in the Secondary School.* National Education Association Project on the Academically Talented Student. (Washington, D. C.: NEA and the Music Educators National Conference, 1960).

17. Herbert Feigl, "Aims of Education for Our Age of Science: Reflections of a Logical Empiricist," *Modern Philosophies of Education,* Fifty-fourth Yearbook of the National Society for the Study of Education (Chicago: The University of Chicago Press, 1955), pp. 325-326.

18. James L. Mursell, *Education for Musical Growth* (Boston: Ginn and Company, 1948), p. 9.

19. Kaplan stresses that only in the school does there exist some equality of opportunity for these values. See Max Kaplan, *Foundations and Frontiers of Music Education* (New York: Holt, Rinehart, and Winston, Inc., 1966), p. 29.

20. "All students should have continuous, rigorous study in breadth and depth in all subject-matter fields." (This specifically includes the arts.) Robert N. Bush and Dwight W. Allen, *A New Design for High School Education* (New York: McGraw-Hill Book Co., 1964), p. 7.

The same concept is applied to the elementary school under such categories as problem solving, skill development, creative expression, and analytical and appreciative response. John U. Michaelis, et al, *New Designs for the Elementary School Curriculum* (New York: McGraw-Hill, Inc., 1967), p. 43.

CHAPTER IV

1. Gestalt and Field theories of learning have gained in influence since approximately 1946.

2. Piaget's theories were initially met with strenuous opposition in the early 1930's. At that time, it must be remembered that the predominant learning theories were those of behavioristic psychologists.

3. Robert M. Gagné, *The Conditions of Learning* (New York: Holt Rinehart and Winston, Inc., 1965).

4. J. P. Guilford, *The Nature of Human Intelligence* (New York: McGraw-Hill Book Company, 1967), p. 63. Used by permission.

5. Whereas early researchers such as Binet (tests of intelligence--1910-1917) and Terman (modifications to Binet intelligence tests and studies of genius--1915-1957) felt that intellect was more or less fixed and not subject to great modification, modern research contradicts this idea. Consequently, intellect and music cognition is subject to change in direct proportion to the kind, quality, and amount of experience obtained by the learner both in and out of school.

6. Woodruff claims that the student's response to a given learning situation varies with the *level of maturity of his motives,* ranging from spontaneous natural curiosity to an intensive pursuit of high life goals. Asahel D. Woodruff, *Basic Concepts of Teaching* (San Francisco, Calif.: Chandler Publishing Company, 1961), p. 207.

7. James L. Mursell, *Education for Musical Growth* (New York: Ginn and Company, 1948).

8. J. P. Guilford, *Intelligence, Creativity and Their Educational Implications* (San Diego, Calif.: Robert R. Knapp, Publisher, 1968), p. 118.

CHAPTER V

1. Benjamin S. Bloom (Ed), *A Taxonomy of Educational Objectives: Handbook I: Cognitive Domain* (New York: David McKay Company, Inc., 1956).

2. Calif. Assn. for Supervision and Curriculum Development, *Goals and Objectives in Music Education* (El Monte, Calif.: CASCD, 1971).

3. From Joseph W. Landon, *How to Write Learning Activity Packages for Music Education* (Costa Mesa, California: Educational Media Press, 1973) pp. 11-12.

4. The term "most" is usually a given percentage, such as 75 percent, 80 percent, or 85 percent of the students.

5. *Ibid,* p. 5.

CHAPTER VI

1. These outmoded notions are delineated by Roy A. Edelfelt in "A New Education and New Models of Teachers," *The Teacher and His Staff: Differentiating Teaching Roles* (Washington, D. C.: The National Education Association, 1969).

2. Glenys G. Unruh and Robert R. Leeper, *Influences in Curriculum Change* (Washington, D. C.: Association for Supervision and Curriculum Development, 1968), p. 40.

3. Bruner says there should be different ways of presenting sequences and provision for some children to "skip" parts while others work their way through--or different ways of "putting things" in any viable curriculum. See Jerome S. Bruner, *Toward a Theory of Instruction* (New York: W. W. Norton and Co., Inc., 1968), p. 71.

4. J. Minor Gwynn and John B. Chase, Jr., *Curriculum Principles and Social Trends, Fourth Edition* (New York: The Macmillan Co., 1969), pp. 1-29.

5. One significant problem of relevancy is found in current attitudes of both parents and students concerning education. Parents tend to emphasize discipline, authority, training for worthy use of leisure, grades, memorization, more homework, and so on--while students want more stress on home and family life, help in planning their own work, sharing of experience, discussion of controversial topics, more creative opportunities (including art and music), and guidance to help them do what they can do best. See Gwynn and Chase, *Op. Cit.,* pp. 95-96.

6. John W. Gardner, *No Easy Victories* (New York: Harper Colophon Books, 1968), p. 2.

7. It has been estimated that music in the typical secondary school (band, chorus, orchestra, etc.) is elected by and serves only approximately 15% of the average total student population. Due to the limited nature of course offerings, most music experiences are designed specifically for. students having the greatest interest or "talent" for performance. Few schools offer courses of general interest in music for the "average" student, although there are some promising trends in this direction throughout the country.

8. Music Educators National Conference, *Experiments in Musical Creativity.* (Washington, D. C.: The Conference, 1966), 87 pages, and California State University, Fullerton, *Annual Reports of the Contemporary Music Projects, 1967, 1968,* Joseph W. Landon (Ed) (Fullerton, California: CSUF, 1967, 1968.

9. This is the fundamental precept of the "spiral of musical concepts." See Ronald B. Thomas, *Manhattanville Music Curriculum Program, USOE No. 6-1999, A Structure for Music Education* (Purchase, New York: Manhattanville College, 1969). and, Bennett Reimer, "New Curriculum Developments in Music Education," in *Influences in Curriculum Change* (Washington, D. C.: Association for Supervision and Curriculum Development, 1968), pp. 59-73.

10. Barbara L. Andress, et al. *Music in Early Childhood* (Washington, D. C.: Music Educators National Conference, 1973).

11. Marilyn P. Zimmerman, *Musical Characteristics of Children* (Washington, D. C.: Music Educators National Conference, 1971).

12. See Lois Choksy, *The Kodaly Method* (Englewood Cliffs, N. J.: Prentice-Hall, Inc., 1974); John Kendall, *Talent Education and Suzuki* (Washington, D. C.: Music Educators National Conference, 1966); Beth Landis and Polly Carter, *The Electic Curriculum in American Music Education: Contributions of Dalcroze, Kodaly, and Orff* (Washington, D. C.: MENC, 1972).

13. Charles H. Benner, *Teaching Performing Groups;* and George L. Duerksen *Teaching Instrumental Music* (Washington, D. C.: Music Educators National Conference, 1972). See also *Bulletin, Council for Research in Music Education* (Urbana, Illinois: Council for Research in Music Education, School of Music, University of Illinois, and, *Journal of Research in Music Education* (Vienna, Virginia: Music Educators National Conference).

14. Karl D. Ernst and Charles L. Gary, *Music in General Education* (Washington, D. C.: Music Educators National Conference, 1965).

15. An interesting new trend is the short-term residency of from three to seven days or more. See Richard Colwell and Carol Schwortz, "Aesthetic Education and the Performing Arts," *Journal of Aesthetic Education,* Vol. 4, No. 2 (April 1970), p. 126.

CHAPTER VII

1. John U. Michaelis, Ruth H. Grossman, Lloyd F. Scott. *New Designs for the Elementary School Curriculum* (New York: McGraw-Hill Book Company, 1967), p. 23.

2. Although these writers stress this concept for the six secondary grades, it also applies to the total spectrum of the school organization. See Robert N. Bush and Dwight W. Allen, *A New Design for High School Education* (New York: McGraw-Hill Book Co., 1964), p. 7.

3. Michaelis et al., *Op. Cit.,* p. 43.

4. Kathryn V. Feyereisen, A. John Fiorino, and Arlene T. Nowak, *Supervision and and Curriculum Renewal: A Systems Approach* (New York: Appleton-Century-Crofts, 1970), p. 171.

5. John I. Goodlad et al, *The Changing School Curriculum* (New York: The Fund for the Advancement of Education, 1966), p. 84.

6. This includes functional space for current programs requiring space of varying size (large, small-group and individual learning areas), study space, areas for seminars and teacher-planning, resource centers, etc.

Note: another characteristic of "new" secondary schools is that of increased size to provide a greater diversity of offerings, broader programs, and services.

CHAPTER VIII

1. Committee for Economic Development, *Innovation in Education: New Directions for the American School.* (New York: CED, 1968), p. 18.

CHAPTER IX

1. William Hullfish and William Pottebaum, "Take On A Digital Assistant: The Computer as a Teaching Aid," *Music Educators Journal,* Volume 57, Number 5 (January, 1971), pp. 83-87.

2. Max Kaplan, *Foundations and Frontiers of Music Education. (New York: Holt, Rinehart, and Winston, Inc., 1966), p. 50.*

3. John D. Hill, "A Study of the Musical Achievements of Culturally Deprived Children at the Elementary School Level (unpublished Doctor's dissertation, University of Kansas, 1968), University of Michigan microfilms, pp. 2738-A and 2739-A.

4. Wilbur Brookover, Jean M. LePere, Don E. Hamachek, Shailer Thomas, and Edsel L. Erickson, *Self-Concept of Ability and School Achievement.* Second Report on the Continuing Study of the Relationships of Self-Concept and Achievement and Final Report on Cooperative Research Project No. 1636. (East Lansing, Michigan: Michigan State University, October, 1965), pp. 2-5.

5. Robert E. Nye and Vernice T. Nye. *Music in the Elementary School, 3rd Ed,* (Englewood Cliffs, N. J.: Prentice-Hall, Inc., 1970), pp. 569-571.

6. William R. Sur and Charles F. Schuller, *Music Education for Teen-Agers.* (New York: Harper and Row, Publishers, 1966), p. 180.

7. Frances Cole, *Music for Children with Special Needs.* (North Hollywood, Calif.: Bowmar Records, Inc., 1965).

8. Jack L. Coleman, et al. *Music for Exceptional Children.* (Evanston, Illinois: Summy-Birchard Co., 1964).

9. Sur and Schuller, *Op. cit.,* pp. 177-188.

10. An IQ of 130 was accepted by Hollingsworth and 140 by Terman as lower limits of gifted students. See Harry Hollingworth, *Mental Growth and Decline* (New York: D. Appleton and Co., 1927); Lewis Terman et al., *Genetic Studies of Genius, Vol I; Mental and Physical Traits of a Thousand Gifted Children.* (Palo Alto: Stanford University Press, 1925).

11. George I. Thomas and Joseph Crescimbeni, *Guiding the Gifted Child* (New York: Random House, 1966), p. 23.

12. This general idea is expressed by Alex S. Osburn in *Applied Imagination, Third Edition* (New York: Charles Scribner and Sons, 1963).

13. Music Educators National Conference, *Experiments in Musical Creativity.* (Washington, D. C.: MENC, 1966).

14. Ronald B. Thomas, *Manhattanville Music Curriculum Program, USOE No. 6-19999, A Structure for Music Education.* (Purchase, N. Y.: Manhattanville College, 1969).

15. Refers to the National Assn. of Secondary School Principals.

16. Mary Val Marsh, *Explore and Discover Music: Creative Approaches To Music Education in Elementary, Middle, and Junior High Schools.* (Toronto, Canada: The Macmillan Co., 1970).

17. Sur and Schuller, *op. cit.*

18. Thomas and Crescimbeni, *Op. cit.,* p. 101.

19. Virginia Hagemann, "Electronic Composition in the Junior High School," *Music Educators Journal* (Vol. 55, No. 3, November 1968), pp. 86-90.

20. E. Thayer Gaston, *Music in Therapy* (New York: MacMillan Co., 1968), p. 7.

21. National Association for Music Therapy, Inc., Lawrence, Kansas.

22. William W. Sears, "Processes in Music Therapy," in Gaston, *Op. cit.* pp. 36-37.

23. Bennett Reimer, *A Philosophy of Music Education.* (Englewood Cliffs, New Jersey: Prentice-Hall, Inc., 1970), pp. 145-6.

24. Max Kaplan, *Music in Recreation: Social Foundations and Practices.* Champaign, Illinois: Stipes Publishing Co., 1955), pp. 59-65.

25. Reimer, *Op. cit.,* p. 164.

CHAPTER X

1. Arthur W. Combs, "An Educational Imperative: The Human Dimension," *To Nurture Humaneness: Commitment for the 70's,* 1970 Yearbook of the Association for Supervision and Curriculum Development (Washington, D. C.: ASCD, 1970), pp. 183-4.

2. From the Lexington State Normal School, 1851.

3. See Edward Bailey Birge, *History of Public School Music in the United States* (Washington, D. C.: Music Educators National Conference), pp. 130-138.

4. Charles E. Silberman, *Crisis in the Classroom, The Remaking of American Education* (New York: Random House, 1970), pp. 183-186.

5. Joseph W. Landon, "Music in Britain's Informal Classrooms: What Does It Suggest for American Education?" (*Music Educators Journal,* Vol. 59, No. 9, May 1973).

6. See also the "Plowden Report"--Central Advisory Council for Education, *Children and Their Primary Schools* (London: Her Majesty's Stationary Office, 1967). One of the important concepts of this report," . . .we know now that play--in the sense of 'messing around' either with material objects or with other children, and of creating fantasies--is vital to children's learning, and therefore vital in school." Thus, "play" is the real work of childhood.

7. United States Department of Health, Education, and Welfare, Office of Education, *Interdisciplinary Model Programs in the Arts for Children and Teachers,* A Summary Report Prepared by the Arts IMPACT Evaluation Team (Washington, D. C.: USOE, March 1973).

8. National Endowment for the Arts, *Artists in Schools,* (Washington, D. C.: U. S. Office of Education, March 1973).

9. U. S. Office of Education, *Schools and Symphony Orchestras: A Summary of Selected Youth Concert Activities* (Washington, D. C.: OSOE, 1971).

10. Thomas H. Carpenter, *Televised Music Instruction* (Washington, D. C.: Music Educators National Conference, 1973).

11. J. Lloyd Trump and Dorsey Baynham, *Focus on Change: Guide to Better Schools* (Chicago: Rand McNally and Company, 1961), pp. 32-45.

12. Robert N. Bush and Dwight W. Allen, *A New Design for High School Education* (New York: McGraw-Hill Book Co., 1964), pp. 52-57.

13. Richard Arends and Don Essig, *A Plan for Studying and Implementing Differentiated Staffing.* (Eugene, Oregon: Eugene Schools, 1970), pp. 12-13.

CHAPTER XI

1. Sunderman, Lloyd F. "Supervisional and Instructional Aspects of Early American Music Education," *Educational Administration and Supervision. (October, 1951), p. 339.*

2. Thomas Tapper, *The Music Supervisor* (Boston: Oliver Ditson Company, 1916), p. 9.

3. Laurence J. Peter and Raymond Hull, *The Peter Principle* (New York: William Morrow and Company, Inc., 1969) pp. 19-27.

4. Robert G. Owens, *Organizational Behavior in Schools* (Englewood Cliffs, N. J.: Prentice-Hall, Inc., 1970), pp. 48-51.

5. William H. Lucio and John D. McNeil. *Supervision: A Synthesis of Thought and Action,* Second Edition (New York: McGraw-Hill Book Company, 1969), p. 82.

6. Daniel E. Griffiths, et al, *Organizations and Human Behavior: Focus on Schools* (New York: McGraw-Hill Book Company, 1969), pp. 371-3.

7. Kimball Wiles, *Supervision for Better Schools* (New York: Prentice-Hall, Inc., 1950), pp. 23-4.

8. This was corroborated during the author's visits in British schools in 1971.

9. See Teacher Education Commission, Music Educators National Conference, *Teacher Education in Music: Final Report* (Washington, D. C.: MENC, 1972).

10. Abbot, Max G. et al, *Organizations and Human Behavior: Focus on Schools* (New York: McGraw-Hill Book Company, 1969), p. 42.

11. Owens, *op. cit.,* pp. 14-15.

12. Elton B. McNeil, *Behavioral Science Frontiers in Education* (New York: John Wiley & Sons, Inc., 1967), p. 254.

13. Roald F. Campbell and Russell T. Gregg (Ed.), *Administrative Behavior in Education* (New York: Harper, 1957), pp. 120-123.

14. Alex Bavelas, *School Administration: Selected Readings* (New York: Thomas Y. Crowell Co., 1968), p. 258.

15. Andrew W. Halpin, *Theory and Research in Administration* (New York: MacMillan, 1966).

16. Roald F. Campbell, John Corbally, and John Ramseyer, *Introduction to Educational Administration,* Third Edition (Boston: Allyn and Bacon, Inc., 1966), pp. 247-249.

17. Wiles, *op. cit.*

18. Snyder, Keith D., *School Music Administration and Supervision,* Second Edition (Boston: Allyn and Bacon, Inc., 1965), pp. 1-25.

19. Raymond H. Ostrander and Ray C. Dethy, *A Values Approach to Educational Administration* (New York: American Book Co., 1968), p. 83.

20. Roald F. Campbell, "Situational Factors in Educational Administration," from Campbell and Gregg, *op. cit.,* pp. 264-266.

21. Halpin, *op. cit.,* pp. 86-7, 124.

22. As reported in Owens, *op. cit.,* p. 170.

23. Halpin, *op. cit.,* pp. 174-181.

CHAPTER XII

1. See Richard Arends and Don Essig, *A Plan for Studying and Implementing Differentiated Staffing* (Eugene, Oregon: Eugene School District 4J, September, 1970), p. 13.

2. Reba M. Burnham and Martha L. King, *Supervision in Action* (Washington, D. C.: Association for Supervision and Curriculum Development, 1961), pp. 31-32.

3. Music Educators National Conference, *The Tanglewood Symposium: Music in American Society,* reprinted in the *Music Educators Journal,* Volume 54, Number 3, November, 1967.

4. Joseph W. Landon, "Music Supervision in California City Schools" (unpublished Doctor's dissertation, The University of Southern California, Los Angeles, 1959), pp. 236-245.

5. Raymond H. Harrison, *Supervisory Leadership in Education* (New York: American Book Co., 1968), p. 146.

6. Roger P. Phelps, *A Guide to Research in Music Education* (Dubuque, Iowa: Wm. C. Brown Co. Publishers, 1969), pp. 8-10.

CHAPTER XIII

1. William H. Curtis, "Program Budgeting Design for Schools Unveiled, with much Work Still to go," *Nations Schools,* Vol. 84, Number 5, November, 1969, p. 40.

2. Oscar Krisen Burros, *Mental Measurements Yearbooks* (Highland Park, New Jersey: The Gryphon Press).

3. Frances M. Andrews and Joseph A. Leeder, *Guiding Junior High School Pupils in Music Experiences.* (Englewood Cliffs, N.J.: Prentice-Hall, Inc., 1953), pp. 262-263.

CHAPTER XIV

1. Available through the Music Educators National Conference, 8150 Leesburg Pike, Vienna, Virginia 22180. Music Industry Council, *The Music Educators Business Handbook* (Washington, D. C.: The Council).

PERMISSIONS

We wish to thank the following persons and/or organizations for permission to quote or use copyrighted materials:

Page 1 – quote from John W. Gardner, *No Easy Victories* (New York: Harper and Row, Publishers, 1968), p. 73.

Page 45 – Figure 6, "The Challenge of Educational Administration in Goal-Modification, in Roald F. Campbell, John Corbally and John Ramseyer, *Introduction to Educational Administration,* Third Edition (Boston: Allyn and Bacon, Inc., 1966), p. 100.

Page 48 – quote from Bennett Reimer, *A Philosophy of Music Education* (Englewood Cliffs, N. J.: Prentice-Hall, Inc., 1970), p. 3.

Page 63 – Figure 9, "Guilford--Structure of the Intellect," in J. P. Guilford, *The Nature of Human Intelligence* (New York: McGraw-Hill Book Company, 1967), p. 63.

Page 126 – quote from John I. Goodlad, "The Educational Program to 1980 and Beyond," *Implications for Education of Prospective Changes in Society,* pp. 47-60. Edited by Edgar L. Morphet and Charles O. Ryan (Denver: Designing Education for the Future, 1967), pp. 323.

Page 146 – quote from Charles E. Silberman, *The Open Classroom Reader* (New York: Vintage Books, 1973), p. 749. Permission from Random House, Inc., copyright owners.

Pages 146-157 (Chapter VIII) – This Chapter in part appears as an article by Joseph W. Landon in the *Music Educators Journal,* April 1974 (Vol. 60, No. 8), pp. 64-69, entitled, "Strategies for Opening the Traditional Classroom." Reprinted portions used by permission of the author and *Music Educators Journal,* Malcolm E. Bessom, Editor (Vienna, Va.: Music Educators National Conference.

Page 159 – quote from James L. Mursell, *Education for Musical Growth* (Boston: Ginn and Company, 1948), p. 283. Permission from Xerox College Publishing, copyright owners.

Page 208 – quote from Ordway Tead, *The Art of Leadership* (New York: McGraw-Hill Book Company, 1935), p. 20.

Page 209 – quote from Thomas Tapper, *The Music Supervisor* (Boston: Oliver Ditson Co., 1916), p. 9. Permission from Theodore Presser & Co., copyright owners.

Page 275 – quote from Lance Morrow, "In Quest of Leadership," *Time* (Vol. 104, No. 3), p. 22. Reprinted by permission from *TIME,* The Weekly Newsmagazine; Copyright Time, Inc. (Note: this is the "cover" story from this issue).

Appendix: Line-drawing floor plan of Fine Arts Building, Highland High School, Bakersfield, California, Kern High School District, Dr. Wesley R. Anderson, Principal. Plan by Whitney Biggar & Associate, Architects.

Line-drawing floor plan of Fine Arts Building, Cajon High School, San Bernardino Unified School District, San Bernardino, California, Dr. Philip A. Allred, Associate Superintendent, Harnish-Morgan and Causey, Architects.

APPENDIX

RESOURCES FOR MUSIC EDUCATION

Music Facilities to be Included in the Physical Plant

Description	Number	Music or Shared	Student Stations	Staff Stations	Special Requirements	When	Comments
Lecture-Recital	1	shared	200	2 tchrs; 3 staff	theatre seating, convertible partitions, sm. stage, sound & projection	Initial plan	Multi-Station TV
*Instrumental studio	1	music	150	1-t; 2-s	Acoustical treat., non-parallel, double ceiling ht. and floor space	"	Near aud. stage
Instrumental storage	2	music	–	–	Inst., lib., uniforms	"	Adj. studio
*Choral studio	1	music, allied arts	150	1-t; 2-s	Accoustical treat., non-parallel, double ceiling ht. and floor space	"	Near aud.
Choral storage	1	music	–	–	Library, robes	"	Adj. studio
**Recording room	2	music	–	–	Visual control of instr. & cho. studios	"	"
Resource center	1	music	12-20	2-4 t & s	Indiv. listening, study, work space program instr., LAPS	"	"
Offices	1-4	music	–	acc. total staff	May be combined with resource center	"	"
**Practice, medium	4	music	6-12	1-t or s	Seminars, small-group ensemble, etc., acc. tr.	"	"
Practice, indiv.-sm.	8-16	music	1-2	–	Acoustical treat.	"	"
Public facilities		shared			Rest rooms, conf.	"	As req'd.
Ancillary areas		music			Repair, sp. storage	"	"
Special Instruction	1-2	music or shared	20-30	1-t; 1-s	Piano (elec.) lab, theory-comp., etc.	Expansion	
Auditorium	1	shared	1200-1500		full stage and lighting facilities	"	Near perf. studios

Legend: t = teacher s = student

* – It is recommended that instrumental and choral facilities not have built-in risers for greater instructional flexibility.
** – recording studios may be combined with medium-practice-seminar rooms.

Based on a secondary school having 1500–2000 students, 2 – 4 music faculty, plus aides and interns.

FIVE-YEAR MASTER PLAN FOR RESOURCES IN MUSIC

Centerpatch Public Schools

	1st Year	2nd Year	3rd Year	4th Year	5th Year
Physical Plant					
New Music-Arts Building					6, 7
Choral Music Room		3			
Instrumental Music Room			4		
Music Classroom	1	2	3, 4	5	
Practice Rooms	5	1, 3	2	4	
Electronic Music Lab	5		1		3
Study-Listening Lab		4	5		
Recital Hall	1			5	6, 7
Auditorium					6
***Equipment**					
New -$5,000; Replace - $2,000					
String Instruments	R-5	R-1	R-3	R-2	N-6, 7
Woodwind Instruments			R-4	R-5	N-6, 7
Brass Instruments		R-2			N-6, 7
Percussion Instruments					N-6, 7
Electronic Piano Lab ($10,000)			5		7
Electronic Guitar Lab ($4,500)	3	4	1		6
Electronic Composition Lab ($3,000)				5	
Listening Equipment ($3,000)	5	2			6, 7

* – See standard equipment list, music.

Schools:
1 – Roosevelt H.S.
2 – Edison H.S.
3 – Kennedy H.S.
4 – Highland H.S.
5 – Westside H.S.
6 – Franklin H.S. (Projected)
7 – Morningside H.S. (Projected)

Phases in the Planning Process for General and Music Facilities

Phase	Primary Responsibility	Secondary Responsibility
1. Educational Plan*	Superintendent and Board	Teachers and staff, status leader
2. General design of school	School architect or consulting architect	Superintendent, principal, Status leader in art
3. Recommend desired educational program	Status leader in music, building principal	(Music Curriculum Team--if available)
4. Determine building for music	Architect	Status leader in music, consulting acoustical engineer, principal
5. Determine site relationship with other educational facilities	Principal, status leader in music	Central office status in other disciplines, architect
6. Draw up working architectural plans and specifications (including needed equipment)	Architect, Assistant superintendent for business affairs	Principal, status leader in music
7. Let, receive, and award bids	Business office, super- and governing board	
8. Staff and equip	Principal	Status leader in music, other music faculty (if available)
9. Conduct instructional program	Music Curriculum Team	Status leader in music

*Note: Final decisions on all phases must be made by the superintendent and governing board.

Operational functions of the music status leader are advisory.

Cajon High School — Theater Building

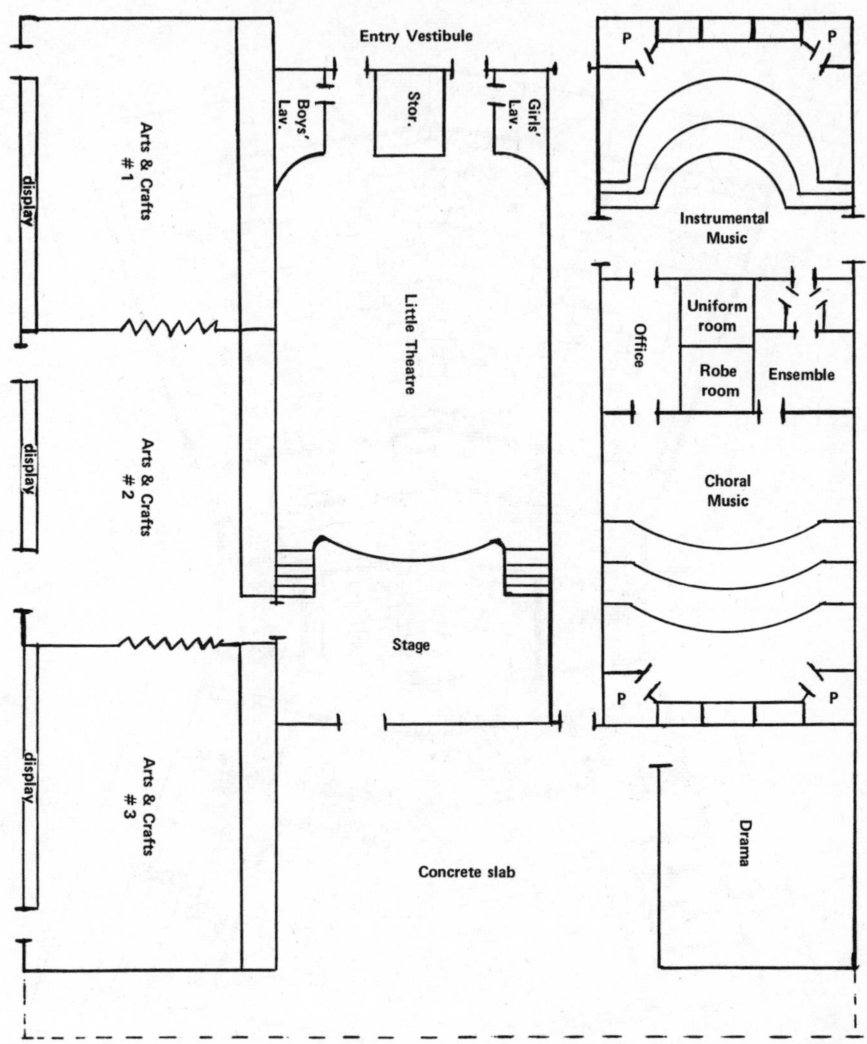

Cajon High School, San Bernardino, California
San Bernardino Unified School District
Harnish-Morgan and Causey Architects

Courtesy Dr. Philip A. Allred, Associate Superintendent of Schools, San Bernardino Unified School District, San Bernardino, California. Used by permission.

Highland High School Art-Music Building

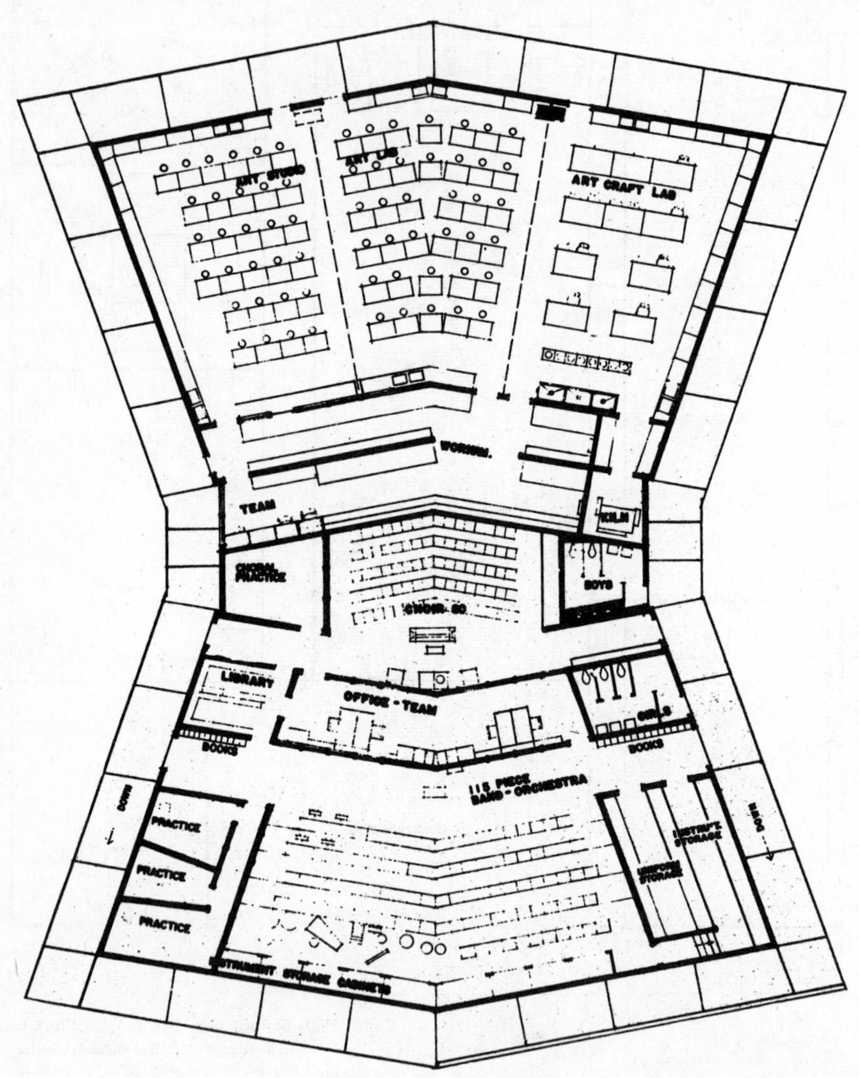

Highland High School, Bakersfield, Calif.
Kern High School District
Whitney Biggar & Associate, Architect

Courtesy Dr. Wesley R. Anderson, Principal, Highland High School, Bakersfield, California. Used by permission.

Formula for Estimating Music Costs

Instrumental Music:

Activity	Cost of Music
Concert Band:	
Marching folios, bandstrations, etc. (Sept.-Nov.)	$2
Daily instruction (sight-reading, technical studies, repertoire development)	$3
Programs (Oct., Dec., Feb., April, June)	$5 av. no. selections= 5-6
Festival Music (Mar.-April)	$2 av. no. selections= 3
Small ensemble and solo music	$1
Total amount per student =	$14*

* Based on: (1) 2 students (av.) per copy of music
(2) average costs of band music:
folios - $3 (each
Bandstrations - $20-$75 (total)
Collections, technical studies, etc. - $3 (ea.)

Activity	Cost of Music
Orchestra:	
Daily Instruction (sight-reading, technical studies, repertoire development)	$6
Programs (comparable to band)	$5 av. no. selections= 5-6
Festivals	$2 av. no. selections= 3
Small ensemble and solo music	$1
Total amount per student	$14**

** Based on: (1) 2 students (av.) per copy of music
(2) average costs of music:
Orchestrations - $35-$100 (total)
Collections - $3-$5 (ea.)
Technical Studies, etc. $3

Activity	Cost of Music
Training Groups:	
Instructional methods & exercises	$4
Supplementary materials & arrangements	$2
Program materials	$2
Total amount per student =	$8***

*** Costs parallel those of band and orchestra, above.

Choral Music:

Daily Instruction (sight-reading, technical studies, repertoire development)	$4
Programs (Oct., Dec., Feb. April, June)	$5 av. no. selections= 10-12
Festival Music (Fall-Spring)	$2 av. no. selections= 3
Solo and ensemble music (including madrigal or vocal ensemble, if not scheduled separately)	$1
Total amount per student	$12****

**** Based on: (1) 2 students per copy of music (av.)
(2) average cost of octavo music = 35¢ per copy

Note: An example of a budget for a high school having the following enrollments in music performance would be:

Band I (Training Group 50 students x $8		= $ 400.00
String Orchestra (Training)	40 x $8	= 320.00
Band II (Concert Band)	120 x $14	= 1680.00
Symphony Orchestra	60 x $14	= 840.00
Boys' Chorus	50 x $12	= 600.00
Girls' Chorus	75 x $12	= 900.00
A Cappella Choir	60 x $12	= 720.00
Total estimated budget		$5460.00

INDEX

K

L

M

Q

R

S

185

226 5 2629